A Poet Offering His Book To A Lady

Reader's Dedication

To my true love: _____

_____

From: _____

The Christian Way to be Happily Married

The Christian Way to be Happily Married

DAVID SANDERLIN, PH.D.

San Diego, CA

Copyright © 2010 by David Sanderlin. All rights reserved. No part of this book may be reproduced in any form or by any means, electronic or mechanical, including photocopying, recording, taping, or by any information storage and retrieval system without the written permission of the author, except for 1) the use of brief quotations in a review, and 2) the reproduction of the worksheet and questions in Appendixes A and B, as indicated at the end of these two appendixes.

Published by Christian Starlight Press
   Christian Starlight Press
   P.O. Box 34078
   San Diego, CA 92163
   www.ChristianStarlightPress.com
   www.TheChristianWaytobeHappilyMarried.com

Book and cover design by 1106 Design

Cover illustration by Lynne Pittard, Lynne Pittard Originals, Inc.
   E-mail: LynnePittardArt@aol.com

ISBN: 978-0-9824396-3-0. Paperback.

LCCN: 2009905263

NIHIL OBSTAT
I have concluded that the materials presented in this work are free of doctrinal or moral errors.
Bernadeane M. Carr, STL
30 October 2009

IMPRIMATUR
In accord with 1983 CIC 827 & 3, permission to publish this work is hereby granted.
+Robert H. Brom
Bishop of San Diego
30 October 2009

The author is grateful for permission to reproduce material from the sources listed below. If there has been any failure to locate and properly credit any copyright owners, please inform the author, and efforts will be made to correct this in future printings.

Front cover illustration, "Two White Doves," by Lynne Pittard. Used by permission of Lynne Pittard, Lynne Pittard Originals, Inc. www.lynnepittard.com.

This permissions list continues on page 247.

"I want you to be happy, always happy in the Lord."
(Paul, letter to the Philippians 4:4)

Author's Dedication

I dedicate this book to my wife, Arnell, and our children, Wendy, John, Michelle, and Kevin, for the happiness that they have brought me in my marriage and family life. They have enabled me to write these upbeat pages on marriage and the family. Arnell is a wonderful person and perfect for me, and Wendy, John, Michelle, and Kevin have always been our pride and joy.

I dedicate this book also to my parents George and Owenita Sanderlin, my brother Johnny, and my sisters Frea and Sheila for the happy childhood I shared with them and for their love and support from their homes nearby and from God's home.

Finally, I dedicate this book to Arnell's family and to the families of Wendy, John, Michelle, and Kevin who have enriched my life and been a source of great happiness for Arnell and me.

David and Arnell with their children and their children's families

Contents

INTRODUCTION	1
PART I: THE CHRISTIAN WAY TO BE HAPPILY MARRIED	13
Chapter 1. Christian Happiness	17
Chapter 2. The Christian Way to Happiness	27
PART II: THE BEGINNING ROMANTIC STAGE OF CHRISTIAN MARRIAGE DISCIPLESHIP	37
Chapter 1. The Emotional Happiness of Romantic Lovers	41
Chapter 2. The Christian Morality Problem with Emotional Happiness	47
Chapter 3. The Emotional Problem with Romantic Love	57
Chapter 4. The Fantasy Problem with Romantic Wisdom	63
PART III: THE CONVENTIONAL NEEDS STAGE OF CHRISTIAN MARRIAGE DISCIPLESHIP	69
Chapter 1. The Conventional Happiness of Needs Lovers	73
Chapter 2. The Christian Morality Problem with Conventional Happiness	81
Chapter 3. The Emotional Problem with Needs Love	93
Chapter 4. The Fantasy Problem with Needs Wisdom	111
PART IV: THE CHRIST-LIKE TRANSFORMING STAGE OF CHRISTIAN MARRIAGE DISCIPLESHIP	125
Chapter 1. The Christian Happiness of Transformed Lovers	129
Chapter 2. Christian Happiness during Hard Times	145
Chapter 3. A Generous but Non-Permissive Marital Love	155
Chapter 4. Virtuous Marriage Conduct	167

Chapter 5. Virtuous Marriage Money Management	185
Chapter 6. Union with God in Marriage & Family Life	193

CONCLUSION   207

APPENDIX A: CHRISTIAN MARRIAGE DISCIPLESHIP CHECK-UP   209

APPENDIX B: GROUP DISCUSSION QUESTIONS   219

NOTES   227

PERMISSIONS   247

ACKNOWLEDGMENTS   249

ABOUT THE AUTHOR   251

Introduction

Have any of you readers fallen in love with a dimple, and then you married the *whole person,* and now you are trying to deal with this?[1] If so, don't panic. Once upon a time in a Garden of Love in a faraway land a young woman and a young man vowed to love and cherish one another for all the days of their lives, and they lived happily ever after, and we Catholics and other Christians can too. This ecumenical Catholic Christian marriage guide is for engaged and married Christians (and non-Christians too!) who believe or at least hope that living happily ever after does not have to be just a fairy tale in our American land, with so many marriages ending in divorce.

It may not be easy to be happily married. Many of us or our friends have suffered from stormy marriage relationships, bitter divorce proceedings, and prolonged child custody battles. The number of children under 18 whose parents have divorced increased in recent decades from under 1% to over 50%.[2] No wonder many young adults have shied away from marriage! One of my college students writes, "I am afraid to be married. I don't want to get divorced. As a child I promised myself I would never put another person through what I had to go through when my parents divorced. To this day that's why I am not married, and that's why I have no children. I have had the same boy friend for ten years."

How can we Christian couples be happily married in what has been called our American Divorce Culture?[3] What is the Christian Way to marriage and family happiness? Communicating well? Resolving conflicts? Dealing with gender, personality, and cultural differences? Kindling the romance?

1

No. These communication and relationship skills have helped many of us a great deal, but they have not always helped enough. Many psychologists and other marriage authorities have been promoting these skills for over half a century now in what has been called our American Psychological Society,[4] but *it is during this very time that divorce rates have skyrocketed!* We Christian couples need something more powerful than psychology's communication and relationship skills. What more do we need?

CHRISTIAN MARRIAGE DISCIPLESHIP

We need to follow Jesus with faith, love, wisdom, and other Christian virtues and gifts. With Christian faith, we believe that Jesus is the Son of God and we trust that he loves and forgives us repentant sinners. With Christian love, we love our partner as much as possible as Jesus loves us, with a love that is always patient and kind (1 Cor. 13:4–7). With this love, we treat our partner well, with patience, kindness, wisdom, and other Christian virtues. *This faithful, loving, virtuous Christian marriage discipleship is the Christian Way to happiness in marriage and family life.*

This Christian Way to marriage and family happiness is good for non-Christians too. It is good for all of us couples to love our partner and treat our partner well, with wisdom, patience, and other Christian virtues. This guide's Christian marriage guidance can be helpful for non-Christians who admire Jesus even though they may not believe that he is the Son of God. Non-Christians could follow Jesus in a limited way as a moral teacher or role model, if not as the Son of God. Surveys show that Americans of all faiths admire Jesus.[5] Mahatma Gandhi says that Jesus belongs to all people.[6]

THE IMITATION OF CHRIST

Are we Christian couples following Jesus as much as we could in our marriage and family life? Maybe. But maybe not. Pope Benedict XVI warns that secularism, materialism, and moral relativism have weakened the discipleship of many Catholics and other Christians in the Western world.[7] Is the Pope right?

We Christian couples can check our Christian discipleship by turning to Jesus and Christian saints and spiritual reformers. Jesus teaches that we should follow him not only by believing that he is the Son of God and trusting that he loves and forgives us repentant sinners, but also by turning away from our sins and amending our life. We turn away from our sins and amend our life in an authentic Biblical sense by becoming like Jesus in our moral character and conduct, with love, wisdom, and other Christian virtues. St. Paul urges the Ephesians "to imitate God [. . .] and follow Christ by loving as he loved you" (Eph. 5:1–2). St. John teaches likewise that "we can be sure that we are in God only when the one who claims to be living in him is living the same kind of life as Christ lived" (1 John 2:5–6). Thomas à Kempis writes in *Of the Imitation of Christ* that we follow Jesus by imitating his life and virtues.[8] Pope John Paul II holds in his theology of the body that the fundamental vocation for all Christians is to follow Jesus by becoming like him in their moral character and conduct.[9]

Jesus calls us Christian couples to become like him not only during prayer, worship, and other religious activities, but also during ordinary marriage and family activities like managing the family money and dealing with the housework. If we do not follow Jesus when we manage the family money and deal with the housework, are we true followers of Jesus? St. Teresa of Avila says that we find Jesus among the pots and pans.

This imitation-of-Christ, pots-and-pans Christian marriage discipleship is the Christian Way to happiness in marriage and family life.

Becoming like Jesus is a tall order! But that's o.k. Many of us couples have already become more like Jesus in our marriage and family life. What's more, some of us may suspect that we could become even more like Jesus, and we may be willing to go for it. We may be willing to go for an even more Christ-like marital love that is even more patient and kind, with little or no anger, fighting, or other hurtful conflict. We may be willing to follow Jesus farther along the Christian Way not only to happiness in marriage and family life, but also to holiness.

CHRISTIAN HOLINESS

We couples can set our sights on holiness. We are already holy in the basic sense of being created in the image of God. But many of us are impure, imperfect images of God, and we are called to become pure, transformed images of God. We are called to become holy in the deep sense of becoming extraordinarily loving, virtuous, Christ-like persons.

At the beginning of this 21st century, Pope John Paul II called for Catholic parishes to provide training in holiness for all parishioners. John

Paul wrote that all the Christian faithful "are called to the fullness of the Christian life and to the perfection of charity." John Paul added that "the time has come to repropose wholeheartedly to everyone this *high standard of ordinary Christian living.*"[10]

CHRISTIAN HAPPINESS

Some of us couples might hem and haw about going for the high standard of becoming like Jesus in our moral character and conduct. We might be afraid that we would have to sacrifice our happiness too much. But we need not be afraid. Becoming like Jesus might require us to sacrifice a worldly happiness at times, but it would not require us to sacrifice a Christian happiness. Christian happiness consists largely of following Jesus virtuously in this life and being united with God in a limited way in this life and then eternally. With this Christian happiness, we follow Jesus virtuously and we are happy at the same time, as we will see (I,1—Part I, Chapter 1, and IV,1–6—Part IV, Chapters 1–6).

St. Paul and many other Christians have envisioned a virtuous Christian happiness in this life. Paul writes to the Philippians: "I want you to be happy, always happy in the Lord. [. . .] Fill your minds with everything that is true, everything that is noble, everything that is good and pure, [. . .] and everything that can be thought virtuous or worthy of praise. [. . .] Then the God of peace will be with you" (Phil. 4:4–9). Pope Benedict XVI teaches that obedience to God is the way to happiness.[11] Benedict says that the virtuous life is the most joyful life.[12]

We Christian couples are called to seek a virtuous Christian happiness, not just a worldly happiness. We would be more likely to seek the Christian happiness if we heard more about it. But many of us hear more about the worldly happiness that is promoted in our American consumer society than the Christian happiness that is prized in our Christian tradition. Some of us seek a worldly happiness more than a Christian happiness without even realizing it. We put our worldly happiness goals ahead of our Christian happiness goal of following Jesus with love, wisdom, and other Christian virtues. Suppose that a Christian stock broker put his worldly happiness goals of making a million dollars in the stock market and buying a multi-million-dollar estate in Beverly Hills ahead of his Christian happiness goal of following Jesus virtuously. He might spend so much time pursuing his worldly happiness goals that he would neglect his wife and children.

Bishop Arthur Brazier, pastor of the Apostolic Church of God in Chicago, says that many couples in his marriage counseling focus on their individual worldly happiness so much that they neglect the needs of their family.[13] Brazier could advise these couples to seek an individual *Christian* happiness that could include pursuing their individual goals, meeting their family's needs, following Jesus virtuously, and being happy all at the same time. But Brazier and many other marriage authorities today do not say enough about Christian happiness.

STAGES OF GROWTH IN CHRISTIAN MARRIAGE DISCIPLESHIP

It may not always be easy to be happy in the Christian sense of becoming like Jesus in our moral character and conduct. But that's o.k. Few of us will become saints today, tomorrow, or by the end of the year. But all of us have the potential to become increasingly loving, Christ-like, virtuously-happy persons gradually over the years, with God's help.

We couples can grow gradually towards Christian ideals of love, happiness, and holiness. Many saints and spiritual reformers have identified beginning, intermediate, and advanced stages of Christian moral and spiritual growth. They have often emphasized growth in love for God during prayer and other religious activities, however, more than growth in marital love for one's partner during ordinary marriage and family activities. This guide applies some of their insights on moral and spiritual growth to everyday marriage and family life. This guide draws from Jesus, St. Paul, St. Thomas Aquinas, St. John of the Cross, St. Thérèse of Lisieux, John Wesley, Dietrich Bonhoeffer, and other saints and spiritual reformers in order to recover and develop a theory of growth in Christian marital love and discipleship that is both faithful to the Christian tradition and relevant for contemporary marriage and family life.

Here's the theory. We couples can grow from a romantic love and wisdom that help make us emotionally happy in a beginning romantic stage of Christian marriage discipleship (Part II of this guide) to a conventional needs love and wisdom that help make us conventionally happy in an intermediate needs stage (Part III) and finally to a Christ-like transforming love and wisdom that help make us virtuously happy in an advanced transforming stage (Part IV). We will focus on growth in love and wisdom, but we will touch upon faith, patience, gratitude, and other Christian virtues too.

Let's not go overboard applying these stages of Christian marriage discipleship to specific persons, including ourselves and our partner. These stages represent broad generalizations that come with many qualifications and exceptions. Still, knowing about these stages could help us know roughly where we are now in our Christian marriage discipleship and where we could go next. We might have trouble if we did not know these things. Author Laurence Peter writes, "If you don't know where you are going, you will probably end up somewhere else."[14]

CONVENTIONAL MARRIAGE GUIDANCE

We Christian couples need plenty of Christian marriage guidance centered around God and virtue in order to get where we are going in our Christian marriage discipleship. We do not get enough Christian marriage guidance from secular marriage authorities today, however. Few of these authorities say much about Christian discipleship, Christian happiness, and Christian virtues. Social critic Barbara Whitehead argues in *The Divorce Culture* that today's mainstream marriage guidance neglects religious and civic virtues that help bind couples together, including the virtues of "forgiveness, modesty, gratitude, loyalty, patience, generosity, and selflessness."[15]

Few secular marriage authorities encourage us couples strongly enough to strive for Christian ideals of love, happiness, and holiness. Many authorities emphasize that most of us cannot help being unloving at times. Psychologists Kinder and Cowan say that marriage can "elicit the most intense feelings of anger, hatred, and even violence."[16] Kinder and Cowan explain that marriage "involves interdependencies and mutual needs, and threats to them can lead to enormous insecurity and retaliatory feelings. Fighting is a *normal and inherent part* [my italics] of any bond that is so meaningful to the parties involved."[17]

I suppose that angry, hateful, and violent fighting could be a "normal" part of "normal" marriages. But this fighting is not an "inherent," inevitable part of all marriages. We couples have the potential to love our partner as Jesus loves us, with no angry, hateful, or violent fighting. Kinder and Cowan do not account adequately for our tremendous human and Christian potential for a Christ-like marital love that is always patient and kind.

Most *Christian* marriage authorities provide more Christian marriage guidance, but not always enough of it. According to Dana Mack in a study of marriage preparation programs for teenagers in over 2,000 public and church middle schools and high schools nationwide, most church school programs offered much the same communications training that was offered in the public school programs, and little else. Mack argues that both the secular and Christian programs needed to go beyond communications training to provide more moral and spiritual marriage guidance.[18]

Donald Browning, Thomas Oden, and some other Christian scholars criticize some of their fellow Christians for "mimicking" current psychological trends and neglecting "their own wisdom traditions."[19] Catholic author Matthew Kelly writes in *Rediscovering Catholicism* that after Vatican II many Catholic priests and educators stopped preaching and teaching about holiness. They thought that holiness was an unrealistic and unattainable ideal that often made people feel guilty, so they tried to make things easier for people by watering down holiness or throwing it out.[20]

Author George Bernard Shaw is even more skeptical about holiness. He writes that Jesus "has not been a failure yet; for nobody has ever been sane enough to try his way."[21]

CHRISTIAN DISCIPLESHIP MARRIAGE GUIDANCE

Let's not pour cold water on Christian ideals of love, happiness, and holiness. I am optimistic about Christianity, including Christian love and marriage. The saints have been extraordinarily loving, Christ-like persons. What's more, we ordinary couples can become increasingly loving, Christ-like persons gradually over the years, with God's help. Let's set our sights optimistically on moral excellence instead of pessimistically on moral mediocrity; on the imitation of Christ instead of living like the rest of the world; on sanctity instead of "normalcy"; and on Christian hopefulness instead of a worldly skepticism. Let's see what we *can* do, with the help of Jesus. Let's not sell ourselves short, and let's not sell Jesus short!

It may help to know that most of us couples are already on the right Christian marriage discipleship track that includes growth from romantic love to needs love to a Christ-like transforming love. What's more, many of us already understand reasonably well how to grow from romantic love to the needs love that many conventional marriage authorities tell us about. We might not understand as well, however, how to grow farther to the Christ-like transforming love that Jesus and many saints and spiritual reformers tell us about. That's where this marriage guide comes in. This guide supplements, enhances, and sometimes corrects today's conventional marriage guidance in order to help couples grow not only from romantic love to needs love, but also from needs love to a Christ-like transforming love. We couples do not hear nearly enough these days about growth from needs love to transforming love.[22]

This guide's Christian growth-centered marriage guidance improves upon today's conventional problem-centered marriage guidance. Many marriage authorities today advise us couples to negotiate and use other communication and relationship skills in order to deal with marital problems and differences effectively. We could use these skills to deal with marital problems and differences, however, without necessarily growing in love, wisdom, and other Christian virtues. Suppose that a couple disagreed about partying and shopping. Suppose that the husband wanted to party more often with his single male and female friends on weekends, and his wife wanted to borrow more money for shopping. The partying husband and shopping wife might negotiate an agreement that the husband could party more often on weekends and his wife could borrow more money for shopping. The husband and wife might be happy with their negotiations, but they would not necessarily be growing in love, wisdom, and other Christian virtues. Who knows, the wife might become a shopaholic, and her husband might commit adultery.

This guide's Christian growth-centered marriage guidance includes practical problem-centered guidance too. We will explore growth in love, wisdom, and other Christian virtues in the practical context of dealing with marital problems and differences. Growing in these virtues is often the best way to deal with marital problems and differences over the long haul. Loving, wise, Christ-like couples usually deal with marital problems and differences better than unloving, foolish, un-Christ-like couples do!

INTEGRATING HAPPINESS & HOLINESS

This guide's Christian marriage guidance is not only growth-centered, but also educational. The word "disciple" means student. We Christian couples are students of Jesus. We need to learn from Jesus about Christian marriage discipleship, including how to integrate happiness and holiness in our marriage and family life.

It may not be easy to learn from Jesus how to integrate happiness and holiness. We may be misled by philosophers, psychologists, and other authorities these days who insist that happiness and holiness often conflict, so we human beings *cannot always be completely happy and completely holy at the same time.*[23]

Jesus, the apostles, and many saints and spiritual reformers, however, tell us couples that we *can* integrate happiness and holiness. Holiness can be our happiness! An Old Testament psalmist prays, "Happy are those who dwell in your house" and "Happy are those who find refuge in you" (Ps. 84:5–6—NAB; see Matt. 5:1–12; John 15:11; 2 Cor. 1:24). Jesus teaches that the poor in spirit, the gentle, the merciful, the peacemakers, and the pure in heart are blessed (Matt. 5:3–9), and many Christians have identified this blessedness with happiness, and rightly so—as we will see throughout this guide.

This guide recovers the teachings of Jesus and many saints and spiritual reformers that true happiness consists of holiness. To recover, defend, and promote this holy Christian happiness—together with a Christian philosophy of life, virtue ethic, and marital spirituality in general—this guide draws not only from the Bible and other Christian classics, but also from many popular and scholarly sources in spirituality, theology, philosophy, psychology, sociology, literature, and other areas. We couples need wise hearts as well as loving hearts in order to understand and follow the holy Christian Way to be happily married in our Psychological Society and Divorce Culture.

ECUMENICAL CHRISTIAN MARRIAGE GUIDANCE

This guide's Christian marriage guidance is also ecumenical. Many of us Christians need ecumenical Christian marriage guidance for the religiously and culturally mixed marriages in our pluralistic and multicultural American society. Journalist Jill Smolowe writes that America has produced "the greatest variety of hybrid households in the history of the world."[24] She notes that if "the daughter of Japanese and Filipino parents marries the son of German and Irish immigrants, together they may beget a Japanese-Filipino-German-Irish-Buddhist-Catholic-American child."[25]

We Christians can dialogue with Jews, Muslims, Buddhists, and other people to develop common ideals of love, wisdom, and other virtues that can strengthen our marriages and families. Pope Paul VI writes that we Catholics want to join with various non-Christian religions in "promoting and defending common ideals in the spheres of religious liberty, human brotherhood, education, culture, social welfare, and civic order."[26]

HOW TO USE THIS GUIDE

It is important for you the readers to apply your understanding of Christian marriage discipleship in general to your own marriage and family life in particular. You can do this informally as you read this guide, or you can do this more systematically by using the "Christian Marriage Discipleship Check-Up Worksheet" in Appendix A at the end of the guide. The worksheet can help you check your Christian marriage discipleship, much as you might check your finances and health.

The worksheet has ten questions about your relationship with your partner on the following ten important aspects of marriage and family life: 1) communication; 2) money; 3) friends and relatives; 4) personality; 5) gender, cultural, and religious differences; 6) sex and intimacy; 7) housework and other family work; 8) education and careers; 9) prayer, worship, and other religious activities; and 10) parenting.

Completing the worksheet could help you and your partner determine where you are following Jesus virtuously now in your marriage and family life, and where you could follow Jesus more virtuously in the future. You and your partner could get ideas for dealing with specific marital problems and differences with love, wisdom, and other Christian virtues.

You could complete the worksheet now and/or later after you have read more of the guide or the whole guide.

There are also discussion questions in Appendix B for use in marriage enrichment workshops, Bible study classes, marriage and family classes, and other groups that deal with marriage, Christian discipleship, Christian spirituality, or other related areas.

This guide's Biblical references are to the New Jerusalem Bible (NJB)[27] unless otherwise noted: NRSV (New Revised Standard Version);[28] REB (Revised English Bible);[29] NAB (New American Bible).[30]

CONCLUSION

The Christian Way for us couples to be happily married is to follow Jesus with love, wisdom, and other Christian virtues during our ordinary marriage and family activities. This virtuous Christian Way to be happily married is timely as well as timeless, for there has been a revival of virtue ethics in recent decades. The time is right for more emphasis upon Christian virtues in our marriage guidance. The time is right for marriage authorities to catch up with many of us couples who have always known that we could strengthen our marriages and families with good, old-fashioned Christian virtues. Some of the virtuous ingredients in popular "recipes" for a happy marriage are 3 cups of love, 2 cups of kindness, 1 cup of courtesy, 4 spoonfuls of hope, 1 pint of faith, and generous portions of patience, respect, and other Christian virtues.

In spite of the recent revival of Christian virtue ethics and the common-sense appeal of Christian virtues, many marriage authorities today continue to emphasize much the same old communication and relationship skills that have been promoted for decades. These marriage authorities do not envision a Christian approach to marriage centered around God and virtue that could transform our marriages and families in this 21st century.

This guide offers Christian marriage guidance for those of you Catholics and other Christians—and non-Christians too—who would like to follow Jesus in your marriage and family life in the authentic Biblical sense of becoming more and more like Jesus in your moral character and conduct, with love, wisdom, and other Christian virtues. *The best thing that you can do for yourself, for your partner, and for your marriage is to follow Jesus in this virtuous Christian way!*

Many of you Christian couples may already be following Jesus with the support of fellow Christians in Bible study classes, prayer groups, lay religious orders, and other groups concerned with Christian discipleship in general. This guide can help you apply your Biblical, prayerful Christian discipleship in general to your marriage and family life in particular. This guide can help you strengthen your Christian *marriage* discipleship.

This guide often addresses married couples, but it is meant for you engaged couples too. The best way to prepare for your marriage is to begin following Jesus now before you marry so you can continue following Jesus after you marry, beginning on the first day of your married life—before it is too late!

We Christian couples can picture our Christian marriage discipleship (or "engagement discipleship") as a mental, emotional, and spiritual journey with Jesus through a Garden of Love in our soul. The Calvinist revivalist preacher Jonathan Edwards (1703–1758) compares a soul that is holy to a garden with beautiful flowers: "Holiness [. . .] made the soul like a field or garden of God, with all manner of pleasant flowers; that is all pleasant, delightful, and undisturbed; enjoying a sweet calm, and the gently vivifying beams of the sun."[31]

It does not matter where we begin our journey with Jesus through the Garden of Love in our soul. We may begin mostly with romantic love, mostly with needs love, mostly with transforming love, or with some combination of these. It matters only that we set out upon this journey. Jesus teaches, "I am the light of the world; anyone who follows me will not be walking in the dark; he will have the light of life" (John 8:12).[32]

Yes, we couples can live happily ever after in our Psychological Society and Divorce Culture, even if we fall in love with a dimple and marry the whole person. We just need to follow Jesus along the Christian Way to happiness and holiness in marriage and family life.

Part I
The Christian Way to be Happily Married

*A*s a Catholic, I believe that marriage is a sacrament that signifies the presence of Jesus. In the sacrament of marriage, Jesus calls us Catholic marriage partners to love one another with a Christian love, not just a worldly love. Jesus calls us to love one another as he loves us, for it is by our love for one another that people will know that we are his disciples (John 13:34–35). The Second Vatican Council (1962–65) declared that the full consummation of the sacrament of marriage requires the mutual exchange of a couple's Christian love for one another, not just a physical act of sexual intercourse.[33] In the sacrament of marriage, Jesus calls us Catholic couples to follow him in a loving Christian marriage discipleship.

To follow Jesus in a loving Christian marriage discipleship, we couples need to understand the primary, overall Christian Happiness goal of this discipleship (Chapter 1 below) and the Christian Way to pursue this goal during the romantic, needs, and transforming stages of this discipleship (Chapter 2).

In this Part I, let's get a bird's eye view of the Christian Happiness goal of Christian marriage discipleship and the Christian Way to pursue this goal. Then let's look more closely at the romantic, needs, and transforming stages of Christian marriage discipleship in Parts II, III, and IV respectively.

chapter 1

Christian Happiness

W E CHRISTIAN COUPLES NEED TO UNDERSTAND the primary, overall goal of Christian marriage discipleship. Where are we going in our journey with Jesus?

THE GOAL OF CHRISTIAN MARRIAGE DISCIPLESHIP

The primary, overall goal of Christian marriage discipleship includes an ultimate goal for eternity and an immediate goal for this life. The ultimate goal for eternity is to be united with God the Father, Son, and Holy Spirit eternally. The immediate goal for this life is to follow Jesus by becoming like him in our moral character and conduct, with love, wisdom, faith, and other Christian virtues and gifts. The immediate goal for this life, in short, is to follow Jesus virtuously.

Following Jesus virtuously helps unite us with God in a limited way in this life, so the immediate goal for this life *includes* the limited union with God that comes with following Jesus virtuously.

The primary, overall goal of Christian marriage discipleship, then, is to follow Jesus virtuously in this life and to be united with God in a limited way in this life and then eternally. The primary, overall goal of Christian marriage discipleship, in short, is God and virtue.

Jesus calls us Christian couples to put the primary God-and-virtue goal of Christian marriage discipleship first, ahead of all our other secondary goals. Sometimes, though, we might put our secondary goals first. A Christian wife put her secondary goal of redecorating the living room ahead of God and virtue. She browbeat her husband into getting a second job on weekends so he could make enough money to redecorate the living room—even though he was already severely stressed out from working overtime on his regular full-time job. The browbeating wife did not respond to her husband lovingly and follow Jesus virtuously. She did not put God and virtue first.

Bernard Haring, Josef Fuchs, and some other Christian theologians characterize the choice to put God and virtue first in our life as a "fundamental option."[34] Christian marriage discipleship is about the fundamental option or choice to put God and virtue first in our marriage and family life, ahead of everything else. When we put God and virtue first, we put ourselves first too, that is, our best, most virtuous, Christ-like self.

Many Christian marriage preparation and enrichment programs do not deal adequately with the primary God-and-virtue goal of Christian marriage discipleship. In the first lesson of a popular Catholic marriage preparation program, Catholic couples are asked to discuss their goals and "dreams" about such things as their talents, careers, and friends. This lesson about goals, however, *does not even mention the most important goal of all,* that is, to follow Jesus virtuously in this life and to be united with God in this life and eternally.[35]

It might seem that most of us Christian couples would already know the primary God-and-virtue goal of Christian marriage discipleship, so we would not need to learn more about it. Maybe. But maybe not. Catholic author Matthew Kelly argues that "the greatest tragedy of modern Catholicism is the dilution and destruction of the goal of the Christian life."[36] Kelly maintains that "the great majority of Catholics do not know the goal of the Christian life."[37]

A Catholic college student did not know the goal of the Christian life. She said, "I'm a Catholic. So the meaning of life for me is just to enjoy ourselves."[38]

Let's not reduce Christian marriage discipleship to "enjoying ourselves." Let's look more closely at the God-and-virtue goal of Christian marriage discipleship. To get the ball rolling, let's see how this goal relates to happiness.

HAPPINESS AS THE PRIMARY GOAL OF HUMAN LIFE

Most of us couples want to be happy, and rightly so. Do God and virtue make us happy?

I use the word "happiness" in the ancient Greek philosophical sense and the traditional Christian religious sense of the primary, overall goal of human life. The primary, overall goal of human life is to be happy. But what is happiness, and what makes us happy? Does pleasure make us happy? Do wealth, power, good looks, and other worldly goods make us happy? Do God and virtue make us happy?

Most of us Christian couples believe that God makes us happy in heaven, with an eternal Christian Happiness. But what about being happy in this life? Does following Jesus virtuously make us happy in this life?

Some of us might not be sure about this. We might identify Christian Happiness with eternal happiness more than with happiness in this life. Many of us Catholics were taught in our Baltimore Catechism years ago that God made us to know, love, and serve him in this life, and to be happy with him in the next life, with a "heavenly" happiness.[39] The Baltimore Catechism did not say enough about Christian Happiness in this life.

Many authorities today, like the Baltimore Catechism in the past, identify Christian Happiness with eternal happiness, but not so much with happiness in this life. On the ABC television special, "The Mystery of Happiness," moderator John Stossel said that "not long ago, most people believed that your only chance for happiness came after you died, if you got to heaven."[40] According to Stossel, most people did not think that they could be happy in this life until about 200 years ago when technology began to make life less "brutal" and more desirable. Then people began to pursue happiness in this life as one of their main goals, and people still do this today.[41]

CONVENTIONAL HAPPINESS

What kind of happiness in this life do we Christian couples pursue these days? It might seem that we would pursue a Christian Happiness. But we do not necessarily do this. Many of us get our ideas about happiness from secular authorities in our Psychological Society and Divorce Culture more than from Jesus, saints, and scholars in our Christian tradition. The speakers on the "Mystery of Happiness" television program discussed above did not even mention Christian Happiness in this life. Many speakers promoted a "new science of happiness" that many social, behavioral, and natural scientists have been developing in recent years. Many of us couples are learning about this new science of happiness from self-help books; public and private schools, including college psychology classes on happiness; magazine articles, such as *Time* magazine's "The New Science of Happiness";[42] academic journals, such as psychology's *Journal of Happiness Studies*; television programs, such as "The Mystery of Happiness"; and many other sources. Today's new "scientific" concepts of happiness are replacing traditional Christian concepts of happiness.[43] Let's look at these new concepts of happiness more closely.

Many happiness authorities in the social, behavioral, and natural sciences are defining happiness as a state of mental and emotional well-being that consists of satisfaction with one's life and pleasant or positive emotions with an absence of unpleasant or negative emotions.[44] I call this a "Conventional Happiness."

The Conventional Way to be conventionally happy is often described in terms of *satisfying our desires for worldly goods*, such as desires for a backyard swimming pool, a rewarding career, and a comfortable retirement.

The Conventional Way to be conventionally happy is described also in terms of *pursuing our goals with sufficient success*. A Christian wife with a goal of becoming the Chief Executive Officer (CEO) of a Fortune 500 company might need to achieve her CEO goal in order to be conventionally happy.

THE SUBJECTIVITY OF CONVENTIONAL HAPPINESS

There are serious problems with this Conventional Happiness. For one thing, this happiness is subjective. We decide for ourselves, subjectively, what makes us happy and whether we are happy. Philosopher Rosalind Hursthouse observes that most philosophers today and most other people believe that happiness is subjective, so "it is for me, not for you, to pronounce on whether or not I am happy, [. . .] and barring, perhaps, cases of advanced self-deception and the suppression of unconscious misery, if I think I am happy, then I am—it is not something I can be wrong about."[45]

Suppose that happiness is indeed something subjective that we cannot be wrong about. Then there is a serious Christian morality problem with this subjective Conventional Happiness. The Christian wife discussed above could decide for herself, subjectively, that she would be happy being the CEO of a Fortune 500 company even if she slept with members of the company's governing board in order to achieve her CEO goal. Then she would be conventionally happy without necessarily following Jesus virtuously or being united with God. God and virtue would be left out of her Conventional Happiness.

God and virtue are not left out of true happiness, including true Christian Happiness. We Christians—together with all other human beings—cannot be truly happy without God and virtue. True happiness is not whatever we happen to say that it is, subjectively. True happiness is what it is, objectively, as a reality of human nature. The reality of human nature is that the primary goal of human life that makes every one of us human beings truly happy is to become virtuous, Christ-like persons in this life and to be united with God in a limited way in this life and then eternally. The primary goal of human life that makes us truly happy, in short, is God and virtue.

We Christian couples are called to seek an objective Christian Happiness centered around God and virtue instead of a subjective Conventional Happiness centered around whatever we happen to think pleases us.

CHRISTIAN HAPPINESS IN THIS LIFE

Let's look at Christian Happiness more closely now, especially the virtue component of this happiness. We can deal later with the union-with-God component of Christian Happiness (IV,6).

St. Thomas Aquinas distinguishes between a perfect Christian Happiness that consists of being united with God eternally and an imperfect Christian Happiness in this life that consists of following Jesus with faith, love, and other Christian virtues.[46] St. Peter refers to a Christian Happiness of this virtuous sort in a letter to the Christian faithful: "You did not see him [Jesus], yet you love him; and still without seeing him, you are already filled with a joy so glorious that it cannot be described" (1 Pet. 1:8). An Old Testament psalmist prays, "Happy are those who dwell in your house!" and "Happy are those who find refuge in you" (Ps. 84:5–6—NAB; see Matt. 5:1–12; John 15:11; 2 Cor. 1:24).

Many Christians have identified Christian Happiness in this life with following Jesus virtuously. St. Augustine identifies the happy life with blessedness.[47] Congregational preacher Henry Ward Beecher (1813–1887) writes that "the happiness of a man consists in finding out the way in which God is going, and going in that way too."[48] Lucille Taylor, a member of the Church of Jesus Christ of Latter-Day Saints, writes that joy and happiness "are virtues that come from within" and they "shine brightest in the light of faith, and in the services of brotherly love."[49] Mother Teresa tells a friend that she is happy being Jesus's "little spouse."[50] A popular Mexican saying refers to a virtuous happiness of this Christian sort: "The kind person and the noble person are familiar with happiness and make others happy as well."[51]

In recent times, some scholars have been recovering concepts of a virtuous happiness in this life not only from the Bible, St. Thomas Aquinas, and other traditional Christian sources, but also from Plato, Aristotle, and other ancient Greek philosophers.[52] Some of us Christian couples may need to develop our understanding of a virtuous Christian Happiness in this life so that we can pursue this Christian happiness instead of going for a subjective, "scientific," morally-problematic Conventional Happiness.

A DEFINITION OF CHRISTIAN HAPPINESS

Let's define Christian Happiness centered around God and virtue. For starters, Christian Happiness is not Conventional Happiness. Christian Happiness is not a state of mental and emotional well-being that consists of life satisfaction and pleasant or positive emotions with an absence of unpleasant or negative emotions. In this Conventional Happiness, God and virtue are often missing or put on the back burners. God and virtue are not missing in Christian Happiness. Christian Happiness is a state of *virtuous* mental, emotional, and *spiritual* well-being that consists of following Jesus virtuously in this life and being united with God in a limited way in this life and then eternally. Christian Happiness, in short, consists essentially of God and virtue.

In this definition of Christian Happiness, I use the word "spiritual" to refer to our experiences of God's presence, such as our experiences of grace, the presence of Jesus, and the indwelling of the Holy Spirit. Sometimes we may be conscious of God's presence and other times we may not be.

We have seen now that God and virtue are *both* the essence of Christian Happiness, as discussed immediately above, *and* the primary, overall goal of Christian marriage discipleship, as discussed in the beginning of this chapter (I,1). So we Christian couples can follow Jesus virtuously in our marriage and family life, be united with God, and be happy all at the same time.

CHRISTIAN HAPPINESS COMPARED TO CONVENTIONAL HAPPINESS

Let's compare Christian Happiness to Conventional Happiness in more detail. Let's see how a middle-aged Christian married couple, Bill and Maria, seek a Conventional Happiness during their vacation in San Diego, California, and let's compare the Conventional Happiness to the Christian Happiness that they should seek instead.

Bill desires to jet-ski with Maria in Mission Bay on the first day of their vacation in order to be conventionally happy, but Maria wants to visit the San Diego Museum of Art with Bill instead. Maria complains, "You have such harebrained ideas. You're no spring chicken. Why don't you act your age?" Bill counterattacks, "You have no sense of adventure. You're such a bore."

Bill and Maria are seeking a Conventional Happiness centered around jet-skiing, art-museum visits, and other worldly goods more than a Christian Happiness centered around God and virtue.

It might seem that we couples could turn to worldly goods *and* to God and virtue as the *two* main sources of our happiness. No such luck! Jesus does not let us take this easy way out. Jesus calls us to put him first as the *one* main source of our happiness. Jesus explains: "No one can serve two masters. He will either hate one and love the other, or be devoted to one and despise the other. You cannot serve God and mammon [worldly goods]" (Matt. 6:24—NAB).

St. Paul writes likewise to the Roman Christians that they cannot serve two masters. Paul explains that they are slaves of God, so they cannot be slaves of sin too:

> You know that if you agree to serve and obey a master you become his slaves. You cannot be slaves of sin that leads to death and at the same time slaves of obedience that leads to righteousness. You were once slaves of sin, but thank God you submitted without reservation to the creed you were taught. You may have been freed from the slavery of sin, but only to become 'slaves' of righteousness (Rom. 6:16–18).

Christian spiritual advisor Henry Foster (1821–1901) teaches likewise that we Christians "cannot afford to be double minded, to have a little of the Spirit of Christ and a little of the spirit of the world."[53] St. Augustine says that "Christ is not valued at all unless he be valued above all."[54]

BILL'S & MARIA'S SELFISHNESS

Most of us couples have some of the spirit of Christ, but we may have some of the spirit of the world too. Let's describe the spirit of the world in terms of selfishness, as Jesus, saints, and spiritual reformers often do. Bill and Maria fight selfishly about the jet-skiing and the art-museum visit. In what sense are they being selfish?

It might seem that Bill and Maria are being selfish in the sense of putting their individual interests and desires ahead of their partner's interests and desires. Bill puts his jet-skiing interests ahead of Maria's art-museum interests, and Maria likewise puts her interests ahead of Bill's interests.

Some Christians have characterized selfishness largely in these terms of putting our interests ahead of other people's interests, but I do not characterize selfishness mostly in this way. Suppose that selfishness was mostly putting our interests ahead of other people's interests. Then it seems that we would often need to sacrifice our interests in order to act unselfishly. But maybe we should not sacrifice our interests as often as we might think. The more we sacrifice our interests, the more we might help other people get *their* way, and then we might contribute to *their* selfishness. We might become permissive doormats, letting people step all over us.

Some psychologists and other authorities today warn us *not* to sacrifice our interests too much. Psychologists Rachael and Richard Heller encourage us to pursue our interests assertively with a "healthy" selfishness in order to develop our individual identity. They warn us not to sacrifice our interests so much that we do not know who we really are. They warn us not to identify ourselves mostly as someone else's son, daughter, husband, wife, and so on.[55]

This "healthy selfishness" is promoted daily in American newspapers, magazines, television programs, and other sources. Here are a few examples from magazine articles and news reports: "Why Selfish is Good" (*The Vauxhall* magazine, Autumn, 2004); "Selfishness: A Good Trait for Soccer Star" (*Plain Dealer*, January 15, 2005); and "Hudson Institute Defends U.S. Selfishness" (*U.S. Abroad.org News*, January 7, 2005).[56]

The Hellers and many other authorities today do distinguish appropriately between a supposedly healthy selfishness and a clearly unhealthy, self-indulgent selfishness. And these authorities do make some good points. But they give selfishness too much of a good name. Selfishness, properly understood, is a negative, unhealthy character trait, not a positive, healthy one. To understand why this is so, let's characterize selfishness not only in terms of our relationship with other people, but also in terms of our relationship with God. Selfishness involves above all putting our interests and our will ahead of *God's* interests and *God's* will—not just ahead of our neighbor's interests and our neighbor's will. After all, our neighbor's interests are sometimes unwise, and our neighbor's will is sometimes unloving. We should not necessarily put our neighbor's interests and will ahead of our own.

Maria should not necessarily put Bill's jet-skiing interests ahead of her art-museum interests in order to act "unselfishly." Bill's interest in pressuring Maria to jet-ski with him is unwise and unloving.

Maria, Bill, and all the rest of us Christian couples should always put God's interests and God's will ahead of our interests and our will. God's interests are always wise, and God's will is always loving. God wants all of us Christian couples to respond to our partner lovingly and follow Jesus virtuously, and we should want these things too. These are our true Christian interests, and we should always put them first.

Bill and Maria do not put their true Christian interests in God and virtue first, ahead of their jet-skiing and art-museum interests. That's why they are acting selfishly.

I will ordinarily use the word "selfishness" in this sense of putting our misguided interests, desires, and will for worldly goods ahead of God's will that we follow Jesus virtuously.

Selfishness is not always sinfulness. With sinfulness, we know that we are being sinful, but we choose to be sinful anyway, with a free choice. We are morally responsible for our sinfulness.

With selfishness, on the other hand, we might not always know that we are being selfish, and we might not always choose to be selfish, with a free choice. Some of us might have been shaped morally during our childhood by such things as misguided parents and what some scholars call an American Culture of Narcissism,[57] so we might be pretty selfish without realizing it. Then we might not be morally responsible for our selfishness. We would be morally responsible, however, for trying to identify and overcome any selfishness that we might have, with the help of Jesus.

In this guide, let's deal with selfishness more than sinfulness. Bill and Maria are selfish, but they are not necessarily sinful in the sense of being morally responsible for their selfishness. Let's leave judgments about people's sinfulness to God.

Bill and Maria might not realize that they are being selfish when they put their jet-skiing and art-museum interests ahead of God and virtue. After all, the jet-skiing and the art-museum visit that they desire are not bad things, and they desire these things for seemingly good reasons. Bill was neglected by his parents during his childhood, so he has low self-esteem. He wants to jet-ski and engage in other adventurous activities in order to bolster his low self-esteem and be happy. He takes pride in himself as an adventurous person.

Maria also has low self-esteem. She wants to visit art museums and engage in other educational activities in order to feel good about herself and be happy. She takes pride in herself as an educated person.

Bill and Maria need to deal with their low self-esteem, but they need to deal with their selfishness too. What's more, dealing with their selfishness could help them build their self-esteem. Suppose that they stopped fighting and started responding to one another more lovingly. Then they could feel better about themselves as more loving, Christ-like persons.

CONCLUSION

We Christian couples are called to seek a Christian Happiness centered around God and virtue instead of a Conventional Happiness centered around worldly goods. Bill and Maria would be much better off during their vacation in San Diego if they sought a Christian Happiness instead of a Conventional Happiness. To seek the Christian Happiness, they would let go of their selfish jet-skiing and art-museum desires in order to be happy responding to one another lovingly and following Jesus virtuously, with or without the jet-skiing and the art-museum visit. They would discuss their jet-skiing and art-museum interests lovingly without being anxious about getting their way. What would they decide to do? It would not matter, as long as they responded lovingly to one another in some reasonable way. They might decide to shop together on the first day of their vacation, to go their separate jet-skiing and art-museum ways on the second day, and to sunbathe together on the third day. They could still do most of the things they enjoyed doing, including jet-skiing and visiting the art museum. They would probably enjoy these things more without the fighting.

Bill, Maria, and all the rest of us couples would lose little and gain a lot by seeking a Christian Happiness instead of a Conventional Happiness, as we will see throughout this guide.

chapter 2

The Christian Way to Happiness

WE CHRISTIAN COUPLES NEED TO understand not only the Christian Happiness goal of Christian marriage discipleship, but also the Christian Way to pursue this goal.

The Christian Way to pursue a Christian Happiness differs significantly from the Conventional Way to pursue a Conventional Happiness. To be conventionally happy, we try to satisfy our desires for worldly goods, such as jet-skiing, art-museum visits, wealth, and power. We could satisfy our desires for worldly goods, however, without necessarily responding to our partner lovingly, following Jesus virtuously, and being united with God. God and virtue are often missing in the Conventional Way to a Conventional Happiness.

God and virtue are never missing in the Christian Way to a Christian Happiness. Christian Happiness consists essentially of God and virtue, including becoming like Jesus in our moral character and conduct, with love, wisdom, and other Christian virtues, as discussed above (I,1). To become like Jesus with love, wisdom, and other Christian virtues, we need to grow in these virtues. Growing in these virtues, then, is the Christian Way to a Christian Happiness. Let's see what St. Paul says about growing in these virtues.

PUTTING AWAY OUR OLD SELF & PUTTING ON A NEW, CHRIST-LIKE SELF

St. Paul discusses growth in Christian virtues in terms of putting away our old selfish, sinful self and putting on a new virtuous, Christ-like self.

Paul writes to the Ephesians, "You should put away the old self of your former way of life, corrupted through deceitful desires, and be renewed in the spirit of your minds, and put on the new self, created in God's way in righteousness and holiness of truth" (Eph. 4:22–24—NAB).

Wouldn't it be great if we could put on a new self without needing to put away our old self? But we cannot do this, and we should not try to do this. We should not try to put on a new self *over* our old self, like a Halloween mask, so that, as Jesus says about the scribes and Pharisees, we are "like whitewashed tombs that look handsome on the outside, but inside are full of dead men's bones and every kind of corruption" (Matt. 23:27).

Why must we put away our old self?

Partly because of Original Sin. As a Catholic, I believe that we human beings are born in a state of Original Sin. Original Sin is not personal sin that we are morally responsible for. Original Sin is a weak and imperfect state of human nature that we are born with. This weak and imperfect state of human nature includes not only an inclination to sin, but also a lack of grace and intimacy with God.[58]

We have an old self not only because we are born with a weak and imperfect human nature, but also because we grow up in a weak and imperfect environment, including our family and our society. Some of us grow up in a nurturing family with loving parents, but few of us grow up in a perfect family, much less in a perfect society. Some of us grow up in a troubled family with misguided parents who may weaken and damage us. Then we may need to put away our old weakened, damaged self in order to put on a new, more virtuous, Christ-like self.

Jesus teaches that we must renounce our [old] self in order to follow him (Matt. 16:24–25), and we must lose our [old] life in order to find our [new] life (Matt. 10:39). Jesus teaches that "unless a wheat grain falls on the ground and dies, it remains only a single grain; but if it dies, it yields a rich harvest" (John 12:24).

PURGATION, OR PURIFICATION

Many Christian saints, spiritual reformers, and mystics discuss putting away our old self and putting on a new self in terms of purgation. Some of them call purgation a beginning stage of Christian moral and spiritual growth that is followed by illumination and then union with God. During the beginning stage of purgation, we begin to be purged of faithlessness, hopelessness, hatred, selfishness, and other moral weaknesses so that we grow in faith, hope, love, and other Christian virtues. St. John of the Cross emphasizes that purgation continues during advanced stages of moral and spiritual growth.[59]

Purgation is often called purification. When we are purged of our moral weaknesses, we are purified, perfected, and transformed mentally, emotionally, and spiritually. We experience an increasingly pure faith, hope, love, and other Christian virtues.

ACTIVELY PURIFYING OURSELVES & PASSIVELY BEING PURIFIED BY GOD

We can play an active or passive role in our purification. We actively purify ourselves with our own human mental and emotional activity. Bill could actively purify his love for Maria by consciously letting go of his selfish jet-skiing desires in order to love Maria unselfishly, without desiring and demanding that she jet-ski with him in return for his love.

We play a passive role in our purification when God purifies us, with little or no purifying activity of our own.

We can separate the active and passive purifications for analytical and discussion purposes, but we cannot always separate them in real life. In real life, God purifies us and we purify ourselves, often at much the same time, so we play both active and passive roles in our purification.

Some contemplatives, mystics, and other Christian authorities on the spiritual life fail to account adequately for the active role that we Christians can play purifying ourselves. These authorities emphasize that we cannot purify ourselves by our efforts alone on account of our fallen human nature and the transcendence of God. These authorities say that we need God to purify us, and they are right about this. But then they go on to overemphasize the passive role that we play in our purification without accounting adequately for the active role that we can play. Psychiatrist Gerald May emphasizes that we human beings cannot do much to purify ourselves morally and spiritually, and he claims that St. John of the Cross and St. Teresa of Avila emphasize this too. May writes that "both John and Teresa pay relatively little attention to the active aspect of the spiritual life because they know from experience that our own autonomous efforts can accomplish very little. They are much more interested in the passive dimension, the work God does within us, seemingly beyond our will and intention."[60]

The fact of the matter is that we human beings can play an important *active* role purifying ourselves morally and spiritually not only during beginning stages of moral and spiritual growth, but also during advanced stages. What's more, St. John of the Cross, St. Teresa of Avila, and many other Christian contemplatives and mystics recognize this, as I have discussed in several scholarly articles on John's mystical theology.[61]

In this guide, let's see what we couples can do actively to purify ourselves, with God's help, during our ordinary marriage and family activities. Let's see how we can actively purify ourselves not only during the beginning romantic stage of Christian marriage discipleship, but also during the intermediate needs stage and the advanced transforming stage. We can have faith and trust that God is always with us spiritually, purifying us, helping us, doing his part, as we will see (IV,6).

ENJOYING A GOOD LIFE WITH PLENTY OF WORLDLY GOODS

Some of us couples might have second thoughts about actively putting away our old self, including selfish desires for jet-skiing, being CEO of a Fortune 500 company, or other worldly goods. We might be afraid that we would have to give up worldly goods too much if we let go of our selfish desires for them. But we do not need to be afraid. Ordinarily we may let go of selfish desires for worldly goods, put away our old self, and have plenty of worldly goods too—within reasonable limits, of course, without too much Las Vegas high rolling, conspicuous consumption,[62] or other extravagances. St. John of the Cross points out that we can let go of selfish desires for worldly goods without necessarily giving up the worldly goods themselves. John explains that it is our selfish desires for worldly goods that sometimes frustrate us, upset us, and prevent us from following Jesus virtuously—it is not the worldly goods themselves, so we may often have plenty of worldly goods.[63]

It is Bill's selfish jet-skiing desires that prevent him from responding to Maria lovingly and following Jesus virtuously—it is not the jet-skiing itself.

St. Paul points out likewise that it is the desire and love for money that is often called the root of all evils—it is not the money itself (1 Tim. 6:10). Ordinarily we may possess money and other worldly goods as long as we do not selfishly desire these worldly goods for our happiness. Ordinarily we may jet-ski, visit art museums, take our children to Disneyland, and enjoy a good life with plenty of worldly goods.

COSTLY GRACE

We have seen that the Christian Way for us couples to pursue the Christian Happiness goal of becoming like Jesus in our moral character and conduct is to put away our old self and put on a new, increasingly virtuous, Christ-like self. We put away our old self and put on a new self with what German Lutheran theologian Dietrich Bonhoeffer calls "costly grace" in his modern spiritual classic, *Discipleship*. Bonhoeffer distinguishes between "costly grace" and "cheap grace." The Christian with cheap grace does not put away his old self enough. He relies upon God to forgive his sins without amending his sinful ways. He does not "live a different life under grace from that under sin!" He lives "like the rest of the world!" His cheap grace is "grace without discipleship, grace without the cross, grace without the living, incarnate Christ."[64]

Christian couples with cheap grace are likely to follow the advice of some conventional marriage authorities who are skeptical about Christian love. These authorities do not advise us couples strongly enough to "live a different life under grace from that under sin." They insist that we cannot help being selfish. Author Toni Poynter advises couples not to expect to improve their behavior very much after they marry. Poynter assures couples that it is o.k. to fight a lot. She explains that married persons often do whatever they want even if their partner objects to this.[65]

It is true that many married persons often do whatever they want, selfishly, come hell or high water. But we loving couples should not do this. We should not call our partner a slob in front of our guests, hog the television set all night, or do whatever else we want in spite of our partner's objections to these things. We should amend our selfish ways after we marry if we have not done so before. Marriage may be our "last, best chance to grow up," as American clergyman Joseph Barth puts it.[66]

Admittedly it does cost us couples something to grow up in our marriage and family life. It costs our old self. We need to put away our old self. But we get a new, more virtuous, Christ-like self in return. That's a bargain, as we will see throughout this guide.

CHRISTIAN MORAL & SPIRITUAL GROWTH

When we couples put away our old self and put on a new self, we do not just remain as we are, living like the rest of the world, with cheap grace. Rather, we grow in faith, love, wisdom, and other Christian virtues. St. Paul praises the Thessalonians for growing in faith and love: "Your faith is growing so wonderfully and the love that you have for one another never stops increasing" (2 Thess. 1:3–4).

We can grow in faith, love, wisdom, and other Christian virtues gradually over the years at our own pace and God's pace. We do not need to become perfectly virtuous, Christ-like persons right now, presto, we're perfect.

It may not be easy to grow morally and spiritually. We should be patient with ourselves. François Fénelon, a Catholic Archbishop and spiritual director (1651–1715), writes in a letter to a friend:

> People who love themselves aright, even as they ought to love their neighbour, bear charitably, though without flattery, with self as with another. They know what needs correction at home as well as elsewhere; they strive heartily and vigorously to correct it, but they deal with self as they would deal with some one else they wished to bring to God. They set to work patiently, not exacting more than is practicable [sic] under present circumstances from themselves any more than from others, and not being disheartened because perfection is not attainable in a day.[67]

STAGES OF GROWTH IN CHRISTIAN MARRIAGE DISCIPLESHIP

It might be easier to be patient with ourselves if we realized that most people grow gradually in love, wisdom, and other Christian virtues, much as they grow gradually in other areas of human development. Scholars have identified stages of growth in thinking skills (Jean Piaget),[68] moral reasoning skills (Lawrence Kohlberg),[69] Christian faith (James Fowler),[70] and other areas.

This guide draws from the Bible and other Christian classics to recover and develop a theory of growth in Christian marriage discipleship that is both faithful to the Christian tradition and relevant for contemporary marriage and family life. The theory is that we Christian couples can grow from a romantic love, wisdom, and happiness during a beginning romantic stage of Christian marriage discipleship (II,1) to a conventional needs love, wisdom, and happiness during an intermediate needs stage (III,1) and finally to a Christ-like transforming love, wisdom, and happiness during an advanced transforming stage (IV,1–6), as noted above (Introduction 5).

Christian romantic lovers and needs lovers do not love their partner with a perfect Christian transforming love, so it might seem that neither romantic love nor needs love is a true Christian love. But most Christian romantic lovers and needs lovers experience Christian love to some extent, so let's deal with romantic love and needs love as stages of growth in Christian marital love. It is still Christian transforming love, however—not romantic love or needs love—that is a perfect or nearly perfect Christian love.

Many of us may not fit neatly into any one of these three stages of Christian marriage discipleship. But it can still help to be aware of these stages, much as it can help to be aware of stages of growth in other areas of human development, such as the Terrible Twos stage of child development. Knowing about the Terrible Twos could help us parents understand where our two-year-old child is now, psychologically speaking, and where he could go next. Likewise knowing about stages of growth in Christian marriage discipleship could help us Christian couples understand where we are now in our Christian marriage discipleship and where we could go next. If we did not know where we could go next, we might not go anywhere. As an old Mexican proverb says, "The person who cannot see ahead will stay behind."[71]

CHRISTIAN PRAYER & WORSHIP

We couples can grow in love, wisdom, and other Christian virtues not only during ordinary marriage and family activities, but also during prayer, worship, and other religious activities. The religious activities are an essential component of Christian marriage discipleship. This guide, however, focuses on the ordinary marriage and family activities.

We can separate religious activities and ordinary marriage and family activities for analytical and discussion purposes, but we cannot separate them in real life. In real life, religious activities and ordinary marriage and family activities often go together. For one thing, religious activities can often help us follow Jesus more virtuously in our marriage and family life.

It would take another book to deal with the ways that prayer, worship, and other religious activities could help us follow Jesus more virtuously in our marriage and family life. Let's look at a few simple ways that prayer could help us do this.

INTENSIVE PRAYER

Let's use a traditional definition of prayer as the raising of our minds and hearts to God, and let's distinguish between intensive prayer and extensive prayer. With intensive prayer, we raise our minds and hearts to God "at particular moments and under particular circumstances."[72] At particular moments and under particular circumstances, we might pray the Our Father or the Rosary.

Intensive prayer can help us couples follow Jesus virtuously in our everyday marriage and family life. Suppose that we said the Our Father and other prayers "intensively" for about ten minutes in the morning. Then we would be committing ourselves to following Jesus virtuously throughout the day, so we would probably be more likely to do so.

Catholic children receiving their first Holy Communion are encouraged to pray every morning that they will be with God during the day. The following morning prayer is included in a child's prayer book published in 1953, *First Steps to Jesus: A New Prayer Book for First Holy Communion*:

> As soon as I awake I say:
> Dear God, I thank You for this day.
> Wherever I go, whatever I do,
> I want to spend this day with You.
> Please, dear God, come into my heart,
> Our day together soon will start
> Bless me ever and ever again!
> I love you, dearest God. Amen.[73]

Here are a few commitments to following Jesus virtuously during the day that we adults could make in our morning prayers: "Thy kingdom come, Thy will be done"; "God, help me forgive others as readily as you have forgiven me" (see Eph. 4:32); "Jesus, help me speak kindly to my mother-in-law today instead of calling her stupid, as I did yesterday."

Of course we Christian couples should follow up our prayerful commitments to following Jesus virtuously during the day by actually doing so. Jesus teaches, "It is not those who say to me, 'Lord, Lord', who will enter the kingdom of heaven, but the person who does the will of my Father in heaven" (Matt. 7:21–22).

EXTENSIVE PRAYER

Extensive prayer, like intensive prayer, can help us Christian couples follow Jesus virtuously during our ordinary marriage and family activities. With extensive prayer, we raise our minds and hearts to God in a general way throughout the day. We may not always be consciously speaking to God or thinking about God, but we love God and we do his will throughout the day, so we live prayerfully in God's presence.[74] Jesus teaches that if we love God and do his will, Jesus and his Father will come to us and be with us: "If anyone loves me he will keep my word, and my Father will love him, and we shall come to him and make our home with him" (John 14:23).

Suppose that a husband was prayerfully raising his mind and heart to God in the general extensive sense of living in the presence of God throughout the day, and suppose that the husband's wife told him that she accidentally dented the fender of his new BMW convertible. The husband could continue prayerfully raising his mind and heart to God by responding to his wife lovingly. He could assure his wife that the dent in the fender did not matter, and he could invite her out for dinner. With his loving response, he would be prayerfully raising his mind and heart to God.

Christian marriage discipleship is profoundly prayerful. When we Christian couples follow Jesus virtuously during our ordinary marriage and family activities, we are prayerfully raising our minds and hearts to God in a general extensive way throughout the day. That's why this guide could help us enrich our prayer life even though the word "prayer" is not often used.

CONCLUSION TO PART I

We have acquainted ourselves briefly with Christian marriage discipleship, including the Christian Happiness goal of this discipleship and the Christian Way to pursue this goal by putting away our old self and putting on a new, increasingly virtuous, Christ-like self. Let's look now at the beginning romantic stage of Christian marriage discipleship.

Part II
The Beginning Romantic Stage of Christian Marriage Discipleship

A PACKET OF GROWING TOGETHER WILDFLOWER seeds reads, "Growing together, ordinary people can perform extraordinary feats." Growing together with Jesus, we ordinary couples can perform the extraordinary feat of becoming like Jesus in our moral character and conduct, with love, wisdom, and other Christian virtues. We can grow from a romantic love, wisdom, and happiness (this Part II) to a conventional needs love, wisdom, and happiness (Part III) and finally to a Christ-like transforming love, wisdom, and happiness (Part IV).

In these Parts II, III, and IV, we separate romantic lovers, needs lovers, and transformed lovers for analytical and discussion purposes, but we cannot separate them in real life. Few romantic lovers experience a 100% romantic love, wisdom, and happiness, with no needs or transforming love, wisdom, and happiness whatsoever. Likewise few needs lovers experience a 100% needs love, wisdom, and happiness, and few transformed lovers experience a 100% transforming love, wisdom, and happiness.

Some of us couples begin our relationship with a good deal of romantic love, wisdom, and happiness. I use the term "romantic love"—as many authorities do—to identify a somewhat selfish and immature love in marriage and other intimate relationships. If our love is more unselfish and mature, we are not romantic lovers in the technical sense that I am using this term, even though we may be very romantic in the conventional sense of whispering sweet nothings into our lover's ear.

Let's look first at some positive aspects of romantic love, wisdom, and happiness (Chapter 1). Then let's look at some problems with this love, wisdom, and happiness, including a CHRISTIAN MORALITY PROBLEM with the Emotional Happiness of romantic lovers (Chapter 2), an EMOTIONAL PROBLEM with romantic love (Chapter 3), and a FANTASY PROBLEM with romantic wisdom (Chapter 4). Romantic lovers need to become aware of these problems in order to nip the problems in the bud. Romantic lovers can overcome these problems by growing to a more mature needs love, wisdom, and happiness (Part III) or, better yet, to a Christ-like transforming love, wisdom, and happiness (Part IV).

chapter 1

The Emotional Happiness of Romantic Lovers

ROMANTIC LOVERS COMMIT THEMSELVES in Holy Matrimony to loving one another not only during good times, but also during bad times. Most of them, however, focus on the good times. They focus on sharing good, fun, romantic times with their partner that help them feel good emotionally, with an emotional happiness. Some psychologists and other authorities today characterize this happiness as a short-term or long-term experience of pleasant or positive emotions with an absence of unpleasant or negative emotions.[75] I call this an Emotional Happiness.

THE ROMANTIC WAY TO BE EMOTIONALLY HAPPY

With romantic love and wisdom, romantic lovers think that the way to be emotionally happy centers around satisfying their desires for worldly goods. Let's identify some different kinds of worldly goods that romantic lovers often pursue for their Emotional Happiness.

Romantic lovers often pursue material goods (for example, money and sex) and immaterial goods (knowledge and friendships). Material goods are often associated closely with man's lower physical, materialistic nature. Immaterial goods are often associated closely with man's higher mental, emotional, and spiritual nature.

Immaterial goods may be psychological (self-esteem), moral (patience), or spiritual (the Christian gift of prophecy). Some immaterial goods are psychological, moral, and spiritual at the same time (Christian transforming love).

The psychological goods may be mental (knowledge) and emotional (joy). The psychological goods may also be internal to us (such as the love that we experience within ourselves) or external to us (such as the love that other people experience for us).

Going back to worldly goods in general, they may also be sustaining or enhancing. Sustaining goods sustain our life. Some sustaining goods are food, water, freedom from acute and chronic pain, and minimally good health. Enhancing goods, on the other hand, promise to enhance and enrich our life in conventional ways. Some enhancing goods are wealth and friendships.

Many Christian authorities on the spiritual life focus on enhancing goods, and we will too. We will deal with minimally good health and other sustaining goods later (IV,2).

Worldly goods may also be apparent or real. An extramarital affair might seem good to a married man, but it would not be a real good. It would be an apparent good.[76]

Worldly goods, then, may be material, immaterial, psychological, moral, spiritual, internal, external, sustaining, enhancing, apparent, real, and the list could go on. Worldly goods, in short, are apparently or really good things that we may possess or experience in this world.

Romantic lovers may desire and pursue all these types of worldly goods for their Emotional Happiness. Many romantic lovers, however, are especially fond of material goods, including money and the material things that money can buy. According to *Kiplinger Magazine*'s 1997 Good Life Index, 5 million Americans went on a cruise in 1997; 3.3 million American homes had hot tubs; Americans had 60 million professional massages; and Americans consumed about 2,200,000 pounds of chocolate.[77] That's the materialistic good life that many romantic lovers desire for their Emotional Happiness!

There is a serious Christian Morality Problem with the Emotional Happiness of romantic lovers, as we will see (II,2). For now, though, let's look at some positive aspects of this Emotional Happiness, together with the romantic love and wisdom that often come with it.

SHARING GOOD TIMES

Many Christian romantic lovers are materialistic, as noted above, but they can still get off to a good start in their Christian marriage discipleship with their romantic love, wisdom, and happiness. They like to share good, fun, romantic times with their partner that help them feel good emotionally, and there is nothing wrong with this. My wife Arnell and I have enjoyed sharing good times for over 46 years now. During our high school and college dating years, Arnell baked snickerdoodles for me, I gave her stocks and other flowers, and once we pedal-boated a pleasant Sunday afternoon away on Mission Bay. I captured our good times in one of my amateur love poems:

> Snickerdoodles, stocks, and pedal boats,
> Were they ever missed?
> The world is full of strange and lonesome things,
> That smile when they are kissed.

We couples may sneak a kiss at the stoplight, walk together through botanical gardens, look at dream houses together, warm up one another's cold ears with our warm hands, and share other fun and romantic times that help us feel good emotionally.[78] We may kindle and rekindle the fun and romance in our relationship for all the days of our lives. That's an important part of treating our partner and ourselves well. That's an important part of Christian marriage discipleship.

POSITIVE-THINKING ROMANTIC WISDOM

Romantic lovers are not likely to share good times with a loving partner if they do not think positively about doing this. They need romantic wisdom of a positive-thinking sort to go with their romantic love. Positive thinkers Jack Canfield and Mark Hansen, authors of *Chicken Soup for the Soul*, advise people to think positively about their relationships and their life in general. Canfield and Hansen say that we all want the best of everything—we might want more money, a more gratifying sexual relationship, or true love.[79] Canfield and Hansen say that we can have all these things if we overcome our fears and think positively about getting them.[80]

Canfield and Hansen tell the positive-thinking success story of a positive thinker, Glenna, who seems to possess some traits of a romantic lover. Glenna was a single mother with three daughters, a house payment, and a car payment. She felt sorry for herself. But then she thought positively about getting the love and happiness that she desired. She put together a scrapbook with pictures of a good-looking man, a woman in a wedding gown and a man in a tuxedo, bouquets of flowers, diamond jewelry, a honeymoon on an island in the Caribbean, a lovely home, new furniture, and a woman vice-president of a large corporation. Soon, sure enough, she met a good-looking man driving a red and white Cadillac, they dated, and they married. Glenna's new husband Jim collected diamonds; Glenna and Jim honeymooned in the Caribbean; they bought a new house with new furniture; and Glenna was promoted to Vice-President of Human Resources in her company.[81] Glenna's positive-thinking romantic dreams came true!

Glenna shared not only good times with Jim, but also a good life of a materialistic sort. She identified the good life closely with material goods. She enjoyed the wedding gown, the flowers, the diamond jewelry, the lovely house with the new furniture, and other material goods.

PRAYERFUL ROMANTIC LOVERS

Many good-times, positive-thinking romantic lovers are not only fun-loving, but also prayerful. They pray in many different ways, much as needs lovers and transformed lovers do. Let's look at some different types of prayer that can help Christian romantic lovers and all the rest of us Christian couples grow in our Christian marriage discipleship.

We can classify prayer according to the purpose of the prayer. The purpose of prayer of adoration is to praise and glorify God. The purpose of prayer of thanksgiving is to express gratitude for our blessings. The purpose of prayer of contrition is to express sorrow for our sins. The purpose of prayer of petition, or intercession, is to ask for blessings for ourselves and others.

We can classify prayer in many other ways. We can distinguish between private prayer and communal prayer. We can distinguish between vocal prayer that involves expressing a prescribed set of words out loud or silently to ourselves (such as the Lord's Prayer) and mental prayer that involves using words spontaneously to express our thoughts, or not using any words at all. We can distinguish between meditation, which is largely mental (thinking), and contemplation, which is largely affective (loving).[82]

Praying in these ways can help Christian romantic lovers and all the rest of us Christian couples strengthen our relationship with God and grow in our Christian marriage discipleship.

Prayer, however, might not always help us grow in our Christian marriage discipleship. St. Francis de Sales points out in his *Introduction to the Devout Life* (1609) that prayer is not always a sign of "true devotion." Francis observes that a man might think that he is devout "because he recites daily a multiplicity of prayers, although immediately afterward he utters the most disagreeable, arrogant, and injurious words in his home and among his neighbors."[83]

St. Francis de Sales and many other Christian authorities on the spiritual life teach that prayer should be an expression of our Christian love for God and neighbor in order to be a sign of true devotion.[84] We Christian couples can strengthen our prayer by growing in love, faith, and other Christian virtues during our ordinary marriage and family activities, as discussed throughout this guide.

CONCLUSION

The good-times romantic love, the positive-thinking romantic wisdom, and the Emotional Happiness covered in this chapter can help some of us Christian couples get off to a good start in our Christian marriage discipleship. Some of us might suffer for years with negative attitudes that we are too fat to share good times with a loving partner, or too short, or too plain-looking. Nonsense! We can share good times with a loving partner for all the days of our lives.

chapter 2

The Christian Morality Problem with Emotional Happiness

ROMANTIC LOVERS CAN BEGIN A LOVING, happy marriage with their romantic love, wisdom, and happiness, as discussed above (II,1). But they should not stop here! They need to deal with the problems with their romantic love, wisdom, and happiness, including the Christian Morality Problem with their Emotional Happiness. The problem is that Emotional Happiness sometimes conflicts with Christian morality, and when it does, romantic lovers sometimes pursue their Emotional Happiness selfishly instead of responding to their partner lovingly and following Jesus virtuously. Bill and Maria pursued their Emotional Happiness selfishly when they fought about the jet-skiing and the art-museum visit during their vacation in San Diego (I,1 above).

EMOTIONAL HAPPINESS/CHRISTIAN MORALITY CONFLICT

Why does Emotional Happiness conflict with Christian morality at times? Partly because Emotional Happiness does not require morality. Many definitions of Emotional Happiness do not even mention morality. Emotional Happiness consists of pleasant or positive emotions with an absence of unpleasant or negative emotions, and that's about it. The problem here is that we could experience pleasant emotions without necessarily being virtuous, Christ-like persons. An alcoholic mother could experience pleasant emotions while getting drunk and letting her young children play unsupervised on the busy street in front of her house. But would she be truly happy?

Most of us couples believe that true happiness must include morality. Most of us hope for a moral, faithful marriage relationship. We do not hope for a series of pleasurable extramarital affairs with little or no fidelity, respect, or other virtues.

Most romantic lovers themselves believe that true happiness must include morality, so they include some morality in their Emotional Happiness. But not always enough morality. Sometimes they pursue their Emotional Happiness selfishly instead of following Jesus virtuously.

THE SELFISH PURSUIT OF AN EMOTIONAL HAPPINESS

Let's say that a romantic lover, Jose, pursued his Emotional Happiness selfishly at times. He felt emotionally happy when his drop-dead gorgeous wife Jessie took his breath away, so he wanted her to look gorgeous practically all the time, including during dinner. He got mad at Jessie when she wore hair curlers at the dinner table, and sometimes he called her a slob and other names.

Why do romantic lovers pursue their Emotional Happiness selfishly at times? Partly because they desire worldly goods so much for their happiness. Many of them are especially fond of money (including the material things that money can buy), power, good looks, and other material goods (II,1), so they pursue these material goods selfishly at times instead of following Jesus virtuously. They put the material goods ahead of God and virtue.

THE SELFISH PURSUIT OF MONEY

Many romantic lovers selfishly pursue money and the things that money can buy in order to be emotionally happy. Some of them do not think that they are being selfish. They think that God wants them to be wealthy or at least prosperous. According to a *Time* magazine poll, 61% of Americans believe that God wants us to be prosperous.[85]

Some Christian romantic lovers who think that God wants us to be prosperous have been influenced by megapastor Joel Osteen and other advocates of today's "Prosperity Theology." One of Osteen's followers, George Adams, rejoices in his growing prosperity: "It's a new day God has given me! I'm on my way to a six-figure income!" Adams adds that he will soon buy his dream house with 25 acres, a barn for horses and ponies for his sons, a pond, and maybe some cattle too. Adams explains, "I'm dreaming big—because all of heaven is dreaming big. [. . .] It's Joel Osteen's ministry that told me. Why would an awesome and mighty God want anything less for his children?"[86]

Jesus is not a Prosperity theologian. Jesus does not call us couples to put away our old self and put on a new, more prosperous self, with a six-figure income and a dream house with 25 acres. Jesus calls us to put on a new, more virtuous, Christ-like self. What's more, St. Paul warns that "'the love of money is the root of all evils' and there are some who, pursuing it, have wandered away from the faith, and so given their souls any number of fatal wounds" (1 Tim. 6:10).

Psychologist Susan Heitler describes a wife Linda and her husband Len who selfishly pursue money and the things that money can buy. Linda and Len fight angrily when they shop for a washing machine. Linda wants an expensive washing machine with many settings, but Len wants a cheaper, more dependable machine. Here is Round One of Linda's and Len's washing machine fight (with Heitler's descriptions and interpretations omitted):

> *Linda:* "I like this one [washing machine] with all the different settings. Let's just buy this one."
> *Len:* "This one is much cheaper, and the manufacturer has a better repair record."
> *Linda:* "But I don't want a washer that limits me to just a couple of options."
> *Len:* "That's foolish if it's going to cost us more money."
> *Linda:* "You never listen to what matters to me!"
> *Len:* "Let's be sensible about this! We have big expenses with the kids."
> *Linda:* "I know we have kids at least as much as you do. You're just being selfish about the machine. You always want things your way."
> *Len:* "What do you want me to do? Buy foolishly and then have no money for other things we need? You're the one who's selfish. How will we pay for all the things the kids need, never mind save for their college!"[87]

Len unreasonably and unlovingly calls Linda's preference for more settings "foolish." It is not necessarily foolish, though, to prefer different settings for different loads.

Linda complains unreasonably and unlovingly that Len "never" listens to her. But surely Len listens to her sometimes. He seems to listen to her during their washing machine fight to some extent, at least. He responds to many of her points. He just does not agree with her. But what's wrong with this? We couples should not blame or belittle our partner for disagreeing with us about washing machines, tattoos, or candidates for the Presidency of the United States. We should let our partner think for himself or herself.

Both Linda and Len unlovingly call each other selfish. They attack each other's character instead of dealing objectively with the pros and cons of the washing machines.

Suppose that Linda and Len dealt with the washing machines reasonably and lovingly. Which washer would they buy?

It would depend. Suppose that Linda and Len were near bankruptcy and the extra settings would not be very useful. Then they might buy the cheaper machine. Suppose, on the other hand, that they could afford the more expensive machine and the extra settings would be very useful. Then they might buy the more expensive machine. For the most part, though, it would not matter which washing machine they bought. Their world would not come to an end if they did not buy the "right" one. Their marriage might come to an end, though, if they continued to fight selfishly about washing machines and other material goods.

Linda and Len experienced the Christian Morality Problem with Emotional Happiness. They fought selfishly for the washing machine of their choice in order to be emotionally happy, so they did not respond to one another lovingly and follow Jesus virtuously.

THE SELFISH PURSUIT OF POWER & CONTROL IN ROMANTIC RELATIONSHIPS

Some romantic lovers struggle selfishly for power and control in their relationship in order to be emotionally happy instead of responding to their partner lovingly and following Jesus virtuously in order to be virtuously happy. They put power and control in their relationship ahead of God and virtue.

In Linda's and Len's washing machine fight discussed above, Len attacked Linda in order to get her to buy the inexpensive washing machine. He tried to control Linda. In other words, he power-struggled with her.

Psychiatrist Aaron Beck describes a power struggle between Laura and her fiancé Fred. Laura is an art instructor in a private day school. She is insecure, and she is afraid that Fred will abandon her. Fred is a computer programmer. He values his independence. He does not want to be controlled by anyone, including Laura.[88]

Laura admired Fred's independence when they first met because she lacked this. But later Fred's independence together with her insecurity fueled conflict in their relationship. Laura often asked Fred to prove that he would never abandon her, but Fred thought that she was trying to control him when she did this. Here is one of Laura's and Fred's power struggles, with their thoughts and other information in brackets:

> *Laura:* Will you stay home tonight? I think I have the flu.
> *Fred:* I'm already committed to visit Joe [a professional colleague].
> *Laura:* [*If he won't do this small favor for me, how can I count on him when I have a major problem?*] You never want to stay home. I very rarely ask you to do anything.
> *Fred:* [*If she insists on keeping me home for such a small thing, what will happen when something big happens—like when we have children? She is completely unreasonable. If I have to give in to her every wish, I won't be able to breathe.*] I'm sorry, but I really have to go.
> *Laura:* [*I can't depend on him. I should get out of the relationship while I can and find somebody I can depend on.*] Go ahead if you want to. I'll find somebody else to stay with me.[89]

Laura and Fred are not communicating with one another honestly, much less lovingly. They are trying to control each other in order to be emotionally happy instead of responding lovingly to each other and following Jesus virtuously in order to be virtuously happy.

THE SELFISH PURSUIT OF GOOD LOOKS

Some romantic lovers pursue good looks selfishly in order to be emotionally happy. There is nothing wrong with the good looks themselves. Romantic lovers may look beautiful or handsome, and they may enjoy this. Romantic lovers may also diet in order to lose weight and look better. It's just the selfish desire and love for good looks that is the problem, not the good looks themselves—much as it is the selfish desire and love for money that is said to be the root of all evils, not the money itself.

Some romantic lovers selfishly want their partner to look beautiful, handsome, or sexy in order to make them feel good emotionally. A balding, slightly overweight, 46-year-old husband did not like his 47-year-old wife Carol's "flabby looks," so he had an affair with a pretty young woman, Michelle.[90]

Some romantic lovers anxiously desire to look beautiful, handsome, or sexy themselves in order to feel good emotionally. They do not accept and love themselves as they are, however they look. They cannot be completely happy with God and virtue—they want good looks too.

Many American women suffer from what psychologist Judith Rodin calls a "normative obsession" with their looks that often begins during their teenage years and sometimes continues during their married life.[91] Psychologist Joan Brumberg describes a typical American girl, Carol, who was obsessed with her looks during high school and college.[92] Carol had friends, dates with popular boys, artistic talent, and good grades. She should have felt good about herself, but she didn't, partly because of her desire to look beautiful. She described herself in her diary as "fat" and "ugly." She weighed herself at least once a day, and she got depressed when she thought she weighed too much. She wrote in her diary one night: "I'm very depressed tonight. Same reason: I'm 120 pounds." A month later she wrote that she was happy because she had lost weight: "I weigh 112. Everything is great for once." About a month later, though, she was unhappy again because she was back up to 120 pounds. She signed her diary entry "Fatty."[93]

Carol tried many diets to lose weight. She smoked cigarettes to suppress her appetite. She gave herself an enema when she felt that her stomach was "out a mile."[94]

Carol needed to let go of her selfish, misguided desire to look beautiful in order to accept and love herself more as she was, whatever she weighed.

American teenage girls in the past were not obsessed with their looks, according to Brumberg. Teenage girls during the 19th century were more concerned about their moral character than their looks, as far as we can tell from their diaries. In their diaries they resolved to improve their moral character, not their looks. In 1892 one girl wrote in her diary: "Resolved, not to talk about myself or feelings. To think before speaking. To work seriously. To be self restrained in conversation and actions. Not to let my thoughts wander. To be dignified. Interest myself more in others."[95]

Maybe some of these 19th-century teenage girls needed to talk more about themselves and their feelings, so maybe they had different problems than teenage girls have today. Still, it seems that the 19th-century girls were not as obsessed with their looks as many teenage girls are today. Many teenage girls today resolve to improve their looks, not their moral character. One girl writes in her diary: "I will try to make myself better in any way I possibly can with the help of my budget and baby-sitting money. I will lose weight, get new lenses, already got new haircut, good makeup, new clothes and accessories."[96]

Some black women worry about their looks. Historically black women were compared to white women on Southern plantations, and later they were compared to white women in advertisements and in the movies. Many black women were told that their skin was too dark, their nose too wide, their lips too thick, and their legs too skinny, so they tried to lighten their skin and change their body type. Later during the "Black is Beautiful" movement, black women learned that black was beautiful, so their skin was not too black after all. But then some black women were told that their skin was not black enough.[97]

Wives who are anxious about their looks need their husband to help them accept and love themselves as they are, however they look. But anxious wives do not always get this loving support.

Wives who are anxious about their looks need the support of their society also, but they do not always get this support from our beauty-conscious American society. Author Naomi Wolf argues that the American diet industry, the cosmetics industry, the cosmetic surgery industry, the pornography industry, movies, talk shows, neighborhood gossip, and other sources promote an American "Beauty Myth" that beauty is a universal quality; that all women should want to be beautiful; and that all men rightly want to possess beautiful women.[98] This Beauty Myth makes many wives even more anxious and unhappy about their looks.

It might seem that *Christian* authorities would support wives who are anxious about their looks. But Christian authorities do not always do this. Some of them help *promote* the American Beauty Myth that beauty is holy and that women should seek it.[99] Some Christians have written books linking beauty with godliness and obesity with sinfulness, such as *God's Answer to Fat—Lose It* and *Help Lord—the Devil Wants Me Fat!*[100]

Other Christians worldwide have contributed to an international Beauty Myth. Javier Abad and Eugenio Fenoy, Catholic authors of *Marriage: A Path to Sanctity*, write that Catholic couples "must try to win each other and fall in love again every day." Abad and Fenoy add that a wife must "try to look as young and as attractive as before while maintaining a certain air of flirtatiousness, mystery and surprise that would captivate and enthrall her husband."[101] Abad and Fenoy claim that St. Josemaria Escriva, the Catholic founder of Opus Dei, has expressed the idea that "women are to be blamed 80% of the time if their husbands go astray: they do not know how to win them each day."[102]

The truth is that husbands have *themselves* to blame for going astray, not their wives. What's more, wives do not have to "win" their husband over every day, and husbands do not have to "win" their wife over either. Truly loving husbands and wives accept and love one another as they are, however they look.

Christian husbands should be happy loving their wife and following Jesus virtuously without desiring and demanding that their wife look trim, attractive, and beautiful in order to "fulfill" herself or to please them. Christian husbands should assure their wife that their love and admiration for her will not go up and down with the bathroom scales. They should assure her that she will always be their beauty queen. They can do these things easily, honestly, and joyfully if they are happy loving their wife and following Jesus virtuously, with or without a drop-dead gorgeous fashion model at their dinner table every night.

There would be more marital love and happiness in our beauty-conscious American society if more of us couples would let go of selfish desires for good-looking bodies in order to be happy responding to our partner lovingly and following Jesus virtuously, with or without beautiful, handsome, or sexy bodies. As an old American proverb says, "Beauty is skin-deep; it is the size of the heart that counts."[103] We couples need beautiful souls for our happiness, not beautiful bodies. What's more, with beautiful souls, we are beautiful persons through and through.

CONCLUSION

Many romantic lovers pursue money, power, good looks, and other material goods selfishly at times instead of responding to their partner lovingly and following Jesus virtuously. They have what I call a *materialistic selfishness*. Their materialistic selfishness weakens not only their marriage relationship, but also their relationship with God, including their prayer. They are likely to pray selfishly at times. George Adams might pray selfishly for a dream house with 25 acres without being happy following Jesus virtuously, with or without the dream house (II,2 above). Linda might pray selfishly for an expensive washing machine with lots of settings without considering Len's washing machine interests much if at all (II,2 above).

We couples are not likely to raise our minds and hearts to God lovingly, wisely, and prayerfully during our ordinary marriage and family activities if we attach our minds and hearts selfishly, unlovingly, and foolishly to dream houses with 25 acres, washing machines with many settings, and other worldly goods. We need to let go of our selfish desires for worldly goods at times in order to follow Jesus not only more virtuously, but also more prayerfully.

When all is said and done about the Christian Morality Problem with Emotional Happiness, romantic lovers should not settle for an Emotional Happiness that often comes with a selfish, shallow, stressful pursuit of wealth, power, beauty, and other material goods. Romantic lovers can seek a Conventional Happiness centered around immaterial psychological and spiritual goods that is more compatible with Christian morality, as we will see (III,1). Better yet, romantic lovers can seek a Christian Happiness centered around God and virtue that is completely compatible with Christian morality (IV,1). For now, though, let's go to the next problem with romantic love, wisdom, and happiness.

chapter 3

The Emotional Problem with Romantic Love

WE COUPLES SHOULD BE AWARE OF THE Emotional Problem with romantic love. There are three main aspects of this problem. First, romantic love is largely an emotion that is not a strong foundation for marriage.

Second, romantic lovers sometimes experience unloving emotions, especially after the honeymoon ends. Romantic lovers turn to one another to satisfy their desires for worldly goods in order to feel good emotionally. They often satisfy one another, but not always. When they frustrate one another, they sometimes feel angry, resentful, or otherwise unloving emotionally. They do not experience a Christ-like transforming love for their partner that is always patient and kind, with no anger, resentment, or other unloving emotions.

Third, romantic lovers do not control their unloving emotions well. Sometimes they repress their unloving emotions, and other times they express them destructively. They do not always deal with their unloving emotions constructively.

AN EMOTIONAL ROMANTIC LOVE

Let's look at the first point that an emotional romantic love is not a strong foundation for marriage. Why isn't it a strong foundation for marriage?

For one thing, emotions are *temporary*. The full heat of an emotion usually lasts for seconds only.[104]

It is true that romantic love *as a whole* is not just a temporary emotion. Romantic love as a whole often includes a willful choice and an intellectual commitment to love our partner even if our loving emotions come and go. The choice and commitment to love our partner usually last longer than a few seconds. But not always that much longer! Sometimes temporary romantic-love emotions fade away, and then the choice and commitment to love go with them. Jason Mesnick, a bachelor on the television show, *The Bachelor*, fell in love with one of the contestants, Melissa Rycroft. He bought her an engagement ring, proposed to marry her, and she accepted—but then he broke up with her six weeks later on the show's final episode. Comedian Richard Lewis says, "When you're in love, it's the most glorious two-and-a-half days of your life."[105] Star Trek medical officer Beverly Crusher told her starship's counselor, Deanna Troi, "I fell in love in a day. It lasted a week. But *what* a week."[106]

Emotions are not only temporary, but also uncontrollable to some extent. The emotion of romantic love often includes uncontrollable bodily changes, such as a rapid pulse, blushing, and breaking into a sweat. A medieval French romance writer, Chrétien de Troyes, describes a woman falling in love uncontrollably: "Love [Cupid] aimed well when he shot his arrow into her heart—often she grew pale and broke into a sweat; in spite of herself she was forced to love."[107]

Emotions are also unreasonable at times, and this includes the emotion of romantic love. Psychiatrist Thomas Moore writes that love is eternally young and "always manifests some of the folly of youth."[108] Someone once said that love is just two fools running after each other.[109]

Romantic love of this emotional, temporary, somewhat uncontrollable, and sometimes unreasonable sort is not a strong foundation for marriage. Let's see why the romantic love of a young married couple, Tim and Samantha, is not a strong foundation for their marriage. Psychologists Howard Markman, Scott Stanley, and Susan Blumberg describe this couple in their book, *Fighting for Your Marriage*.

TIM'S & SAMANTHA'S EMOTIONAL ROMANTIC LOVE

Tim and Samantha experience a good deal of romantic love for one another that is centered around sharing good times that help them feel good emotionally. One evening Tim and Samantha looked forward to enjoying a baseball game together. They experienced loving feelings for one another when they left for the game, but their loving feelings did not last long. On the way to the game, Tim's mother called Tim on his mobile phone, and Tim talked with her for a long time. Samantha had been upset with Tim's mother in the past for butting in on Tim and Samantha during their times together, so Samantha got mad at Tim for talking with his mother for such a long time, and Tim got mad at Samantha in return. Here is Tim's and Samantha's angry fight:

> *Samantha:* Why do you always let her [Tim's mother] interfere with our relationship? This is our evening out.
> *Tim:* (*really hot under the collar*) There you go again, blasting me when we're going out to have fun for a change.
> *Samantha:* (*sounding indignant*) Well, I didn't know we were planning on bringing your mother with us.
> *Tim:* (*words dripping with sarcasm*) Ha, ha. Real funny, Sam.[110]

Markman, Stanley, and Blumberg rightly point out that Tim and Samantha should have dealt with the mother-in-law problem ahead of time instead of waiting for events like the telephone call to trigger the problem.[111] But there are obviously deeper problems here, including Tim's and Samantha's emotional romantic love itself. For one thing, Tim's and Samantha's loving feelings for one another are temporary. Their loving feelings turn into angry feelings when Tim talks with his mother on the phone for a long time. Tim's and Samantha's angry feelings might even turn into feelings of hatred in the future if Tim and Samantha continue getting mad at each other about things like this. St. Francis de Sales points out in his *Introduction to the Devout Life* that anger can turn into hatred, especially if we let the sun set on our anger (see Eph. 4:26).[112]

VOLATILE LOVE/HATE RELATIONSHIPS

Since love can turn into anger and anger can turn into hatred, love and hatred are often called the two closest emotions.[113] The French moralist François de La Rochefoucauld (1613–1680) observes, "If we judge love by the majority of its results, it rather resembles hatred than friendship."[114] Author George Bernard Shaw points out, "When we want to read of the deeds that are done for love, whither do we turn? To the murder column; and there we are rarely disappointed."[115]

Romantic love seldom ends in murder, but it often does end in divorce.

ANXIETY

Romantic lovers experience all sorts of unloving, un-Christ-like emotions at times, ranging from anxiety and regret to the anger and hatred discussed above. With respect to anxiety, many Christian romantic lovers are anxious about the money, power, good looks, or other material goods that they desire for their Emotional Happiness. They may think that their anxieties about material goods have little to do with Christian marriage discipleship, but they are wrong. Jesus teaches that we Christians should not be anxious about food, clothing, and other sustaining goods, much less about wealth, power, good looks, and other enhancing goods (Matt. 6:25). Anxiety about enhancing goods in particular is an unloving, un-Christ-like emotion that prevents us from being completely happy loving God and following Jesus virtuously, with or without wealth, power, good looks, or other enhancing goods. We anxiously desire the enhancing goods too, in addition to God and virtue.

Let's deal here with anxiety about enhancing goods, especially enhancing material goods. We can deal later with anxiety about minimally good health and other sustaining goods (IV,2).

Sociologist Barry Schwartz discusses the anxiety and other negative emotions that many Americans experience when they shop for material goods. Schwartz calls these negative emotions unpleasant and unhealthy. I call these negative emotions unloving and un-Christ-like too. When we shop anxiously for material goods, we are not completely happy loving God unconditionally and following Jesus virtuously, with or without the material goods. We want the material goods too, in addition to God and virtue.

Schwartz discusses the unpleasant emotions that American shoppers often experience in the broad context of his theory about the paradox of choice in our prosperous American society. The paradox is that having more choices in most areas of our life is often bad for us, not good for us.[116]

To defend his theory, Schwartz points out that we prosperous Americans have more choices than ever before in our shopping, education, entertainment, careers, relationships, religion, and most other areas of life. Schwartz notes that his neighborhood supermarket has 85 varieties of crackers to choose from, 285 varieties of cookies, 65 juice "box drinks" for children, 230 soup offerings, 120 different pasta sauces, 175 different salad dressings, 275 varieties of cereal, and his list goes on.[117] Having more choices in our shopping and other areas of our life, however, is often bad for us, according to Schwartz. We are likely to experience anxiety, regret, or other unpleasant emotions at times in our efforts to deal with all our choices. In short, we are likely to suffer from an overload of choice.[118]

Let's see what Schwartz says about one unpleasant, unhealthy, unloving emotion, regret of a selfish sort, that many American shoppers experience.

REGRET

According to Schwartz, we Americans may experience regret in our shopping and other areas of our life if we "make a decision and it doesn't turn out well" or if we "find an alternative that would have turned out better."[119] We may experience anticipated regret if we worry ahead of time about how we would feel if our decision did not turn out well or if another decision turned out better. With this anticipated regret, we may worry so much about making bad decisions that we put off making decisions. Anticipated regret can make it hard to make decisions in the first place.[120]

We may experience postdecision regret if our decision does not turn out well or if we learn that a different decision would have turned out better. Postdecision regret in the area of shopping is often called "buyer's remorse." Postdecision regret makes decisions harder to enjoy after we make them.[121]

Linda and Len (II,2 above) might have experienced anticipated regret worrying about how their washing machine decision would turn out. They might have experienced postdecision regret if the washing machine that they bought did not work well or if they learned that another washing machine would have worked better.

We may regret shopping decisions also if we consider what economists call "opportunity costs." The opportunity costs of an option include the loss of the opportunities that would have come with another option.[122] The opportunity costs of buying the expensive washing machine discussed above would include the money that Linda and Len would have saved by buying the cheaper washer. Suppose that Linda and Len would have saved $300 on the cheaper washer's purchase price and about $40 a year on the lower operating and maintenance costs. Then the opportunity costs for buying the expensive washer would have been $300 plus about $40 a year for as long as Linda and Len used the washer.

Linda and Len might regret buying the expensive washing machine if they took the opportunity costs into account. Suppose that a few months after buying the washer, they could not pay the rent for their apartment, so they were evicted. Then they might have regretted buying the expensive washer.

We may regret shopping decisions also if we compare the results of our decisions to the results that we had expected or desired.[123] Suppose that Linda had planned to use the expensive washer with the extra settings to wash her silk lingerie, but the washer did not work well for the lingerie. Linda might have regretted buying the washer.

We may regret shopping decisions also if we compare our shopping experiences with other people's shopping experiences.[124] Suppose that Linda's and Len's washer did not work as well as the washer that their neighbors bought a few weeks later for less money. Linda and Len might have regretted buying the washer.

Schwartz discusses many more reasons why some Americans regret their shopping decisions about washing machines and other material goods, but let's not flog a dead washing machine. The point is that some Americans experience a good deal of regret in their desirous pursuit of the material goods that they think they need in order to be emotionally happy. And regret is just the tip of the unpleasant, unloving emotional iceberg! Some Americans experience anxiety, frustration, anger, and other unpleasant, unloving emotions for many of the same reasons discussed above.

CONCLUSION

Should romantic lovers settle for an emotional, roller-coaster romantic love with wild emotional ups and downs, loving and hating, blowing hot and cold? Should romantic lovers settle for an emotional romantic love of a temporary, somewhat uncontrollable, often unreasonable, and volatile sort? Heavens no! The husband Jude in Thomas Hardy's novel, *Jude the Obscure*, reflects that his life and his wife Arabella's life were both ruined "by the fundamental error of their matrimonial union: that of having based a permanent [marriage] contract on a temporary feeling."[125]

Romantic lovers can work out the Emotional Problem with their romantic love by growing to a conventional needs love or, better yet, to a Christ-like transforming love, as we will see (III,1–3; IV,1–2). For now, let's go to the next problem with romantic love, wisdom, and happiness.

chapter 4

The Fantasy Problem with Romantic Wisdom

THE FANTASY PROBLEM WITH ROMANTIC WISDOM is that romantic lovers with romantic wisdom sometimes fantasize about themselves, their partner, and their relationship instead of dealing with themselves, their partner, and their relationship realistically and wisely. Romantic lovers with rose-colored glasses sometimes fantasize that their romanticized partner will make them emotionally happy by satisfying their desires for worldly goods in a romantic fantasyland. But their *real* partner in this *real* world will not always satisfy them, and then they are likely to be disappointed, upset, unloving, and unhappy. They need to deal with their partner more realistically and wisely in order to strengthen their relationship and follow Jesus more virtuously. And they often need to deal with themselves more realistically and wisely too!

Of course there is nothing wrong with harmless fantasies that romantic lovers do not take too seriously. This chapter deals only with harmful fantasies that some romantic lovers take too seriously.

ROMANTIC FANTASIES ABOUT MR. & MISS WONDERFUL

Many romantic lovers are not aware of the Fantasy Problem with their romantic wisdom. The romantic lover Glenna discussed above (II,1) was not aware of the Fantasy Problem with her positive-thinking romantic wisdom. After all, her positive-thinking romantic dreams were coming true. She thought positively about meeting the handsome, wealthy man of her dreams, and then, presto, a handsome, wealthy man drove by in a red and white Cadillac, they dated, they married, and, it seemed, they would live happily ever after. Or would they? Just how realistic is this?

Maybe not too realistic. Psychologists Gwendolyn Grant and Audrey Chapman say that black women often think positively about meeting a handsome, wealthy, loving man—a Mr. Wonderful—much as Glenna did. But few of these women discover Mr. Wonderful driving by in a red and white Cadillac a few weeks later. Many of the women never find their dream man. What is the result of their "positive thinking"? Disappointment. Withdrawal. Depression. An inability to build a loving relationship with an average man.[126]

Grant and Chapman do not call black women's fantasizing about Mr. Wonderful "positive thinking." They call it "soap opera thinking" and the "female fantasy trap."[127]

Of course Glenna did meet and marry her Mr. Wonderful. But would she live happily ever after with him?

I wouldn't know, and probably Glenna wouldn't know either. Glenna fantasized mostly about Mr. Wonderful's good looks, wealth, and other external material goods, as many romantic lovers do. Glenna did not think much about Mr. Wonderful's inner moral character. She did not seem to realize that a handsome man may just be good in the face, as the Apaches say.

Glenna needed to think more realistically and more wisely not only about Jim's moral character, but also about her own moral character. Probably she and Jim both had character weaknesses that could weaken their relationship as well as character strengths that could strengthen it. What would happen to their relationship if selfishness, jealousy, dishonesty, or other character weaknesses emerged after the honeymoon ended?

Glenna and Jim probably did not know what would happen. It seems that they had not thought much about their character weaknesses, much less dealt with them. They did not seem to realize that "during courtship there is sweetness and later comes reality," as the Mexicans say.[128]

ROMANTIC FANTASIES ABOUT BEING EMOTIONALLY HAPPY

Romantic lovers with romantic wisdom fantasize not only about Mr. or Miss Wonderful, but also about being happy with Mr. or Miss Wonderful, with an Emotional Happiness. They think that they are happy when they feel good emotionally while sharing good times with their dream guy or dream girl (II,1 above). Are romantic lovers truly happy, though, just because they feel good emotionally during their good times? Let's say that romantic lovers Raul and Celeste Gonzales felt good emotionally while they were dining out and laughing together. Would they be truly happy?

According to some authorities today, Raul and Celeste probably would be truly happy if they felt good emotionally. These authorities identify happiness mostly with pleasant emotions (II,1 above). On the ABC television show, "The Mystery of Happiness," Thomas Bouchard, Richard Davidson, and other psychologists discussed twin sisters Barbara Herbert and Daphne Goodshed as models of happiness because the sisters felt good when they laughed and giggled, and they laughed and giggled a lot.[129] Anthropologist Helen Fisher compared the giggling happiness of these "giggle twins" with the hooting happiness of chimpanzees. Fisher said that chimpanzees are happy when they laugh and hoot, much as the giggle twins were happy when they laughed and giggled. Fisher suggested that the chimpanzees and the giggle twins might have similar "happiness" genes.[130]

Should we couples strive for an emotional, feel-good, giggling, hooting, chimpanzee-like happiness? Heavens no! True happiness is much more profound and complex than this. Giggling and laughter can cover up anxiety, insecurity, hostility, and other mental and emotional distress. What lies deep in our souls beneath our giggling and laughter? What happens if we have serious personal problems or marital problems?

Romantic lovers often need to deal with their problems in order to be truly happy. Suppose that when Raul was dining out and laughing with Celeste, he was afraid that she was having an affair. He did not want to deal with this problem, though, so he drowned out his fears by drinking more brandy. He might have felt good while he was dining out, drinking brandy, and laughing with Celeste, but would he have been truly happy?

Not according to philosopher Robert Nozick. Nozick argues that pleasant emotions by themselves are not enough for our happiness. To be truly happy, according to Nozick, many of us want our pleasant emotions to be based on reality. We do not want to live in a delusion.[131] Surely Raul would not want to live in a drunken delusion that Celeste loved him faithfully if in fact she was betraying him and did not really love him.

Suppose that happiness was mostly just pleasant emotions. Then happy people might be self-delusional. Psychologist Richard Bentall studied people who were considered happy based on today's emotional "feel-good" standards. These people overestimated their control over their environment. They gave unrealistically positive evaluations of themselves, and they believed that other people shared these evaluations. In short, they were self-delusional. But that's a serious psychiatric disorder. That's not true happiness.

ROMANTIC AVOIDANCE OF PROBLEMS

Fantasizing romantic lovers are not truly happy just because they feel good while sharing good times with their romanticized partner in a romantic fantasyland. They often need to deal with their problems in order to be truly happy with their real partner in this real world. They need to deal most of all with any major character weaknesses or other moral problems that are preventing them from responding to their partner lovingly and becoming increasingly Christ-like, virtuously-happy persons.

Unfortunately romantic lovers often avoid dealing with their problems, especially their moral problems. Maybe they are too busy trying to keep up with the Joneses to deal with their problems. Maybe they lack the self-confidence to deal with their problems. Maybe they grew up in a dysfunctional family, and they think that their problems just come with the territory of being human, so they cannot do much about them. Maybe they believe the skeptical marriage authorities who insist that married couples cannot help experiencing anger, rage, and other primitive emotions at times. There are many reasons why romantic lovers often avoid dealing with their problems.

Suppose that we couples become aware of problems that could threaten our love and happiness. Suppose that we become aware of jealousy, controlling behavior, or serious disagreements about whether to have children. We should deal with the problems promptly instead of avoiding them. If we are not yet married, we should deal with the problems before we marry instead of waiting until afterwards. If we do not at least begin to deal with the problems before we marry, what makes us think that we will do so afterwards? And what makes us think that our partner will do so?

PROBLEMS AS OPPORTUNITIES FOR CHRISTIAN MORAL & SPIRITUAL GROWTH

We couples do not need to break out into a cold sweat if problems in our relationship come to light. We can approach many of our problems as opportunities for responding to our partner more lovingly, helping our partner respond to us more lovingly, and growing together in love, wisdom, and other Christian virtues. A Biblical author urges fellow Christians to welcome their problems as opportunities for moral and spiritual growth:

> You will always have your trials but, when they come, try to treat them as a happy privilege; you understand that your faith is only put to the test to make you patient, but patience too is to have its practical results so that you will become fully-developed, complete, with nothing missing (Jas. 1:2–4).

We couples do not have to look at problems fearfully as stumbling blocks that prevent us from being emotionally happy. We can often look at problems hopefully as stepping stones that can help us respond to our partner more lovingly and become increasingly Christ-like, virtuously-happy persons. The only difference between a stumbling block and a stepping stone is the way we use them, as an old American proverb says.[132]

Romantic lovers can use the Christian Morality Problem with their Emotional Happiness, the Emotional Problem with their romantic love, and the Fantasy Problem with their romantic wisdom as stepping stones to a greater love, wisdom, and happiness than they have known before.

CONCLUSION TO PART II

Many romantic lovers desire and pursue a materialistic good life in order to be emotionally happy more than they desire and pursue God and virtue in order to be virtuously happy. These romantic lovers do not always put God and virtue first, ahead of money, power, beauty, and other worldly goods.

Romantic lovers need to put away their old, materialistic Romantic Self and put on a new, less materialistic, more mature Needs Self or, better yet, a new, more virtuous, Christ-like Transformed Self.

Let's go to Part III to see how romantic lovers can grow from their romantic love, wisdom, and happiness to a more mature needs love, wisdom, and happiness. Before we do this, though, some of you readers might choose to check your Christian marriage discipleship at this time. You could look especially for any romantic aspects of Christian marriage discipleship that have been covered in this Part II. Do any of these romantic aspects of Christian marriage discipleship apply to your discipleship?

To check your Christian marriage discipleship, complete the Christian Marriage Discipleship Check-Up Worksheet in Appendix A. Completing the worksheet could help you apply the material covered in this Part II to your use of money, communications, and other areas of your married life. You and your partner might get some good ideas for dealing with marital problems and differences in these areas.

If you complete the worksheet in Appendix A at this time, you could consider both the positive and negative aspects of the romantic love, wisdom, and happiness covered in this Part II. On the positive side, you could consider this question:

1) To what extent do you share good times with your partner in a fun, loving, positive-thinking marriage relationship (covered in this Part II, Chapter 1)? Explain your answer with examples from your marriage experiences.

On the negative side, you could consider these three questions:

1) Do you experience the Christian Morality Problem with the Emotional Happiness of romantic lovers to some extent (II,2)? In other words, do you sometimes pursue money, power, good looks, or other worldly goods selfishly instead of responding to your partner lovingly and following Jesus virtuously? Explain your answer with examples from your marriage experiences.

2) Do you experience the Emotional Problem with romantic love to some extent (II,3)? In other words, do you love your partner to some extent with an emotionally volatile, hot-and-cold, roller-coaster romantic love? Explain your answer with examples from your marriage experiences.

3) Do you experience the Fantasy Problem with romantic wisdom to some extent? In other words, do you fantasize about yourself, your partner, or your relationship at times instead of dealing with yourself, your partner, or your relationship realistically and wisely (II,4)? Explain your answer with examples from your marriage experiences.

Part III
The Conventional Needs Stage of Christian Marriage Discipleship

Romantic lovers could grow directly from their romantic love, wisdom, and happiness to a Christ-like transforming love, wisdom, and happiness. Many of them, however, grow first to a conventional needs love, wisdom, and happiness.

Romantic lovers do not have to go for the whole kit-and-caboodle of a Christ-like transforming love in one fell swoop. They can set their immediate sights on growing from their romantic love to a more mature needs love. But this does not mean that they should turn a blind eye to transforming love. They should keep transforming love in their sights. For one thing, many of them *could* love their partner with transforming love to some extent, at least. What's more, striving for transforming love could help them grow in their marital love even if they fell short of their lofty transforming-love goal. British historian Arnold Toynbee points out that it is a "profoundly true and important principle of life that the most likely way to reach a goal is to be aiming not at that goal itself but at some more ambitious goal beyond it."[133]

American politician Carl Schurz observes, "Ideals are like stars; you will not succeed in touching them with your hands, but like the seafaring man on the desert of waters, you choose them as your guides, and, following them, you reach your destiny."[134]

In this Part III, let's look at the needs love, wisdom, and happiness that can be stepping stones to the Christ-like transforming love, wisdom, and happiness that is our destiny in this life. Let's look first at some positive aspects of needs love, wisdom, and happiness (Chapter 1). Then let's look at some problems with needs love, wisdom, and happiness, including the Christian Morality Problem with the Conventional Happiness of needs lovers (Chapter 2), the Emotional Problem with needs love (Chapter 3), and the Fantasy Problem with needs wisdom (Chapter 4).

chapter 1

The Conventional Happiness of Needs Lovers

IN ORDER TO BE CONVENTIONALLY HAPPY with needs love and wisdom, romantic lovers need to work out the Christian Morality Problem with their Emotional Happiness, the Emotional Problem with their romantic love, and the Fantasy Problem with their romantic wisdom. As they work out these problems, they gradually put away their old Romantic Self and put on a new, more mature Needs Self. They gradually become needs lovers.

In this chapter, let's see how needs lovers work out the Christian Morality Problem with the Emotional Happiness of romantic lovers (Section A of the chapter), the Emotional Problem with romantic love (Section B), and the Fantasy Problem with romantic wisdom (Section C).

A. WORKING OUT THE CHRISTIAN MORALITY PROBLEM WITH EMOTIONAL HAPPINESS

The Emotional Happiness of romantic lovers sometimes conflicts with Christian morality, and when it does, romantic lovers sometimes pursue their Emotional Happiness selfishly instead of following Jesus virtuously. This is the Christian Morality Problem with the Emotional Happiness of romantic lovers (II,2 above). Needs lovers work out this problem by seeking a Conventional Happiness that is more compatible with Christian morality. Let's look at this Conventional Happiness.

The Conventional Happiness of needs lovers includes not only feeling good emotionally (an Emotional Happiness), but also being satisfied with one's life mentally. In order to be conventionally happy, needs lovers try to satisfy their desires for worldly goods—much as romantic lovers try to satisfy their desires for worldly goods in order to be emotionally happy (II,1–2 above). So how do needs lovers and romantic lovers differ in their desirous, worldly pursuit of happiness? Why is the Conventional Happiness of needs lovers more compatible with Christian morality than the Emotional Happiness of romantic lovers?

For one thing, romantic lovers and needs lovers *desire different types of worldly goods* for their happiness. Romantic lovers desire more material goods, such as beachfront homes, while needs lovers desire more immaterial psychological and spiritual goods, such as friendships and spiritual feelings of inner peace during prayer. The desires of needs lovers for friendships and other immaterial psychological and spiritual goods are often more compatible with Christian morality than the desires of romantic lovers for beachfront homes and other material goods. Desiring friendships for one's happiness is often more praiseworthy, morally speaking, than desiring beachfront homes.

THE INTRINSIC GOALS OF NEEDS LOVERS COMPARED TO THE EXTRINSIC GOALS OF ROMANTIC LOVERS

Let's compare not only the *desires* of needs lovers and romantic lovers, but also the *goals* of these lovers. When needs lovers pursue their goals, they often try to satisfy their desires too, so goal-pursuit and desire-satisfaction often go together.

Many authorities today are discussing the way to be conventionally happy in terms of goal-pursuit more than desire-satisfaction. Psychologist Robert Emmons holds that pursuing meaningful goals with sufficient success can contribute significantly to one's happiness, that is, one's "subjective well-being."[135] Emmons points out that goals "provide a sense of meaning and purpose in life."[136] Philosopher Tim Mulgan describes goals likewise as "our chosen pursuits, projects, and endeavours, which give life much of its meaning and purpose."[137]

Needs lovers pursue their goals in order to be conventionally happy, much as romantic lovers pursue their goals in order to be emotionally happy. So how do needs lovers and romantic lovers differ in the pursuit of their goals? Why are the goals of needs lovers more compatible with Christian morality than the goals of romantic lovers?

Romantic lovers and needs lovers pursue different types of goals, much as they desire different types of worldly goods. Romantic lovers pursue extrinsic goals most of all. Two types of extrinsic goals are materialistic goals and power goals. Materialistic goals reflect desires for wealth, good looks, and other material goods, and power goals "reflect a desire to influence others and have an impact on them."[138]

Needs lovers, on the other hand, pursue intrinsic goals most of all. Three types of intrinsic goals are intimacy goals, personal growth goals, and generativity goals, according to Emmons. Intimacy goals "reflect a concern for establishing deep and mutually gratifying relationships."[139] A husband might have an intimacy goal of forgiving his wife for flirting with one of his friends at an office party two years ago.

Personal growth goals reflect desires for personal growth. A wife might have a personal growth goal of becoming more patient with her forgetful husband.

Generativity goals involve "creating, giving of oneself to others, and having an influence on future generations."[140] A husband and wife might have a generativity goal of improving the education in their local schools not only for their children, but also for future generations.

The intrinsic goals of needs lovers are often more compatible with Christian morality than the extrinsic goals of romantic lovers. It is often more praiseworthy, morally speaking, to pursue friendships and other intrinsic goals than to pursue wealth and other extrinsic goals. Let's look more closely at these extrinsic and intrinsic goals.

THE EXTRINSIC GOALS OF ROMANTIC LOVERS

Many romantic lovers pursue mostly materialistic goals, power goals, and other extrinsic goals. They pursue the American Dream of becoming wealthy, powerful, famous, good looking. But this American Dream may be a nightmare, according to Emmons and some other scholars. Many of us Americans are *not* wealthy, powerful, famous, good looking, and the like, and we may *never* be. Many of us struggle at times with rent-gouging landlords, oppressive bosses, weight problems, and other blemishes and bruises of ordinary life. Happiness would be rare indeed if we needed wealth, power, fame, good looks, and other material goods for our happiness.

Pursuing mostly extrinsic goals is not likely to make us happy. On the contrary, pursuing mostly extrinsic goals is likely to diminish personal well-being, according to many research studies.[141] People with mostly extrinsic goals experience more anxiety, depression, and other mental disorders than people with more intrinsic goals experience.[142] People with mostly extrinsic goals often focus on the external world and neglect their inner mental, emotional, and spiritual well-being.

There is more bad news about extrinsic goals. Americans who pursue the American Dream of being wealthy, powerful, famous, good looking, and the like might not be that happy *even if they achieved their goals!* Many newly-wealthy lottery winners said that one year after winning the lottery, they were no happier than they had been before. Some of them were less happy. Some of them lost their friends, and others divorced.[143]

Wealth cannot buy happiness. Sociologist Barry Schwartz points out that increases in a country's wealth over the poverty level have little effect on people's happiness. The average Japanese is nearly ten times wealthier than the average Pole, but Japanese are not happier than Poles.[144]

Suppose that romantic lovers put the American Dream on the back burners of their marriage and family life. Suppose that they stop pursuing mostly wealth, power, good looks, and other extrinsic goals. What kinds of goals should romantic lovers and all the rest of us couples pursue for our happiness?

THE INTRINSIC GOALS OF NEEDS LOVERS

We should pursue mostly intimacy goals, personal growth goals, generativity goals, and other intrinsic goals, according to Emmons and many other scholars.[145] People with mostly intrinsic goals report higher levels of well-being than do people with mostly extrinsic goals.[146]

The point here is not that we should *never* pursue extrinsic goals. The point is that we should not pursue *only* these goals or *mostly* these goals. A married couple might rightly pursue a materialistic goal of making $100,000 in the stock market together with an intimacy goal of strengthening their relationships with their children. Achieving the $100,000 stock-market goal by itself, however, would not necessarily make them happier. Money cannot buy happiness. But achieving the $100,000 stock-market goal could help the couple achieve their intimacy goal of strengthening their relationships with their children. The $100,000 might enable them to stop working overtime, and they might use the extra time to strengthen their parent-child relationships. Then it would be the stronger relationships with their children that would make them happier, not the $100,000 by itself.

We can see now that needs lovers work out the Christian Morality Problem with the Emotional Happiness of romantic lovers to a great extent by seeking a Conventional Happiness centered around intimacy goals, personal growth goals, and other intrinsic goals. The intrinsic goals of needs lovers are often more compatible with Christian morality than the extrinsic goals of romantic lovers.

The intrinsic goals of needs lovers, however, are not always compatible with Christian morality. Suppose that a needs lover pursued a personal growth goal of improving his communication skills in order to win more arguments with his wife and get what he wanted most of the time. This personal growth goal would not be compatible with Christian morality.

We will find that a new Christian Morality Problem comes into the picture with the Conventional Happiness of needs lovers (III,2). For now, though, let's see how needs lovers work out the next problem with romantic love, wisdom, and happiness.

B. WORKING OUT THE EMOTIONAL PROBLEM WITH ROMANTIC LOVE

Romantic love is largely a temporary, often uncontrollable, and sometimes unreasonable emotion that is not a strong foundation for marriage. This is the Emotional Problem with romantic love (II,3 above). Needs lovers work out this problem by growing in a needs love for their partner that is more stable, self-controlled, and reasonable emotionally.

It might seem that needs lovers do not work out the Emotional Problem with romantic love. Needs lovers turn to one another to satisfy their desires for worldly goods in order to be conventionally happy, much as romantic lovers turn to one another to satisfy their desires for worldly goods in order to be emotionally happy. Needs lovers and romantic lovers often satisfy one another, but not always. Sometimes they frustrate one another. Then both the needs lovers and the romantic lovers are likely to feel angry, bitter, or otherwise unloving emotionally. So it might seem that needs lovers and romantic lovers are not much different emotionally.

Needs lovers and romantic lovers are different emotionally, however. It is true that both needs lovers and romantic lovers experience unloving emotions at times. But needs lovers deal with their unloving emotions better than romantic lovers do. Needs lovers usually deal with their unloving emotions constructively instead of repressing them or expressing them destructively. Needs lovers usually treat their partner reasonably well in their external conduct even if they do not feel like doing so emotionally. Their needs love is more self-controlled and reasonable than romantic love.

Suppose that the romantic lover Samantha discussed above experienced more needs love for her husband Tim on their way to the baseball game (II,3). Then she might still be mad at Tim for talking with his mother for a long time on the phone, but she would not express her anger destructively. She would not angrily "blast" Tim for talking with his mother. She would not say sarcastically, "I didn't know we were bringing your mother with us." She would express her anger much more constructively. She might tell Tim that she was mad at him for talking with his mother for a long time, and she might suggest that she and Tim enjoy the baseball game now and discuss the phone call sometime during the next few days.

EMOTIONAL MANAGEMENT TECHNIQUES

Needs lovers often use emotional management techniques to control the ways that they act upon their unloving emotions. Needs lovers may use stretching exercises, calming down during interpersonal conflicts, speaking and listening non-defensively, validating their partner's emotions, and other helpful techniques.

In a stretching exercise, needs lovers list some of their minor frustrations with their partner, such as their partner's fast driving. Then their partner chooses a few items from their list, and their partner does what they want even if he or she does not feel like doing so.[147]

To calm down during interpersonal conflicts, needs lovers try deep breathing, timeouts, and the like.

To speak and listen non-defensively, needs lovers listen to their partner carefully and respond to their partner's concerns instead of mostly just defending their own interests.

To validate their partner's emotions, needs lovers listen to their partner empathetically and assure their partner that they respect his or her feelings and consider them valid. Then their partner would be more likely to express his or her feelings honestly in the future without being afraid of upsetting them.

Needs lovers clear up the Emotional Problem with romantic love, then, by controlling the ways that they act upon their unloving emotions in their external conduct. Their needs love is more self-controlled and reasonable than romantic love.

Let's go now to the next problem with romantic love, wisdom, and happiness.

C. WORKING OUT THE FANTASY PROBLEM WITH ROMANTIC WISDOM

Romantic lovers with romantic wisdom sometimes fantasize about themselves, their partner, and their relationship instead of dealing with themselves, their partner, and their relationship realistically and wisely. This is the Fantasy Problem with romantic wisdom (II,4 above). Needs lovers work out this problem by growing in a conventional needs wisdom that is more realistic and insightful than romantic wisdom.

Needs lovers with needs wisdom deal with their problems more realistically and wisely than romantic lovers do. Needs lovers do not avoid dealing with their problems, as romantic lovers often do. Needs lovers often welcome their problems as opportunities to respond to their partner more lovingly; strengthen their relationship; grow in love, wisdom, and other Christian virtues; and deepen their relationship with God.

Dealing with problems realistically helps needs lovers build what psychologist Harville Hendrix calls a healthy "conscious marriage" instead of an unhealthy "unconscious marriage." Couples in a conscious marriage are usually conscious of their problems, and they usually deal with them realistically. Couples in an unconscious marriage, on the other hand, are often unaware of their problems, and they often fail to deal with their problems realistically.[148]

Hendrix describes a conscious marriage. He writes that in a conscious marriage "you realize that your love relationship has a hidden purpose—the healing of childhood wounds"; "you create a more accurate image of your partner"; "you learn to value your partner's needs and wishes as highly as you value your own"; "you embrace the dark side of your personality"; "you search within yourself for the strengths and abilities you are lacking"; and "you become more aware of your drive to be loving and whole and united with the universe."[149]

These characteristics of a conscious marriage reflect a conventional needs wisdom that is often compatible with Christian values. Suppose that we Christian couples in a conscious marriage embrace the dark side of our personality. We could be humbly acknowledging our old self, including our selfishness and sinfulness. Suppose that we search within ourselves for the strengths and abilities that we are lacking. We could be searching for the love, wisdom, and other Christian virtues that we are lacking. This needs wisdom could help many of us grow in our Christian marriage discipleship.

On the other hand, this needs wisdom could sometimes hold us back in our Christian marriage discipleship. Suppose that we searched within ourselves for the strengths and abilities that we were lacking. We might search for an assertiveness that we were lacking so we could pursue our goals selfishly without giving much consideration to our partner's goals. We might become *more* selfish and unloving, not less so.

We will find that a new Fantasy Problem comes into the picture with needs wisdom (III,4). But the point here is that needs lovers work out the Fantasy Problem with romantic wisdom by growing in a more realistic, insightful needs wisdom that helps them build a conventional conscious marriage.

CONCLUSION

Romantic lovers can work out the Christian Morality Problem with their Emotional Happiness, the Emotional Problem with their romantic love, and the Fantasy Problem with their romantic wisdom by growing from their romantic love, wisdom, and happiness to a more mature needs love, wisdom, and happiness. Romantic lovers can make some good progress in their Christian marriage discipleship by putting away their old Romantic Self and putting on a new, more mature Needs Self.

chapter 2

The Christian Morality Problem with Conventional Happiness

THE CONVENTIONAL HAPPINESS OF NEEDS LOVERS is more compatible with Christian morality than the Emotional Happiness of romantic lovers (III,1 above). But there is a lingering Christian Morality Problem with Conventional Happiness. The problem is that this happiness sometimes conflicts with Christian morality, and when it does, needs lovers sometimes pursue their Conventional Happiness selfishly instead of responding to their partner lovingly and following Jesus virtuously. They put their Conventional Happiness ahead of God and virtue.

CONVENTIONAL HAPPINESS/CHRISTIAN MORALITY CONFLICT

Why does Conventional Happiness conflict with Christian morality at times? Partly because Conventional Happiness does not require morality. Conventional Happiness consists of feeling good emotionally and being satisfied with one's life mentally, and that's about it (I,1 and III,1 above). The problem here is that we could feel good emotionally and be satisfied with our life mentally *without necessarily treating our partner well and without necessarily being virtuous, Christ-like persons*. A political power broker could feel good emotionally and be satisfied with his life mentally without necessarily treating his wife well and without necessarily being a virtuous, Christ-like person.

Robert Emmons identifies the following goal-conflicts that I would say involve conflict between Conventional Happiness and Christian morality:

1) "Make people like me" [Conventional Happiness] vs. "Live a 'godly' life" [Christian morality];[150]
2) "Make myself happy" [Conventional Happiness] vs. "Ease others' lives" [Christian morality];[151]
3) "Appear more intelligent than I am" [Conventional Happiness] vs. "Always present myself in an honest light" [Christian morality];[152]
4) "Have as much fun as possible" [Conventional Happiness] vs. "Make life easier for my parents" [Christian morality].[153]

Theoretically needs lovers could choose Christian morality over their Conventional Happiness in cases of Conventional Happiness/Christian morality conflict. They could act morally even if they were not completely happy doing this. And often they do choose Christian morality over their Conventional Happiness. But not always. They desire certain worldly goods for their Conventional Happiness so much that they cannot always resist the temptation to pursue these worldly goods selfishly instead of following Jesus virtuously.

Let's look more closely at this selfishness aspect of the Christian Morality Problem with the Conventional Happiness of needs lovers.

THE PSYCHOLOGICAL & SPIRITUAL SELFISHNESS OF NEEDS LOVERS

The Christian Morality Problem with the Conventional Happiness of needs lovers is like the Christian Morality Problem with the Emotional Happiness of romantic lovers, but it is not the same. Romantic lovers selfishly desire wealth, power, sex, and other material goods most of all in order to be emotionally happy, so they need to deal above all with their materialistic selfishness (II,2 above). Needs lovers, on the other hand, do not struggle with selfish desires for material goods nearly as much as romantic lovers do. Needs lovers selfishly desire friendships and other immaterial psychological and spiritual goods most of all in order to be conventionally happy, so they need to deal above all with their psychological and spiritual selfishness. Let's look at their psychological and spiritual selfishness more closely.

SELFISH DESIRES FOR PSYCHOLOGICAL GOODS

Most of us couples realize that our desires for wealth, power, and other *material* goods can be selfish. We can be greedy for money, 42-inch plasma television sets that descend from the ceiling, and other material goods. We may not realize as much, however, that our desires for *psychological* goods and other immaterial goods can be selfish too. We can be greedy for thoughtfulness, admiration, and other external psychological goods that we desire from other people. We may be upset with others and respond less lovingly to them if they frustrate our desires for their thoughtfulness, admiration, and other psychological goods. A wife Briana was upset with her husband Shaun when he "thoughtlessly" paid the electric bill late for two months in a row; when he "thoughtlessly" left the milk out on the breakfast table again; and when he "thoughtlessly" forgot to pick up the balloons for their child's birthday party. Briana's selfish desires for thoughtfulness from Shaun on these occasions prevented her from responding to Shaun lovingly and following Jesus virtuously.

Would Briana have to be upset and unloving on these electric-bill, breakfast-milk, and birthday-balloon occasions? Not at all. She should not expect or desire Shaun to be perfect. She should let go of her selfish desires for Shaun to act "thoughtfully" on these occasions in order to accept and love him more as he is—imperfect, occasionally forgetful, and maybe a little thoughtless at times too.

It is important to understand that Briana could respond to Shaun lovingly on these occasions *without being too permissive.* She could stand up assertively for her interests in the electric bill payments, the breakfast milk, and the birthday balloons—as we will see in an upcoming chapter on non-permissive marital love (IV,3). For now, though, let's just say that Briana could respond to Shaun lovingly and still do something about the electric bill payments, the breakfast milk, and the birthday balloons. She could propose to handle the electric bill payments herself, for example. Whatever she did, though, she could do it in a loving Christian way without fuming, fretting, and flying off the handle. Shaun would probably appreciate her love and understanding. He might even be more loving and understanding in return.

NEEDY DESIRES FOR PSYCHOLOGICAL GOODS

Needs lovers desire thoughtfulness or other psychological goods a little selfishly at times in order to be conventionally happy, as discussed above. What's more, needs lovers sometimes think that they *need* these psychological goods in order to be conventionally happy. Needs lovers are a little needy at times. But they are not nearly as needy as dysfunctional lovers. Some dysfunctional lovers think that they need their partner's thoughtfulness, attention, love, and other psychological goods so much that they could not live without these things. Some dysfunctional lovers would do almost anything for their partner in order to get the thoughtfulness, attention, love, and other psychological goods that they think they need. A beautiful middle-class black woman wanted so badly to be loved that she let her lovers abuse her. She said that one of her husbands "literally beat three babies out of me." She explained why she stayed with him: "I wanted to love him and be loved by him, and so I vowed to take care of him."[154]

This black woman could not let go of her selfish, needy desires for love and other psychological goods from the men in her life. Her desires were part of an illusion that these men would make her happy. There is a Korean word, "won," for desirous illusions like this. "Won" is an inability or an unwillingness to let go of our desires for certain worldly goods even though these desires are causing us great suffering. People with "won" cannot let go of such things as an abusive lover or an old love affair.[155]

Some "Generation Me" couples (born from 1970 to 2005) are especially likely to suffer from selfish, needy desires not only for psychological goods, but also for material goods. Psychologist Jean Twenge points out that many psychologists, educators, parents, and other authorities in recent decades focused on building the self-esteem of Generation Me children. These authorities taught the children that they were the greatest, so they deserved the best of everything, including fine food, fashionable clothes, friendships, and other material and psychological goods. Some Generation Me children learned their self-esteem lessons well, so they think that they deserve the best of everything. But few of them will get the best of everything in this real world, so many of them are likely to be frustrated, upset, and unhappy a good deal of the time.[156]

NARCISSISTIC DESIRES FOR PSYCHOLOGICAL GOODS

In some cases, needy, selfish desires for thoughtfulness, attention, love, and other psychological goods from others can be symptoms of a narcissistic personality disorder, which is a serious mental illness. Narcissists desire love and other psychological goods from others so much that they are never satisfied. They do almost anything to get the love and other psychological goods that they desire.

Some Generation Me couples might have narcissistic tendencies. According to Twenge, the results of a Narcissistic Personality Inventory completed by over 15,000 college students between 1987 and 2006 indicate that Generation Me students are significantly more narcissistic than students in previous generations.[157]

Let's take these questionnaire results with a grain of salt. Many Generation Me students were taught to use a psychological language of self-esteem that might have made them sound narcissistic in their questionnaire responses. But they might not have been any more narcissistic than students in previous generations who were often taught to use a traditional Christian language that might have made them sound unselfish. People often say what they have been taught to say. In a recent research study, supposedly liberated husbands claimed to share the housework with their wife, while traditional husbands said that housework is a woman's job. The "liberated" husbands talked a good liberated housework game, but they spent only about four more minutes a day for housework than the traditional husbands did.[158]

SELFISH DESIRES FOR SPIRITUAL GOODS

We couples can desire spiritual goods selfishly, much as we can desire psychological goods selfishly. St. John of the Cross warned some Catholic Carmelite friars and nuns and other "spiritual persons" in 16th-century Spain that their desires for spiritual goods were sometimes selfish, including their desires for pleasant spiritual feelings of inner peace during their prayer. These "spiritual persons" were disappointed when they did not experience pleasant spiritual feelings during their prayer. Some of them blamed God for this. They were not content to love God unconditionally without desiring and demanding pleasant spiritual feelings in return. John wrote that these friars and nuns "wander about in search only of sweetness and delightful communications from God. Such an attitude is [. . .] the indication of a 'spiritual sweet tooth'."[159]

We couples should not selfishly desire only sweetness and delightful communications from our partner any more than Catholic friars and nuns should selfishly desire only sweetness and delightful communications from God. We should accept and love our partner as he or she is, even when our partner is not being his or her usual sweet self.

SELFISH GOALS

We couples may need to put away selfish desires for psychological and spiritual goods in order to respond to our partner more lovingly and follow Jesus more virtuously, as discussed above. We may need to put away also selfish *goals*. A young college student identified some of his selfish goals: "Make my girlfriend feel guilty when she talks to guys" and "Avoid letting my girlfriend know I am in contact with other girls."[160] This young man put away his selfish goals to some extent during the next five years. He married his girlfriend and set new goals of keeping her happy and spending time with his family.[161]

Most of us couples realize that we may pursue materialistic goals, power goals, and other extrinsic goals selfishly. We may not realize as much, however, that we may pursue intimacy goals, personal growth goals, and other intrinsic goals selfishly—much as we may pursue psychological and spiritual goods selfishly, as just mentioned. Let's see how a Christian husband, Garrett, pursued his intrinsic intimacy and personal growth goals selfishly instead of responding to his wife Nicole lovingly and following Jesus virtuously.

GARRETT'S SELFISH INTIMACY & PERSONAL GROWTH GOALS

Garrett works about 50 hours a week as a financial advisor to help support Nicole and their three young children. Garrett says that he needs to play golf five times a week in order to pursue his intimacy and personal growth goals of renewing his college golfing friendships, reducing stress, and developing and enjoying his God-given golfing talents. Nicole, however, asks Garrett to give up his golfing and spend more time with their children in order to help her raise them well. Garrett has been spending only about five hours a week with the children, mostly during meals. Nicole says that Garrett has a Christian moral responsibility to spend more time with their children, and Garrett agrees. But he still wants to play golf five times a week in order to be conventionally happy. He must choose between his conventional golfing happiness and Christian morality, including his parenting responsibilities.

It's a no-win, Catch-22 situation for Garrett. On one hand, if he chooses his golfing happiness, he will sacrifice his Christian morality to some extent. But if he chooses Christian morality, he will sacrifice his golfing happiness to some extent.

Garrett chooses his golfing happiness. He continues playing golf five times a week without spending any more time with his children.

A SUBJECTIVE CONVENTIONAL HAPPINESS

It might seem that Garrett could play golf twice a week, spend more time with his children, and be conventionally happy too. Maybe. But Garrett might not be happy with this compromise. He might insist that he needed to play golf at least five times a week, minimum, in order to spend enough time with his college golfing friends, to reduce enough stress, to play well enough to enjoy playing, and, in short, to be conventionally happy. Then his conventional golfing happiness would still conflict with Christian morality.

Conventional Happiness can and often does conflict with Christian morality. Why? Partly because Conventional Happiness is subjective.[162] We decide for ourselves, subjectively, whether we are happy in the conventional sense of feeling good emotionally and being satisfied with our life mentally, as discussed above (I,1). So Garrett could insist that he needed to play golf five times a week in order to be happy, and his wife Nicole could say that she needed to do a little husband-swapping, and who knows what else people might say that they needed for their happiness.

Many proponents of this subjective Conventional Happiness claim to "measure" our happiness with questionnaires that ask us how happy we are and what makes us happy. Then they accept our subjective judgments about our happiness without questioning our judgments much if at all.[163] In a typical "scientific" research study on happiness, social scientists Shaver, Lenauer, and Sadd asked 2,500 American women to rate their happiness on a 7-point scale from 1 (very happy) to 7 (very unhappy).[164] Then these researchers accepted the women's subjective judgments about their happiness without questioning the judgments much if at all.

But did all these women know for sure how happy they were? And did they all know what true happiness is?

Not by a long shot! Philosophers, psychologists, and all the rest of us human beings have disagreed about the nature of happiness for centuries, so we rightly question people's ideas about happiness, including their subjective judgments about their own happiness. Suppose that one woman in the "scientific" happiness research study discussed above felt good emotionally during an extra-marital affair, so she reported subjectively that she was "very happy" (1). But was she really "very happy"? Maybe she felt guilty about her affair, so she did not feel *that* good emotionally, and she was not *that* satisfied with her life mentally. But she might not have wanted to admit this to herself, much less to the researchers.

Suppose, on the other hand, that this woman did *not* feel guilty about her affair. Suppose that she was indeed very happy in the conventional subjective sense of feeling good emotionally and being satisfied with her life mentally. Well, so what! This subjective, feel-good, adulterous happiness would be nothing to write home to mother about. Happiness is supposed to be a great thing that most of us couples want for ourselves and our children. But would we want this subjective, feel-good, adulterous happiness for ourselves and our children?

We couples should not cheapen happiness by saying that happiness is whatever we or anyone else happens to say that it is, subjectively. True happiness is what it is, objectively, and true happiness requires morality.

Fortunately some philosophers, theologians, and other authorities today are recovering ancient Greek and traditional Christian concepts of an objective, virtuous happiness in this life that not only requires morality, but centers around it, as discussed above (I,1).[165] Christian Happiness in this life, as I see it, is an objective mental, emotional, and spiritual state of being a virtuous, Christ-like person in our moral character and conduct, and being united with God in a limited way. With respect to being a virtuous, Christ-like person, virtuous, Christ-like people all have the same fundamental virtues of faith, love, and wisdom that fulfill all of us human beings. The faith, love, and wisdom come with hope, patience, kindness, honesty, and other virtues, for there is a unity of the virtues, according to St. Paul (1 Cor. 13:4–7), St. Thomas Aquinas, and other Christians.[166]

Christian Happiness in this life, in short, is an objective state of virtuous mental, emotional, and spiritual well-being that fulfills all of us human beings.

SELFISH MORAL CHARACTER

To be virtuously happy in this life, we couples need to be virtuous, Christ-like persons not only in our external conduct, but also in our inner character. Jesus calls us to become like him not only in our conduct, but also in our character. Jesus rebuked the scribes and Pharisees, "Alas for you, scribes and Pharisees, you hypocrites! You who clean the outside of cup and dish and leave the inside full of extortion and intemperance. Blind Pharisee! Clean the inside of cup and dish first so that the outside may become clean as well" (Matt. 23:25–26).

Saints, sages, and spiritual reformers in the world's great religions have taught likewise that we need to cleanse and purify our heart, mind, and soul on the inside in order to be clean on the outside as well. Thomas à Kempis writes in *Of the Imitation of Christ*, "Whenever a man desires anything inordinately, at once he is disquieted within himself. The proud and the covetous are never at rest."[167] Lao Tzu, legendary founder of Taoism, teaches in the *Tao Te Ching*, "There is no crime greater than having too many desires; There is no disaster greater than not being content; There is no misfortune greater than being covetous."[168]

Christians who selfishly covet certain worldly goods for their Conventional Happiness are not only somewhat selfish in their character; they are also likely to be somewhat conflicted and ambivalent. Robert Emmons explains that we human beings are often conflicted when "we cannot have or do all that we desire because often our desires themselves are mutually exclusive."[169] Garrett was conflicted. His desires to play golf five times a week *and* to spend more time with his children were mutually exclusive. He could not completely satisfy both of these desires.

Garrett was also ambivalent in the sense of having "opposing feelings towards the same objects."[170] Garrett felt good about golfing five times a week because this made him conventionally happy. But he felt bad about golfing five times a week because he upset his wife, neglected his children, and failed to follow Jesus virtuously when he did this.

Selfish, conflicted, ambivalent, and otherwise mentally and emotionally troubled needs lovers do not always follow Jesus virtuously as the one main source of their happiness. They desire certain worldly goods for their Conventional Happiness in addition to God and virtue. They try to serve two masters, God and worldly goods, with a little of the spirit of Christ and a little of the spirit of the world (I,1). This is the Christian Morality Problem with the Conventional Happiness of needs lovers.

STRIPPING AWAY MATERIALISTIC, PSYCHOLOGICAL, & SPIRITUAL SELFISHNESS DURING A DARK NIGHT OF THE SOUL

To overcome the Christian Morality Problem with Conventional Happiness—and the Christian Morality Problem with Emotional Happiness—we couples need to strip away materialistic, psychological, and spiritual selfishness, as discussed throughout this chapter.[171] St. John of the Cross teaches that we strip away selfishness and become increasingly virtuous, Christ-like persons during a dark night of the soul. John's dark night includes a beginning night of the senses and an advanced night of the spirit. During the beginning night of the senses, we are purged mostly of materialistic selfishness. During the advanced night of the spirit, we are purged mostly of psychological and spiritual selfishness.

We play both active and passive roles during the nights of the senses and the spirit, so there is an active night of the senses, a passive night of the senses, an active night of the spirit, and a passive night of the spirit. Let's focus on the active nights of the senses and the spirit.

GROWTH FROM ROMANTIC LOVE TO NEEDS LOVE DURING THE ACTIVE NIGHT OF THE SENSES

To grow from romantic love to needs love, romantic lovers need to strip away their materialistic selfishness most of all. They need to let go of selfish desires for jet-skiing, recreational drugs, or other material goods in order to respond to their partner more lovingly and follow Jesus more virtuously.[172] They need to put away their old, materialistic Romantic Self in order to put on a new, less materialistic, more mature Needs Self. They can do this, with God's help, during the beginning active night of the senses.

Romantic lovers strip away their materialistic selfishness most of all during the active night of the senses, but they can strip away some of their psychological and spiritual selfishness too. We can separate layers of materialistic, psychological, and spiritual selfishness for analytical and discussion purposes, but we cannot separate them in real life. In real life, most of us need to deal with materialistic, psychological, and spiritual selfishness during every stage of our moral and spiritual growth, as St. John of the Cross often points out.[173]

STRIPPING AWAY PSYCHOLOGICAL & SPIRITUAL SELFISHNESS DURING THE ACTIVE NIGHT OF THE SPIRIT

When romantic lovers strip away enough of their materialistic selfishness during the beginning active night of the senses, they become needs lovers. Then they may be ready to strip away more of their psychological and spiritual selfishness, with God's help, during the advanced active night of the spirit. Then they may be ready to grow farther from their needs love to a Christ-like transforming love.

During the active night of the spirit, needs lovers continue stripping away their materialistic selfishness, as St. John of the Cross points out.[174] Most of all, though, they strip away their psychological and spiritual selfishness. They let go of selfish desires for thoughtfulness from their spouse, pleasant spiritual feelings during their prayers, or other psychological and spiritual goods in order to respond to their partner more lovingly and follow Jesus more virtuously. They gradually put away their old Needs Self and put on a new, more Christ-like Transformed Self.

CONCLUSION

We couples must choose between desiring and pursuing a Conventional Happiness centered around worldly goods, and desiring and pursuing a Christian Happiness centered around God and virtue. To pursue a Christian Happiness, we need to let go of selfish desires for material, psychological, and spiritual goods in order to be happy responding to our partner lovingly and following Jesus virtuously, with or without these worldly goods. St. John of the Cross teaches that the more strongly we desire worldly goods for our happiness, the less strongly we will desire God and virtue. John explains:

> [Some people] are so engrossed in the things, riches, and affairs of this world that they care nothing about the fulfillment of the obligations of God's law. [. . .] Their appetite and joy is already so extended and dispersed among creatures—and with such anxiety—that they cannot be satisfied. The more their appetite and thirst [for worldly goods] increases, the further they regress from God, the fount which alone can satisfy them. [. . .] These greedy persons fall into thousands of kinds of sins out of love for temporal goods, and the harm they suffer is indeterminable.[175]

The more intensely we couples desire and seek a Conventional Happiness centered around worldly goods, the less fervently we will desire and seek a Christian Happiness centered around God and virtue. God and virtue will play second fiddle to worldly goods. This is the Christian Morality Problem with Conventional Happiness.

Needs lovers can work out the Christian Morality Problem with Conventional Happiness by desiring and seeking a virtuous Christian Happiness that does not conflict with Christian morality, as we will see (IV,1). The point here, though, is simply that there is a serious Christian Morality Problem with the Conventional Happiness of needs lovers.

chapter 3

The Emotional Problem with Needs Love

THERE IS AN EMOTIONAL PROBLEM WITH NEEDS LOVE. The problem is that needs lovers sometimes experience anger, resentment, or other unloving emotions that weaken their marital love. They do not love one another perfectly with a Christ-like transforming love that is always patient and kind, with no anger, bitterness, or other unloving emotions.

A SELF-CONTROLLED NEEDS LOVE

Many psychologists and other authorities today do not believe that there is an Emotional Problem with needs love that can be worked out. These authorities believe that most if not all of us human beings cannot help feeling anger, resentment, or other unloving emotions at times, so we are not morally responsible for these feelings. Parenting authority Stephen Vannoy claims that we "have every right" to feel angry or whatever we feel because feelings "can't be argued about."[176] The editors of the *Ladies' Home Journal* write that anger is a "normal, expected, and acceptable emotion," so we should give ourselves permission to be angry.[177] Psychologist Theodore Rubin holds that love often *includes* anger instead of excluding it. Rubin writes that love and anger are not mutually exclusive because we can get deeply angry at people we love.[178]

Certainly many of us do get deeply angry at people we love. But this does not necessarily mean that it is morally good to do so.

Rubin, Vannoy, and many other authorities today argue that we are morally responsible for controlling the ways that we act upon anger in our external conduct, but we are not morally responsible for the angry feelings themselves. These authorities advise us to accept our angry feelings and express them "constructively" instead of repressing them or expressing them destructively. Psychologist Harville Hendrix praises a husband and wife for accepting their anger and expressing it "constructively." The wife brags that her husband "had already learned to accept his own anger in his therapy group, but he hadn't accepted *mine*. Now he has. I yell and I scream and I'm still loved."[179]

These authorities make some good points about anger and other negative emotions. We couples *should* "permit ourselves to be angry" in the sense of permitting ourselves to be ourselves. We should accept ourselves as we are instead of pretending to be someone we are not. If we are angry, we should acknowledge our anger honestly; then we can deal with it.

These authorities are right also that we are morally responsible for controlling the ways that we act upon anger and other negative emotions in our external conduct. It is better to express anger "constructively," for example, than to express it destructively.

SELFISH OR SINFUL ANGER

These authorities are wrong, however, about anger and other negative emotions being morally acceptable. Usually anger is not morally acceptable. Jesus teaches that "anyone who is angry with his brother will answer for it before the court" (Matt. 5:22). James writes in a Biblical letter that "human anger does not promote God's justice" (Jas. 1:20—REB). Thomas à Kempis writes in *Of the Imitation of Christ* that a person with true love and humility cannot feel angry at people.[180] In the Christian tradition, anger is one of the Seven Deadly Sins, together with sloth, lust, pride, envy, gluttony, and greed.[181]

Jesus, James, and Thomas à Kempis are referring in the passages above to sinful anger that is not morally acceptable and that we are morally responsible for. They are not referring to special types of anger, such as righteous anger (which is morally acceptable) and suppressed anger (which we might not be morally responsible for). A husband might not be morally responsible for his suppressed anger that developed during his childhood with abusive parents. But he should still deal with this anger not only for his wife's sake, but also for his own sake, including his own mental, emotional, and spiritual well-being.

The fact of the matter is that most anger is sinful or at least selfish. Selfish anger and sinful anger are not compatible with Christian transforming love that is always patient and kind, with no anger, resentment, or other unloving emotions (1 Cor. 13:4–7).

EMOTIONAL NEEDS-LOVE CONFLICT

It could help to be aware of the times when we couples are most likely to experience anger or other unloving emotions. Then we could be better prepared to deal with these emotions.

Many of us are likely to experience unloving emotions when our desires for worldly goods conflict internally within ourselves or interpersonally with our partner. At these times, we may have trouble satisfying all of our conflicting desires, so we may feel frustrated, irritated, angry, or otherwise upset and unloving emotionally.

Let's say that a Christian husband Cory's strong desire to send his children to Christian schools conflicted internally with his equally strong desire to live within his means without borrowing money. He could not enroll his children in Christian schools without borrowing $20,000, so he could not satisfy both of his conflicting desires. Because of this, he was irritated with his wife Jodi for not working part-time to help pay for enrolling their children in Christian schools. He was mad at himself for not making enough money to send their children to Christian schools. He was upset with God for turning a deaf ear to his prayerful request for help sending his children to Christian schools. His unloving emotions weakened his love for Jodi, his self-love, and his love for God.

Cory experienced also interpersonal conflict with Jodi that stirred up unloving emotions. Cory's strong desire to send his children to Christian schools conflicted interpersonally with Jodi's equally strong desire to send the children to public schools. Cory and Jodi fought angrily about this issue.

Many authorities point out that conflicting desires, goals, and needs are especially troublesome in marriage and other intimate relationships because the partners desire so much from each other for their happiness. Psychologists Kinder and Cowan explain that "when you want a person to be your lifelong companion, you are linking your happiness and emotional well-being to him or her. And if your mate does things that threaten that bond, you are likely to respond in the same way anyone does when the basic sense of security is shaken—with anxiety, anger, and even rage."[182]

CHRISTIAN TRANSFORMING VIRTUES COMPARED TO CONVENTIONAL SELF-CONTROLLED VIRTUES

With the emotionally-stormy needs love described above, we couples are not completely transformed emotionally so that we love our partner with a Christ-like transforming love that is always patient and kind. Needs love is not a Christian *transforming* virtue. But this does not necessarily mean that needs love is not a virtue at all. Many philosophers and other authorities today would say that needs love is a *self-controlled* virtue. They would point out that needs lovers control the ways that they act upon their unloving emotions in their external conduct even though they still experience the unloving emotions themselves at times. Needs lovers express their anger and other unloving emotions constructively, for example, instead of destructively. They usually treat their partner reasonably well in their external conduct even if they do not feel like doing so emotionally. They have self-control.

Many philosophers today characterize virtue more in terms of self-control than transformation, as Catholic philosopher Robert Sokolowski points out. Sokolowski argues that our modern self-controlled virtues are weak compared to ancient Greek and traditional Christian transforming virtues. The transforming virtues transform us emotionally so that we experience loving, reasonable emotions with an absence of unloving, unreasonable emotions. The modern self-controlled virtues do not transform us this much emotionally.[183]

We couples can learn about the transforming character of love and other Christian virtues not only from Jesus, St. Thomas Aquinas, and other Christians, but also from some non-Christians, including the ancient Greek philosopher Aristotle. Aristotle identifies six types of people: 1) the godlike person (comparable to the perfectly transformed lover), 2) the virtuous person (somewhat like the transformed lover); 3) the self-controlled person, called the "continent" person (somewhat like the needs lover); 4) the person lacking in self-control, called the "incontinent" person (somewhat like the romantic lover, even though most romantic lovers have a good deal of self-control); 5) the vicious person, and 6) the brutish person.[184] Aristotle observes that godlike and brutish persons are rare, so he focuses on the other four types of people.

According to Aristotle, the self-controlled person is not completely transformed emotionally in the sense of being reasonable emotionally. His emotions, desires, and other inclinations sometimes conflict with his reason. He has self-control, however, so he usually overcomes his conflicting inclinations and acts reasonably.[185]

Suppose that a self-controlled husband Michael was jealous of his wife Hiroko for laughing at another man's jokes. With self-control, Michael would not *act* jealously by telling Hiroko not to laugh. But he would still *feel* jealous even though he knew that his jealous feelings were not reasonable. He would be a self-controlled person, but not a virtuous person. Self-control is not a virtue, according to Aristotle.[186]

The virtuous person, on the other hand, is reasonable emotionally, according to Aristotle. The virtuous person's emotions, desires, and other inclinations do not conflict with his reason. A virtuous husband would not feel jealous if his wife laughed at another man's jokes. His emotions would be reasonable as well as his actions.

The virtuous person is not only reasonable emotionally, but also loving. St. John of the Cross teaches that Christian love transforms a person emotionally so that the person "rejoices only in what is purely for God's honor and glory, hopes for nothing else, feels sorrow only about matters pertaining to this, and fears only God."[187] With these four loving emotions of joy, hope, sorrow, and fear that are directed towards God, John holds that the virtuous person loves God with all his heart, all his soul, and all his strength, including his emotions.[188]

TRANSFORMING OUR EMOTIONS WITH OUR REASON & WILL

Jesus calls us couples to love our partner with an emotionally-pure, Christ-like transforming love, but do we have the human potential to do this? Yes. According to St. Thomas Aquinas, we can transform ourselves emotionally with our reason and will, with God's help. Aquinas writes that our emotions are "subject to the command of the reason and will."[189]

Aquinas does not claim that we can *completely* transform ourselves emotionally with our reason and will. Aquinas distinguishes between the involuntary, irrational elements of our emotions and the voluntary, rational elements.[190] The involuntary, irrational elements of our emotions are the purely physical elements. The emotion of jealousy, for example, includes involuntary, purely physical elements, such as rapid breathing, that we cannot ordinarily control directly with our reason and will. We are not morally responsible for transforming the involuntary, purely physical elements of our emotions.

We can potentially control the voluntary, rational elements of our emotions, however, and we are often morally responsible for doing so. The emotion of jealousy, for example, includes voluntary, rational elements, such as thoughts and feelings of jealousy, that we can potentially control with our reason and will. Suppose that a wife felt angry with her husband for forgetting to pick up a birthday cake for their son's birthday party. The wife could reason that she should not get mad about this, and she could desire and choose willfully to stop feeling angry.

Sometimes it might seem that we cannot control our emotions directly with our reason and will. A five-year-old girl might not be able to stop feeling afraid of the darkness in her bedroom—at least not when she was five years old. But she would have the potential to overcome her fear of the darkness in her bedroom gradually over the years as she matured emotionally. Most of us mature emotionally as we grow from infancy to adulthood. We overcome fears of the dark, temper tantrums, and other childish emotions. During our Terrible Twos, some of us might have thrown temper tantrums if we had not been given Cap'n Crunch's Crunch Berries for breakfast. Hopefully we adults would not throw temper tantrums like this.

TRANSFORMING OURSELVES EMOTIONALLY WITH CHRISTIAN LOVE & WISDOM

We couples need a *loving* will and a *wise* intellect in order to transform ourselves emotionally. More specifically, we need the Christian virtues of love that transforms our will and wisdom that transforms our intellect. With Christian love for God and neighbor, we *desire* willfully to be loving and reasonable emotionally. With Christian wisdom, we *reason* wisely that we should be loving and reasonable emotionally, and we *understand* how to be loving and reasonable emotionally. Then with Christian love once again, we *choose* willfully to be loving and reasonable emotionally.

With Christian love, the jealous husband Michael discussed above could desire willfully not to feel jealous when his wife Hiroko laughs at another man's jokes. With Christian wisdom, he could reason wisely that he should not feel jealous, and he could understand how to stop feeling jealous. Finally with Christian love once again, he could choose willfully to stop feeling jealous. He could stop feeling jealous about things like this gradually over the years, at least, if not right away.

We couples can transform ourselves emotionally with Christian love and wisdom. St. Augustine writes in *The City of God* that our emotions are morally good if our love is good, and our emotions are morally evil if our love is evil.[191] St. Thomas Aquinas teaches that our emotions are morally good to the extent that they are reasonable, and they are morally evil to the extent that they are unreasonable.[192]

Some philosophers, theologians, and other authorities today realize that we human beings have the potential to transform ourselves emotionally and that we are often morally responsible for doing so. Catholic ethicist G. Simon Harak argues in *Virtuous Passions* that we are morally responsible for becoming virtuous emotionally.[193]

Let's see how Christian love and wisdom could help a husband Don stop feeling angry with his wife Jaimee and start feeling more love and compassion for her instead. Don is mad at Jaimee for using his toothbrush after he asked her three times last week not to use it. With Christian love for Jaimee, Don could desire to stop feeling mad at her in order to love her more virtuously, with loving feelings instead of angry feelings. Then with Christian wisdom, Don could come up with wise reasons for not being mad at Jaimee. He could reason that Jaimee might not have intended to ignore his toothbrush requests. Maybe she was worrying about serious problems at work, so she was not aware that she was using his toothbrush. If so, she would need Don's love and compassion, not his anger.

Suppose, on the other hand, that Jaimee used Don's toothbrush spitefully to get back at him for using her hairbrush the day before. Then wouldn't it be reasonable for Don to get mad at Jaimee?

Not by a long shot! Suppose that Jaimee did use Don's toothbrush spitefully. Then she would not have been feeling good about her relationship with Don. In this case, she would need Don's love and understanding even more. A loving response from Don might comfort her like sunshine after rain, to borrow a phrase from Shakespeare.[194]

We couples need to realize that marriage can be like a long trip in a tiny rowboat, as author David Reuben puts it. Reuben explains that "if one passenger starts to rock the boat, the other has to steady it; otherwise they will go to the bottom together."[195]

We couples can row our marriage boat together with compassion, joy, and other loving feelings for one another, or we can risk going to the bottom together with animosity, bitterness, and other unloving emotions.

Suppose that our partner rocks our marriage boat at times in emotionally stormy marriage waters. The stormy waters provide us with golden opportunities to love our partner not only during the good, calm times, but also during the bad, stormy times. In the Disney movie *Mulan*, the Chinese Emperor praises the young Chinese girl Mulan for her great love for her father and her Chinese nation during difficult times. The Emperor says, "The flower that blooms in adversity is the greatest flower of all."

TRANSFORMING OUR BODY AS WELL AS OUR HEART, MIND, & SOUL

We couples can transform our heart, mind, and soul, including our emotions, with love, wisdom, and other Christian virtues, as discussed above. And that's not all. We can transform our body also in a limited way. More specifically, we can transform our *sensory experiences* of sight, hearing, smell, taste, and touch to some extent. It is true that we cannot transform the involuntary, purely physical elements of our sensory experiences, much as we cannot transform the involuntary, purely physical elements of our emotions. A hungry child, for example, could not help being hungry, and he could not prevent his stomach from growling. But he could stop complaining about being hungry, forget about his hunger for a while, and wait patiently for dinner. In this case, the child's patience, wisdom, and other Christian virtues would modify his total mental, emotional, and sensory experience of being hungry.

St. John of the Cross holds that we can purify and transform our sensory experiences to some extent with love, wisdom, and other Christian virtues. John writes that the person transformed by love and other Christian virtues "orders the body according to God." This person "rules and governs the [...] senses according to God and directs their actions towards Him."[196]

Pope John Paul II holds likewise in his theology of the body that love, continence, and other Christian virtues transform not only our external conduct, but also our inner character, including our sensory and emotional experiences. John Paul writes that the Christian virtue of continence helps "guide the whole sensual and emotive sphere" of the human person towards God.[197]

John Paul dwells at length on the transformation of sensory sexual experiences. He explains the teaching of Jesus that "whoever looks at a woman to desire her [lustfully] has already committed adultery with her in his heart [...] (Mt. 5:28)."[198] John Paul holds that the virtue of continence enables people to refrain from committing adultery not only in their external conduct, but also in their inner character, including the voluntary, rational elements of their sensory and emotional experiences. A continent married man would not desire a woman lustfully in his sensory and emotional experiences. He would be free of inner sexual and emotional "tensions," as John Paul puts it.[199]

A Christian husband needed to be transformed sexually and emotionally when he had an affair with a gorgeous woman on his church fund-raising committee. He was "flattered" by the woman's attention and thrilled by her "fantastic" sex.[200] He needed to end the affair not only externally in his conduct, but also internally in his character, including the voluntary, rational elements of his sensory and emotional experiences. He needed to stop lusting after the woman not only in his mind, heart, and soul, but also in his body.

RIDDING OURSELVES OF ANGER WITH WISE CHRISTIAN REASONING

Let's look more closely now at transforming ourselves emotionally. Let's see how Christian wisdom can help us rid ourselves of one particular unloving emotion, that is, anger. Let's look at some wise Christian reasons for not being angry with our partner. These reasons can help motivate us not to get mad at our partner. Most of these reasons apply not only to anger, but also to resentment, bitterness, envy, hotheadedness, and other unreasonable, unloving emotions.

Why is it usually unreasonable for us couples to get mad at our partner?

For starters, anger can undermine our physical health and even kill us. In *Anger Kills*, psychiatrist Redford Williams and his wife Virginia point out that angry people are especially susceptible to ulcers, heart disease, and other health problems.[201]

Anger can kill us in other ways too. According to a news report, a woman and her husband fought angrily over a cigarette. She shot and killed him.

Anger can hurt us mentally and emotionally as well as physically. It is not pleasant to feel angry. A Hindu philosopher writes,

> Why, sir, do you get angry at someone who is angry with you? What are you going to gain by it? How is he going to lose by it? Your physical anger brings dishonor on yourself; your mental anger disturbs your thinking. How can the fire

in your house burn the neighbor's house without engulfing your own?[202]

Anger can hurt us even if we express our anger constructively. Redford Williams challenges the conventional psychological advice that we should express our anger constructively instead of repressing it or expressing it destructively. Williams agrees that it is better to express our anger constructively than to repress it or express it destructively. But he points out that other alternatives are often overlooked. For one thing, we could simply stop being angry. Better yet, we could not get mad in the first place. Williams explains that expressing our anger keeps it alive, even if we express it constructively.[203]

Our anger hurts other people as well as hurting us. People do not feel good bearing the brunt of our anger. They may feel unloved, misunderstood, disrespected, intimidated, controlled, verbally abused, or who knows what else. We seldom make them feel accepted, loved, and cherished when we get mad at them.

Sometimes we may think that our anger is reasonable, but usually we should think again. St. Francis de Sales observes in his *Introduction to the Devout Life* that "there was never an angry man that thought his anger unjust." Francis advises his readers not to be angry even if they think their anger is reasonable: "It is better [. . .] to find the way to live without anger, than to pretend to make a moderate and discreet use of it."[204] Here Francis criticizes the fashionable "anger management" theories of his times.

SUPPOSEDLY REASONABLE ANGER

Many authorities today say that anger is often reasonable. But when is this so?

Not nearly as often as we are led to believe. Redford and Virginia Williams point out correctly that anger kills, but then they backtrack and say that anger is "relatively harmless" for "non-hostile" people who become only mildly angry when others mistreat them.[205] The Williamses argue that anger is justified "on a purely rational, objective basis" when we or other people are treated "unjustly." The Williamses give the following examples of "unjust" conduct that would justify anger: 1) a driver cuts in front of us on the freeway; 2) a co-worker keeps interrupting us after we have asked him not to; 3) our spouse gives us cooking instructions while we are cooking dinner after we have asked him not to; 4) our spouse forgets one of our phone messages; 5) our spouse writes a big check on our joint account in order to buy a new car, but she does not consult us.[206]

It might seem reasonable to be angry with these people, especially the car-buying spouse. But it would not be reasonable. Why not? For starters, these people are ordinary, imperfect people, and ordinary, imperfect people do not act perfectly all the time. It is unrealistic to expect them to act perfectly all the time.

What's more, suppose that we did get mad at imperfect people for acting imperfectly at times. Then we would get mad again and again in this imperfect world, and all of our supposedly mild, justifiable anger would hurt us mentally, emotionally, and physically, as discussed above. It is not reasonable to hurt ourselves day in and day out with all this anger.

And that's not all. When we get mad at imperfect people for acting imperfectly, we are not accepting and loving them as they are, as imperfect human beings.

The fact of the matter is that most anger undermines our happiness even if the anger is mild and supposedly justifiable. When we are angry, we are not completely happy in the conventional sense of feeling good emotionally, much less in the Christian sense of following Jesus virtuously. Anger is usually an unpleasant, un-Christ-like emotion. Brigham Young University professor Terry Warner observes that harboring anger, resentment, and other self-destructive emotions makes no sense. Warner wonders:

> Why don't we get fed up with the wretchedness of being angry, resentful, irritated, vindictive, petty, humiliated, offended, or whatever, and say to ourselves, "Living like this stinks! Who wants to wallow around in pain? I'm quitting! I'm tossing out these afflicting feelings—packing them around is ruining my life!"[207]

SELFISH, UNLOVING ANGER

Let's look at one of the examples of the mild, supposedly justifiable anger that Redford and Virginia Williams envision. According to the Williamses, a husband would justifiably be angry with his wife Mary if she forgot to give him a phone message about an important conference. The Williamses say that the husband should remind Mary that she promised to give him all his phone messages, and then she broke her promise. The Williamses suggest that the husband could say,

Mary, you and I agreed that you would let me know about all the calls I received. Mr. Jones tells me that he left a message with you the other day, yet I never heard about his call. As a result, I missed hearing about a conference. I want you always to let me know about every call I get. Is that something you can do in the future?[208]

The Williamses say that the husband is being reasonable when he asks Mary to give him all his phone messages without ever forgetting a message. But the husband is not being reasonable, much less being loving. He unreasonably expects Mary to remember every single one of his phone messages for the rest of their married life together. He warns Mary unlovingly that she had better not forget any of his phone messages ever again, or else! He does not assure Mary that he will always accept, love, and cherish her just as she is—even if she forgets one of his phone messages from time to time. He does not tell Mary lovingly, "Don't worry about forgetting the phone message about the conference. No problem. I forget things sometimes too. You're great! I love you so much!"

The husband blames Mary for making him angry, but he should blame himself. *He* is the one who is getting mad, not Mary. *He* is morally responsible for his anger, not Mary. *He* is the one who should stop being angry in order to respond to Mary lovingly, follow Jesus virtuously, and be happy.

The husband could respond to Mary lovingly and still deal with his phone messages in practical ways. He could talk with Mary lovingly about his phone messages without being mad at her. If it would help, Mary could have callers leave their messages on the answering machine instead of taking the messages herself.

In any case, it does no good for the husband to get mad at Mary about the phone messages. As a couple old American proverbs say, anger usually punishes itself and profits nobody.[209]

LOOKING CHARITABLY FOR THE BEST IN OUR PARTNER

It is not reasonable to be angry with ordinary, imperfect people when they mistreat us, as discussed above. It is even less reasonable to get mad at these people when *we think* that they are mistreating us, but we are wrong. Unfortunately this happens all too often in marriage and other intimate relationships. Some couples rush to one-sided, sexist, unfair, or otherwise faulty negative judgments about their partner, and then they get mad at their partner because of this!

We can avoid rushing to mistaken negative judgments about our partner by looking for the best in our partner instead of the worst. If we look for the worst in our partner, we are more likely to judge our partner harshly and unfairly, and then we may be angry, resentful, or otherwise unloving emotionally. If we look for the best in our partner, on the other hand, we are more likely to judge our partner compassionately and charitably, and then we may be compassionate, upbeat, and otherwise loving emotionally.

A husband looked for the worst in his wife when she did not want to cook dinner one night. He complained angrily that she did not care about him. But there could have been many reasons why she did not want to cook dinner that night. Maybe she was tired from a long day at work.

We couples can look for the best in our spouse, much as we can look for the best in our guests. The Navajo Indians say, "Always assume your guest is tired, cold, and hungry, and act accordingly."[210]

St. Thomas Aquinas looked for the best in people. One day one of Thomas's friends called Thomas to come see a flying ox outside the window. Thomas rushed to the window and looked out for the flying ox. Then Thomas's friend cried out gleefully, "What a fool you are, Thomas, for thinking that an ox could fly." Thomas replied, "I would rather think that an ox could fly than that you would lie."[211]

Virtuous couples habitually look for the best in their partner, but they see the worst too. They help their partner deal with any serious character weaknesses if their partner is willing and able to do this. They do not love their partner permissively, as we will see (IV,3).

CHRISTIAN ANGER PREVENTION

Suppose that we couples reason wisely that most anger is unreasonable and unloving, as discussed above. Then we would be motivated not to be angry in the first place. We could deal with anger more effectively with this Christian anger *prevention* than we could with today's conventional anger management techniques. Let's see why this is so.

With Christian anger prevention, we couples do not get mad at ourselves or our partner in the first place, so there is no anger to hurt us or our partner. With anger management techniques, on the other hand, we struggle to manage our anger whenever it flares up, day in and day out, year in and year out, for the rest of our life together. We may not be liberated from anger and other hurtful emotions until the day that we or our partner dies. And even then we may not be liberated from these hurtful emotions. The epitaph for a husband named Walter might apply to us too: "Here lies my darling husband, Walter. May he rest in peace until we meet again."[212]

Let's face the facts. Every minute we are angry, we lose 60 seconds of happiness, as an old American proverb says.[213]

We may lose even more than 60 seconds of happiness for every minute we are angry. We may suffer from the consequences of our anger for days, months, and even years. We may suffer from health problems, like headaches and heart attacks. We may suffer from relationship problems, like divorce and child custody battles. As an old American proverb says, anger is a brief madness, but it can do damage that lasts forever.[214]

Yes, anger can do damage that lasts forever. Anger can damage our soul. Anger can hold us back from following Jesus virtuously in this life and from being united with God in this life and eternally.

HURTFUL NEEDS-LOVE CONFLICT

Marriage authorities who believe that anger is inevitable in marriage and other intimate relationships usually believe that fighting also is inevitable. Psychologists Markman, Stanley, and Blumberg write in *Fighting for Your Marriage* that marital conflict is unavoidable, so if we couples want to have a good marriage, we had "better learn to fight right."[215]

Today's fashionable fighting-right marriage guidance could help romantic lovers express anger and other unloving emotions "constructively" and fight "fairly" with supposedly healthy marital conflict instead of expressing these emotions destructively and fighting unfairly with unhealthy marital conflict. This fighting-right marriage guidance, however, would not help needs lovers as much as it could help romantic lovers. Many needs lovers already express anger and other unloving emotions "constructively" and fight "fairly" with supposedly healthy marital conflict, so they do not need to learn how to do these things. Now they need to learn how to become even more loving emotionally, with little or no anger, fighting, or other hurtful conflict. They need to learn how to grow from their emotionally-volatile, fair-fighting needs love to a stable, emotionally-pure, Christ-like transforming love. They need more Christian marriage guidance.

MODEL NEEDS LOVERS

Conventional marriage authorities today do not provide enough Christian marriage guidance that covers growth from needs love to transforming love. Supposedly model couples described in most marriage guides experience anger, fighting, and other hurtful conflict on a permanent, ongoing basis. Psychologist Harville Hendrix describes a "model" couple, Greg and Anne, who "have managed to create a marriage that satisfies each individual's need for healing and wholeness."[216] When Greg's and Anne's needs and desires conflict, they negotiate their differences with fair fighting and other communication skills.

Let's look at one of Greg's and Anne's fair fights. In this fight, Anne noticed that Greg was not wearing his wedding ring. She felt hurt, angry, and betrayed. Instead of "stewing" about this, though, she conveyed her feelings to Greg right away. She said,

> I'm really hurt that you're not wearing your ring. A ring is a visible sign to other people that we're married, and it's really important to me. I'm really upset. I don't know what it means that you're not wearing it. I don't like it, and I want you to wear it.[217]

Greg replied sensitively, "It makes sense that you feel that way. I understand that you're angry." Days later Greg explained that he took off his wedding ring to get back at Anne for using her maiden name without asking him how he would feel about this. He had felt hurt by that.[218]

Greg and Anne did not resolve their problem right away. Anne said that the important thing was that "we both got our feelings out. We listened to each other. We defused all the bad energy. And we're not angry any more. Before, we would have gotten obsessed about it and gone on and on."[219]

Greg and Anne demonstrated commendable needs love and wisdom in their fair fighting over Greg's wedding ring. But they could have been more loving and wise. Anne used her maiden name without asking Greg how he would feel about this. Greg then retaliated childishly by taking off his wedding ring. Anne then felt hurt, angry, and betrayed even though she had not even asked Greg why he was not wearing his wedding ring. She was not treating Greg fairly by rushing to the harsh emotional judgment that Greg was betraying her, and then getting mad at him because of this. The fact of the matter is that Anne did not know whether or not Greg was betraying her. Who knows, maybe Greg gained weight recently, and he took his ring to the jeweler to be sized.

Greg and Anne experienced conflict on a continuing basis. Anne said that working things out with Greg is the hardest thing that she has ever done.[220]

Greg and Anne could have dealt with their wedding-ring problem more effectively with Christian transforming love and wisdom than they did with their needs love and wisdom. With transforming love and wisdom, Anne would have been happy being a virtuous, Christ-like person without being uptight about Greg's wedding ring. She would have dealt with the wedding ring situation lovingly from the start, considering Greg's interests as well as her own. She would not have felt hurt, angry, and betrayed when she noticed that Greg was not wearing his ring. She would not have jumped to negative emotional judgments about Greg without asking for his point of view first. She would probably have asked Greg about the ring, listened compassionately, and responded sensitively to his concerns about her maiden name. She still could have told Greg that she would like him to wear the ring. She could have looked out for her interests as well as for Greg's interests.

With Christian transforming love and wisdom, Anne and Greg would have prevented the wedding-ring and maiden-name problems from coming up in the first place. They would have dealt with these matters lovingly and wisely from the start.

Greg, Anne, and the rest of us couples can work out the Emotional Problem with needs love by growing to a Christ-like transforming love that is not weakened by unloving emotions, as we will see (IV,1–4). The main point in this chapter, though, is simply that there is a serious Emotional Problem with needs love. Needs lovers sometimes experience unloving emotions that weaken their marital love significantly.

CONCLUSION

We couples should not take lightly the anger, fighting, and other hurtful conflict that sometimes come with needs love. Conflict can weaken and even destroy a marriage. John Taylor observes that his marriage "wasn't hellish; it was simply dispiriting. My wife, Maureen, and I didn't hate each other; we simply got on each other's nerves. We had just, over the years, each accumulated a store of minor unresolved grievances."[221] Taylor's wife

Maureen said that she and John fought more and more over the years, and finally they divorced.[222]

It is true that marital conflict can be "healthy" in the conventional needs-love sense of "defusing bad energy" so that we couples do not feel angry any more, as Anne puts it. But it is the elimination of the anger and the resolution of the conflict that is healthy, not the anger and conflict itself. Webster's dictionary does not define conflict as a healthy encounter. Webster's dictionary defines conflict as a "hostile encounter" and a "strife for mastery." In a survey of Miramar College students, most of the students said that if they were married, they would like to deal with marital problems and differences peacefully. An Iranian student said that if two people loved each other, "they would solve any disagreements very lovingly and sweetly!"

My wife Arnell recalled recently that she had been impressed by what I said during our first year of marriage when we disagreed about what television show to watch. I said that we could make our marriage whatever we wanted it to be. We could deal with our differences lovingly without arguing about getting our way. That's what we have tried to do, and it has worked well.

chapter 4

The Fantasy Problem with Needs Wisdom

THERE IS A FANTASY PROBLEM WITH NEEDS WISDOM. The problem is that needs lovers with needs wisdom fantasize about being conventionally happy, much as romantic lovers with romantic wisdom fantasize about being emotionally happy. Realistically, though, romantic lovers and needs lovers are often not as happy as they fantasize they will be.

The fantasies of romantic lovers and needs lovers are fanciful, deceptive images of reality. Romantic lover Jose discussed above was deceived by his fanciful image of his drop-dead gorgeous wife Jessie as a source of his dinnertime happiness (II,2). The real Jessie was not always a source of his dinnertime happiness. The real Jessie often dined with hair curlers, frayed and faded sweats, and greasy white facial cream that hardened into a ghastly white mask that a mime might wear on Halloween. Jessie the drop-dead gorgeous dinnertime beauty queen was Jose's romantic fantasy.

NEEDS-WISDOM FANTASIES ABOUT CONVENTIONAL HAPPINESS

Needs lovers with needs wisdom sometimes fantasize that they will be conventionally happy by satisfying many of their desires for worldly goods. But their desires are often frustrated in this real world with all the natural disasters, injustice, crime, cruelty, computer viruses, sand traps, and the like. Then needs lovers sometimes experience disappointment, regret, or other mental and emotional distress that undermines their Conventional Happiness significantly.

Members of Generation Me (born from 1970 to 2005) may be especially likely to fantasize about satisfying their desires for wealth, fame, or other worldly goods. According to Jean Twenge, many members of Generation Me expect unrealistically

> to go to college, to make lots of money, and perhaps even to be famous. Yet this generation enters a world in which college admissions are increasingly competitive, good jobs are hard to find and harder to keep, and basic necessities like housing and health care have skyrocketed in price.[223]

Twenge argues that the gap between what young people desire and what they have is greater now in the beginning of the 21st century than it has ever been.[224]

The gap between what some members of Generation Me desire and what they have shows up in their pursuit of life's simple pleasures, such as a relaxing dip in a hot tub. A young Generation Me woman in a comic strip on a billboard at Universal Studios in Hollywood complains to her boy friend, "Oh Andy, [. . .] the hot tub overflowed and ruined my cell phone. Then the cappuccino maker exploded and the top on the convertible is stuck [. . .] AGAIN!" The title for the billboard comic strip is "LA Angst."

This young Generation Me woman was not as happy as she fantasized that she would be with her hot tub, cell phone, cappuccino maker, convertible, and other worldly goods.

NEEDS-WISDOM FANTASIES ABOUT NEEDS LOVE

Needs lovers with needs wisdom fantasize not only about their Conventional Happiness, as discussed above, but also about their needs love. It might seem that they view their needs love realistically without fantasizing about it. After all, they admit that they get mad at their partner at times, with a good deal of marital conflict. Aren't they being realistic about this?

Yes, to some extent. Needs lovers acknowledge their anger, fighting, and other conflict somewhat realistically. But then they sometimes go on to fantasize that their anger is "constructive," their fighting is "fair," and their conflict is "healthy."[225] Some of them fantasize that their conflict can lead to such "positive" things as a "liberating" divorce that is supposedly desirable not just for them, but for their children too. Many needs lovers pick up fantasies about divorce from some psychologists, sociologists, and other authorities today who characterize divorce largely as a positive, liberating, growth experience.[226] These authorities make some good points, but they do not account adequately for the problems that often come with divorce.

Needs-wisdom fantasies about "constructive" anger, "fair" fighting, and other supposedly healthy conflict reflect part of the truth about needs love, but not the whole truth. Certainly it *is* better for us couples to express our anger "constructively" and to fight "fairly" with supposedly healthy conflict than it would be to express our anger destructively and to fight unfairly with unhealthy conflict. But this is not the whole truth about needs love, including the anger, fighting, and other conflict that sometimes come with needs love. The whole truth about anger includes the facts that most anger is unloving, unwise, and hurtful; that we couples have the potential to rid ourselves of selfish or sinful anger; and that we are often morally responsible for doing this (III,3 above).

THE REALISM OBJECTION TO CHRISTIAN LOVE

Some psychologists and other authorities defend needs love by attacking the Christian ideal of transforming love. These authorities maintain that most if not all of us human beings cannot help feeling anger, resentment, or other unloving emotions at times, so there is nothing wrong with this, as long as we deal with these emotions constructively. These authorities object that it would be unrealistic to strive for an anger-free, emotionally-pure Christian transforming love in marriage and other intimate relationships. I call this the REALISM OBJECTION to Christian love.

Physician John Jacobs raises the Realism Objection to love of an unconditional, transforming Christian sort in his book, *All You Need Is Love and Other Lies about Marriage*. According to Jacobs, most people who think that they have discovered unconditional love are young, naive, or involved in a dependent relationship with an emotionally-troubled person.[227] Along these same lines, Catholic authors Wilkie Au and Noreen Cannon warn their readers *not* to believe that people who seem to be consistently generous, kind, and charitable really are that way. Au and Cannon say that these people *must* be repressing the dark side of their personality, for no one could be that perfect. Au and Cannon add that these people who seem "too good to be true" may irritate us because we know intuitively that they are "hiding their true feelings and reactions so that others will admire them."[228]

Once again, let's not be misled by today's marriage skeptics. The Realism Objection to Christian love does not hold water. It is true that many people who claim to have experienced unconditional love *are* young, naïve, and/or co-dependent, and many people who seem to be consistently generous, kind, and charitable *are* "hiding their true feelings and reactions so that others will admire them." These people are not saints. But so what? We have understood for centuries that people who do "good works" in order to be admired by others are not saints. St. John of the Cross writes that some Christians

> do not perform them [good works] unless they see that some gratification or praise will result from them. [. . .] Some want praise for their works; others, thanks; others talk about them and are pleased if this person or that or even the whole world knows about them. [. . .] The Saviour in the Gospel compares this to sounding the trumpet, which is the practice of vain men, and He declares that as a result they will not receive a reward from God for their works [Mt. 6:2].[229]

The fact that many people are not saints does not mean that there are no saints. The Realism Objection to Christian love does not account for the fact that there are saints who *do* experience a Christ-like transforming love for God and neighbor.

Au, Cannon, Jacobs, and other skeptical marriage "experts" probably discourage some of us Christian couples from trying to "live the same kind of life as Christ lived." But that's a shame. Let's not be discouraged. American author Robert Heinlein tells us how to listen to "experts" like these. He says, "Always listen to experts. They'll tell you what can't be done and why. Then do it."[230]

CHRISTIAN OPTIMISM ABOUT LOVE

Jesus calls us couples to do it, that is, to love our partner as Jesus loves us: "This is my commandment: love one another, as I have loved you" (John 15:12).

Christian saints have loved their neighbors as Jesus loves us, and we couples can too—especially if the saints are our heroes, heroines, and role models. My mother Owenita Sanderlin wrote in one of her Catholic parenting articles that if parents work at it, the saints can become their children's heroes and heroines.[231] The saints have always been my heroes and heroines.

Christian saints may not be heroes and heroines for as many Christians today as they have been in the past. Catholic theologian Karl Rahner comments on the passing of the saint from Catholic piety.[232] Christian scholars Alasdair MacIntyre and John Coleman observe that we have lost a vocabulary of sanctity and virtue in our modern American society.[233] This guide aims to help recover our Christian vocabulary of sanctity and virtue in order to help couples strengthen their marriages and families with love, wisdom, and other Christian virtues.

THE PERFECTIONIST OBJECTION TO CHRISTIAN LOVE

There is a PERFECTIONIST OBJECTION to Christian love as well as a Realism Objection. Some critics of Christian love object that desiring and striving for a Christ-like transforming love prevents us from accepting and loving ourselves as we are, imperfect human beings, incapable of such a perfect love. What's more, if we strive for such a perfect love, we will surely fail, frustrate ourselves, and damage our self-esteem. In short, we will be immature perfectionists. This is the Perfectionist Objection to Christian love.

It is true that some couples who strive for a Christ-like transforming love *are* immature perfectionists. They may not have been accepted and loved by their parents or adult guardians during their childhood, so they may be longing for acceptance and love not only from other people, but also from themselves. They may try to be perfect in order to get the acceptance and love that they desire. They may strive for such things as a perfectly clean house and a perfect anger-free love in order to "earn" acceptance and love from themselves and others. But they should not strive for these perfect things in order to get the acceptance and love that they desire. They should accept and love themselves as they are, however untidy, angry, or otherwise imperfect they may be. God accepts and loves them as they are, and they should too.

The fact that some people who strive for a Christ-like transforming love are immature perfectionists does not mean that all people who do this are immature perfectionists. We can distinguish between an immature perfectionism and a mature pursuit of moral excellence. The Perfectionist Objection to Christian love does not account adequately for a mature pursuit of moral excellence. Let's see why this is so.

A MATURE PURSUIT OF MORAL EXCELLENCE

With a mature pursuit of moral excellence, we couples desire and strive for perfection in the area of morality, but not necessarily in morally-neutral areas, such as housecleaning. In the area of morality, we try to become like Jesus in our moral character and conduct, and there is nothing wrong with this. Jesus calls us to be morally perfect, even as our heavenly Father is morally perfect (Matt. 5:44–48). We rightly try to become increasingly virtuous, Christ-like persons, as best we can, with God's help.

AN IMMATURE PERFECTIONISM

With an immature perfectionism, on the other hand, we desire and strive for perfection mostly in morally-neutral areas, such as housecleaning, and sometimes there is a problem with this. The problem is that desiring and striving for perfection in morally-neutral areas can prevent us from responding to our partner lovingly and following Jesus virtuously. Let's see how a wife Laura's desirous pursuit of perfection in the area of dishwashing prevented her from responding to her husband Fred lovingly and following Jesus virtuously.

Laura wanted Fred to put the dishes away "properly" or "perfectly" after he washed them in order to please her. She complained to their marriage counselor:

> The only area I have control over is the kitchen. There's a right way and a wrong way to do things. He [Fred] never puts away the dishes properly on the shelf. He mixes the tall glasses and the short glasses and the cups. And he won't stack the dishes properly in the dishwasher. [. . .] He doesn't really care about *how* he does it [the job]. [. . .] Basically, he doesn't think much of me.[234]

Laura should not selfishly desire and demand that Fred put the dishes back "properly" or "perfectly" in order to please her. Laura should let go of her selfish, perfectionist dishwashing desires in order to be happy responding to Fred more lovingly and following Jesus more virtuously. She should accept and love Fred as he is, even when he mixes the tall glasses, short glasses, and cups.

Many members of the audience in an Oprah Winfrey show dealing with perfectionism were perfectionists mostly in their housecleaning, looks, cooking, or other morally-neutral areas. One woman said that "a house can never be too clean, even if it means spending every day, all day, cleaning it."[235] Another woman tried to reconstruct her face with nine plastic surgeries.[236]

We couples may need to let go of selfish perfectionist desires for such things as a perfectly clean house, "perfectly" arranged glasses and cups, and a perfect 300 game in bowling in order to be happy responding to our partner lovingly and following Jesus virtuously, without or without these "perfect" things.

We should not selfishly desire and demand perfection in housecleaning and other morally-neutral areas in order to be happy, as discussed above, but what about *pursuing* perfection in these areas? May we pursue perfection in housecleaning, dishwashing, bowling, or other morally-neutral areas that interest us—as long as we do not desire and demand perfection in these areas for our happiness?

Yes, sometimes we may pursue perfection in morally-neutral areas. The Lexus automobile company pursues perfection in the building of their automobiles, and why shouldn't they? And why shouldn't we couples pursue perfection in morally-neutral areas that interest us? Why shouldn't we try to bowl a perfect 300 game if we would enjoy doing this? There is nothing morally wrong with a perfect 300 game in bowling or other worldly goods. It is our *selfish desires* for the perfect game or other perfect worldly goods that often frustrate us and prevent us from following Jesus virtuously—it is not the perfect worldly goods themselves.

MARLA'S IMMATURE PURSUIT OF MORAL PERFECTION

We couples rightly strive for perfection in the area of Christian morality, as discussed above. But we should not desire and demand Christian moral perfection right now, pronto, according to our timetable. We should be content trying to become more like Jesus gradually over the years, as best we can, with God's help.

A perfectionist wife Marla tried to love her husband Peter with a perfect anger-free love before she was mentally and emotionally prepared to do this. She wanted Peter to approve of her, so she tried to be morally perfect in order to impress him. She often got mad at him, but she did not want him to know this, so she hid her anger instead of acknowledging it honestly and dealing with it constructively. She finally did acknowledge her anger in a counseling session with Peter and their counselor, Harville Hendrix. She said that she had been mad at Peter one night when she told him about an important dream and he did not listen. She recalled:

> I didn't like it that you weren't paying any attention to me. [. . .] (Whispers.) Oh, God. There's like this big wall in my head against being angry. [. . .] (Shouts.) I won't tell you about my angry feelings. (She begins to cry.) You never listen anyway. [. . .] I want you to listen to me when I'm really being me, and not trying to be perfect. [. . .] (Cries.) I'm so afraid of getting angry at you. [. . .] (Sobbing.) If I get angry at you . . . you're going to hate me! [. . .] And I'm afraid you'll think I'm *stupid*. [. . .] (Loudly.) It doesn't make sense! I know I can get angry. I know I have that right. [. . .] I have a right to be angry! (Louder.) I have a right to be angry![237]

We couples need to be ourselves. Suppose that we could not help being mad at our partner at times. That would be o.k. We could acknowledge our anger and deal with it constructively instead of repressing it or expressing it destructively.

What if we *already* acknowledge our anger and deal with it constructively, however, with a self-controlled needs love for our partner? Now we would not grow mentally and emotionally by acknowledging our anger and dealing with it constructively because we would already be doing this. Now we would grow mentally and emotionally by gradually ridding ourselves of our anger and, better yet, by not getting mad in the first place. Now striving for an anger-free Christian transforming love could be a mature pursuit of moral excellence.

ST. THÉRÈSE OF LISIEUX'S MATURE PURSUIT OF MORAL EXCELLENCE

Some marriage authorities give the impression that desiring and striving for such perfect things as a Christ-like transforming love would *always* be objectionably perfectionist for *everyone*. But this is not so. Many saintly Christians have achieved a perfect or at least a nearly perfect Christian love. St. Thérèse of Lisieux, a French Carmelite nun, recalls in her *Autobiography* (1898) that in her early twenties it was easy for her to love others with perfect charity, but it had not always been easy. During her late teens she had struggled with mild feelings of annoyance that had tainted her love for others. She recalls an incident in her convent:

> I was in the washhouse near a sister who constantly splashed me with dirty water as she washed the handkerchiefs. My first impulse was to draw back and wipe my face so as to show her I would like her to work with less splashing. Then I at once thought how foolish I was to refuse the precious gifts offered me so generously and I was very careful not to show my annoyance. In fact, I made such efforts to want to be showered with dirty water that after half an hour I had genuinely taken a fancy to this novel kind of aspersion, and I decided to turn up as often as I could to that lucky spot where so much spiritual wealth was freely handed out.[238]

Thérèse was not an immature perfectionist during her late teens when she struggled with mild feelings of annoyance. Thérèse was becoming a saint.

OVERCOMING IMMATURE PERFECTIONISM BY PURSUING MORAL EXCELLENCE

A mature pursuit of moral excellence is *not* an immature perfectionism. In fact, a mature pursuit of moral excellence is often *the best way to overcome an immature perfectionism!* To pursue moral excellence, we need to let go of selfish perfectionist desires for perfect worldly goods in order to be happy following Jesus virtuously, with or without these perfect things. We need to let go of desires for such things as perfectly-cooked meals, with no greasy barbecued chicken; a perfectly clean car, with no candy wrappers under the front seats; a perfect front lawn, with no weeds or brown spots; and the list of perfectionist desires, frustrations, anxieties, and the like could go on.

To achieve moral excellence, some of us couples may need to put away our old Perfectionist Self in order to put on a new, more virtuous, Christ-like Transformed Self.

THE SELF-ACCEPTANCE OBJECTION TO CHRISTIAN LOVE

There is a third objection to Christian love that often comes with the Realism and Perfectionist Objections discussed above. This is the SELF-ACCEPTANCE OBJECTION. Some critics of Christian love argue that most of us couples would not be accepting ourselves as we are, imperfect human beings, if we tried to grow from needs love to a Christ-like transforming love. These critics emphasize that we should accept ourselves as we are, however sinful and un-Christ-like we may be.

Certainly we should accept ourselves as we are. But in what sense should we accept ourselves as we are? Critics with the Self-Acceptance Objection to Christian love do not account adequately for a distinction between a complacent self-acceptance and a humble Christian self-acceptance. With a complacent self-acceptance, we accept ourselves as we are without trying to improve ourselves much if at all. We say that God accepts and loves us as we are, so we should do this too. We are "self-satisfied" in a negative way (Rom. 12:16).

With a humble Christian self-acceptance, on the other hand, we accept ourselves as we are, but we try to improve ourselves too. Our self-acceptance includes a humble commitment to amend our life as best we can, with the help of Jesus.

A COMPLACENT SELF-ACCEPTANCE

Some couples complacently accept themselves as they are without trying to improve themselves much if at all. What's more, they often expect their partner to accept them as they are—even when they mistreat their partner! They may mistreat their partner, shrug their shoulders, and say, "Nobody's perfect," or, "I'm only human." American journalist Sydney Harris (1917–1986) observes that "a person who is going to commit an inhuman act invariably excuses himself by saying, 'I'm only human, after all'."[239]

A woman in the 1997 music video "Bitch," performed by Meredith Brooks, associates being human with being a bitch at times. She asks her partner to accept her as she is even though she is a bitch at times. She sings, "I can't change. [. . .] I'm a bitch. [. . .] I'm a child. I'm a mother. I'm a sinner. I'm a saint. [. . .] I do not feel ashamed. Take me as I am."[240]

Should this singer's partner take her as she is, even if she is a bitch at times and will not change? Yes and no. Yes, he should accept her in his heart, mind, and soul. But no, he should not accept her bitchy conduct. He should not permit her to mistreat him without standing up against this. He should try to help her become a more loving, Christ-like person to the extent that she is willing and able to do this.

Suppose that we ourselves are the bitchy or bastardy ones. Should we excuse our bitchiness or bastardness because "nobody's perfect"? Should we sweep our selfishness and sinfulness under the rug, shrug our shoulders, and tell our partner, "I'm only human, after all"?

Unfortunately some Christian authorities today encourage us to sweep a good deal of our selfishness and sinfulness under the rug. But this is not new. St. Teresa of Avila recalls in the *Book of Her Life* that she paid too little attention to her venial sins during her early twenties, as Catholic author Ralph Martin has pointed out.[241] Teresa writes that she was misled by some priests who gave her the "liberal" and "permissive" advice that "what was venial sin [. . .] was no sin at all" and "what was serious mortal sin [. . .] was venial."[242] Teresa recalls that this advice harmed her greatly for more than seventeen years until a Dominican Father [Vincente Barron] enlightened her about the seriousness of venial sins.[243]

St. Teresa emphasizes the seriousness of both venial and mortal sins in her *Way of Perfection*. She advises her Carmelite sisters to be "most careful not to commit venial sins." She advises the sisters also to "have such a fixed determination not to offend the Lord that you would rather lose a thousand lives, *and be persecuted by the whole world,* than commit one mortal sin."[244]

We couples should try to improve *ourselves* most of all, not other people, including our partner. Some of us try to improve our partner more than we try to improve ourselves. We see the splinter in our partner's eye, but not the plank in our eye (Matt. 7:3–5).

An Islamic Sufi sage, Nulla Nasrudin, recalls that when he was young, he prayed to Allah for the strength to change the world. Then in mid-life he realized that he had not changed anyone, so he prayed for the strength to change those close to him. Finally in his old age he realized that he still had not changed anyone. Now he prayed for the strength to change himself.[245]

Catholic spiritual director François Fénelon emphasizes the importance of improving ourselves. He writes,

> Nothing is more perilous to your own salvation, more unworthy of God, or more hurtful to your ordinary happiness than being content to remain as you are. Our whole life is given us with the object of going boldly on towards the heavenly home. The world slips away like a deceitful shadow, and eternity draws near. Why delay to push forward? While it is time, while your merciful Father lights up your path, make haste and seek his kingdom![246]

THE COURAGE TO PUT AWAY OUR OLD SELF & PUT ON A NEW SELF

It takes courage to seek God's kingdom. It takes courage not only to accept our old sinful self, but also to put away our old sinful self in order to put on a new, more virtuous, Christ-like self. But that's what Jesus calls us to do. Jesus teaches that we need to renounce ourselves in order to follow him (Luke 9:23), and we need to lose our life in order to save it (Luke 9:24). St. John of the Cross teaches that we need to pass through a dark night of the soul in order to be united with God. Taoist Lao Tzu teaches that "the Way of illumination seems dark [. . .] higher virtue seems empty, great purity seems ignominious, broad virtue seems insufficient."[247]

It takes courage to change ourselves for the better. In William Faulkner's short story, "Barn Burning," a young boy Sarty summoned the courage to rebel against his abusive father and leave his dysfunctional family in order to become a better person. Sarty left everything that he had known for the unknown. At the end of the story, he sat during the night with "his back toward what he had called home" and "his face toward the dark woods." Then shortly before dawn he walked toward the dark woods "within which the liquid silver voices of the birds called unceasing," and he did not look back.[248]

Some of us couples may need to summon the courage to walk away mentally and emotionally from the familiar places in our childhood and the comfortable places in our soul that we have called home in order to walk with Jesus through the dark Christian woods that lead to a greater love and happiness than we have known before.

What do we couples need for this journey with Jesus in addition to courage, faith, love, and other Christian virtues and gifts?

We need the *commitment* to following Jesus that comes with these virtues and gifts. We need to commit ourselves faithfully, lovingly, and wisely to following Jesus wherever he leads us—even if he leads us to embrace our spouse lovingly and joyfully when she burns the pot roast, bounces three checks in one week, and (God forbid!) forgets to tell us about an important phone message.

An anonymous medieval Christian mystic describes the commitment to following Jesus wherever he leads us in terms of following a "gentle stirring of love" in our heart. The mystic writes,

> You may confidently rely on this gentle stirring of love
> in your heart and follow wherever it leads you, for it is your

sure guide in this life and will bring you to the glory of the next. This little love is the essence of a good life and without it no good work is possible. Basically, love means a radical personal commitment to God. This implies that your will is harmoniously attuned to his in an abiding contentedness and enthusiasm for all he does.[249]

CONCLUSION TO PART III

We Christian couples do not have to settle for a conventional needs love, wisdom, and happiness that come with such things as "constructive" anger, "fair" fighting, and other supposedly healthy conflict. We can grow to a Christ-like transforming love, wisdom, and happiness. To see how we can do this, let's go to the Christ-like transforming stage of Christian marriage discipleship (Part IV).

Before we go to Part IV, some of you readers may choose to check your Christian marriage discipleship at this time by looking for the needs aspects of this discipleship that have been covered in this Part III. The Christian Marriage Discipleship Check-Up Worksheet in Appendix A can help you do this. Completing the worksheet can help you apply the material in this Part III to your family finances, housework, and other areas of your marriage and family life. You and your partner might get some good ideas for dealing with problems and differences in these areas.

If you complete the worksheet in Appendix A at this time, you may consider both the positive and negative aspects of needs love, wisdom, and happiness. On the positive side, you could consider these three reflection questions:

1) To what extent do you seek a Conventional Happiness centered around intimacy goals, personal growth goals, and other intrinsic goals instead of seeking an Emotional Happiness centered around materialistic goals, power goals, and other extrinsic goals (covered in this Part III, Chapter 1, Section A)? Explain your answer with examples from your marriage experiences.

2) To what extent do you control the ways that you act upon anger, animosity, or other negative emotions in your external conduct so that you treat your partner reasonably well even if you do not feel like doing so (III,1B)? Explain your answer with examples from your marriage experiences.

3) To what extent do you deal with yourself, your partner, and/or your relationship more realistically and insightfully than romantic lovers do (III,1C)? Explain your answer with examples from your marriage experiences.

On the negative side, you could consider these three reflection questions:

1) To what extent do you experience the Christian Morality Problem with the Conventional Happiness of needs lovers (III,2)? In other words, to what extent do you pursue a Conventional Happiness selfishly at times instead of responding to your partner lovingly and following Jesus virtuously? Explain your answer with examples from your marriage experiences.

2) To what extent do you experience the Emotional Problem with needs love (III,3)? In other words, to what extent do you experience anger, resentment, or other negative emotions that weaken your love for your partner, for yourself, or for God? Explain your answer with examples from your marriage experiences.

3) To what extent do you experience the Fantasy Problem with needs wisdom (III,4)? In other words, to what extent do you "fantasize" somewhat unrealistically and wishfully about yourself, your partner, or your relationship instead of acknowledging and dealing with real problems with yourself, your partner, or your relationship?

Part IV
The Christ-Like Transforming Stage of Christian Marriage Discipleship

IN THIS PART IV, LET'S BEGIN WITH a bird's eye view of Christian transforming love, wisdom, and happiness (Chapter 1). Then let's look at some important aspects of this love, wisdom, and happiness, including being happy following Jesus virtuously during hard times (Chapter 2); loving our partner generously, but not too permissively (Chapter 3); treating our partner and ourselves well, with virtuous marriage conduct (Chapter 4); managing our family money lovingly and wisely (Chapter 5); and being united with God by our Christian marital love (Chapter 6).

chapter 1

The Christian Happiness of Transformed Lovers

THERE IS A CHRISTIAN MORALITY PROBLEM with the Conventional Happiness of needs lovers, an Emotional Problem with needs love, and a Fantasy Problem with needs wisdom (III,2–4 above). Needs lovers can work out these problems by growing from their needs love, wisdom, and happiness to a Christ-like transforming love, wisdom, and happiness. As they work out these problems in bits and pieces, sometimes with two steps forward and one step backwards, they gradually put away their old Needs Self, and they put on a new, more virtuous, Christ-like Transformed Self. They gradually become transformed lovers. Let's call them transformed lovers in this chapter.

WORKING OUT THE PROBLEMS WITH NEEDS LOVE, WISDOM, & HAPPINESS

We began to see in Part III how transformed lovers work out the problems with needs love, wisdom, and happiness. They work out the Christian Morality Problem with the Conventional Happiness of needs lovers by seeking a virtuous Christian Happiness that does not conflict with Christian morality, as we will see in this chapter.

Transformed lovers clear up the Emotional Problem with needs love by growing in a Christ-like transforming love that is not weakened by animosity, bitterness, or other unloving, un-Christ-like emotions. With the transforming love, their marital love is extraordinarily patient and kind, with no bitterness, resentment, or other unloving, un-Christ-like emotions.

Transformed lovers clear up the Fantasy Problem with needs wisdom with their more realistic, insightful transforming wisdom. With transforming wisdom, they understand how to be happy by following Jesus virtuously, with a virtuous Christian Happiness, not just a worldly Emotional Happiness or Conventional Happiness.

In this chapter, let's look more closely at the transforming love, wisdom, and happiness that we have touched upon briefly throughout this guide. Let's begin with Christian Happiness.

CHRISTIAN HAPPINESS

With a Christian Happiness in this life, we couples are happy following Jesus virtuously and being united with God, with or without a conventionally good life with plenty of worldly goods. Could we really be happy with God and virtue, though, without possessing lots of worldly goods too? There seems to be plenty of virtue in this Christian Happiness, but is there enough happiness?

THE GOOD LIFE & MEANINGFUL LIFE OBJECTIONS TO CHRISTIAN HAPPINESS

It might seem that there is not enough happiness in Christian Happiness. Many psychologists, philosophers, and other authorities in modern times argue that God and virtue are not sufficient for our happiness. They say that most if not all of us human beings need a "good life" with plenty of worldly goods *in addition to or instead of God and virtue.*[250] I call this the GOOD LIFE OBJECTION to virtuous happiness in general and virtuous Christian Happiness in particular.

Many of these same authorities have raised also a MEANINGFUL LIFE OBJECTION to Christian Happiness. They say that we have important individual interests, projects, talents, goals, and the like that we need to pursue with sufficient success in order to achieve an individually meaningful, truly happy life. So God and virtue are not sufficient for our happiness.

The Good Life and Meaningful Life objections to Christian Happiness are similar, so let's combine them. According to the combined Good/Meaningful Life Objection to Christian Happiness, desiring and pursuing this happiness would often prevent us from achieving a good, meaningful, truly happy life. We might have to sacrifice our individual interests too much at times in order to respond to our partner lovingly and follow

Jesus virtuously. A husband might have to sacrifice his interest in getting a college degree in order to work full-time to support his wife and children, and he might not be completely happy doing this.

The Good/Meaningful Life Objection to Christian Happiness does not stand up to Christian scrutiny. Let's see why this is so.

LETTING GO OF SELFISH DESIRES FOR WORLDLY GOODS WITHOUT GIVING UP THE WORLDLY GOODS THEMSELVES

The Good/Meaningful Life Objection to Christian Happiness does not account adequately for the fact that we couples need to let go of our selfish desires for worldly goods in order to be happy following Jesus virtuously, with or without these worldly goods—*but we do not necessarily need to give up the worldly goods themselves!* St. John of the Cross points out that it is our selfish desires for worldly goods that often upset us and prevent us from following Jesus virtuously—it is not the worldly goods themselves, as discussed above (I,2). Ordinarily we may relax in a hot tub, apply for admission to Harvard, and pursue other worldly goods as long as we do not selfishly desire, demand, and depend upon these worldly goods for our happiness. Ordinarily we may follow Jesus virtuously and possess plenty of worldly goods too.

A LOVING CHRISTIAN MOTIVATION TO PURSUE A GOOD, MEANINGFUL LIFE

It is all very well to say that we couples *could* follow Jesus virtuously and possess plenty of worldly goods too, but would we actually do this? It might seem that we would not be motivated to get worldly goods for ourselves and our partner if we did not desire the worldly goods for our happiness. Why would we be motivated to go out for dinner and a movie, for example, if we did not desire the dinner and the movie for our happiness? What would motivate us?

Christian love would motivate us, together with compassion, kindness, and other Christian virtues. With Christian love for our partner and for ourselves, we are motivated to treat our partner and ourselves well, and this involves getting things that interest us, not things that do not interest us. Christian love could motivate a couple to buy an antique Victorian sofa that interested them instead of buying a barbed wire collection that did not interest them.

It might seem that Christian love would not motivate a couple to buy an antique Victorian sofa that interested them because they *would not be interested in the sofa in the first place!* They would be happy loving one another and following Jesus virtuously, with or without the sofa. So why would they be interested in the sofa if they did not desire it for their happiness?

To answer this question, let's distinguish between desirous interests that come with Conventional Happiness and desireless interests that come with Christian Happiness. With desirous interests, we are interested in something, such as an antique Victorian sofa, as an essential source of our Conventional Happiness. We would not be completely happy without the sofa. We might be frustrated, disappointed, or otherwise mentally and emotionally upset if we could not get the sofa.

With desireless interests, on the other hand, we are interested in something, such as an antique Victorian sofa, as something that would please us, but that is not necessary for our happiness. We would be happy following Jesus virtuously, with or without the sofa.

I call desireless interests "preferences." Most of us have preferences for certain worldly goods that interest us even though they are not necessary for our happiness. I prefer playing tennis to bowling, but I do not need to play tennis this week to be happy. Still, my preference for playing tennis could motivate me to play tennis this week instead of bowling.

A Christian preferential motivation might seem weak compared to a conventional desirous motivation. With a desirous motivation, we desire certain worldly goods for our Conventional Happiness, so we are strongly motivated to get them. With a preferential motivation, on the other hand, we do not desire certain worldly goods for our Christian Happiness, so it might seem that we would not be strongly motivated to get them.

Christian preferential motivation is strong, however. This motivation is strengthened with love, compassion, and other Christian virtues. With Christian love for our partner and for ourselves, we are strongly motivated to treat our partner and ourselves well, and this includes getting things that interest us, not things that do not interest us. Christian love is a powerful motivator.

ENJOYING WORLDLY GOODS UNSELFISHLY

Suppose that love, compassion, kindness, and other Christian virtues would motivate us couples to get an antique Victorian sofa, a tennis club membership, and other worldly goods that interested us and our partner. It still might seem that we would not *enjoy* these worldly goods that much if we did not desire them for our happiness. Why would we enjoy having an antique Victorian sofa if we did not desire the sofa for our happiness?

To answer this question, let's distinguish between a selfish joy that often comes with Conventional Happiness and an unselfish joy that often comes with Christian Happiness. St. John of the Cross distinguishes in this way between enjoying worldly goods selfishly and possessively ("possessive joy") and enjoying worldly goods unselfishly and non-possessively ("non-possessive joy"). With possessive joy, we enjoy worldly goods that we desire for our happiness. If we cannot get these worldly goods, we are likely to be frustrated and not completely happy.[251] Many children enjoy candy, toys, and other worldly goods possessively, and then they are frustrated and unhappy when they cannot have them.

With non-possessive joy, on the other hand, we enjoy worldly goods that interest us, but we do not desire these worldly goods for our happiness, so we are not frustrated and unhappy if we do not get them. We might enjoy watching a beautiful sunset tonight non-possessively without desiring to see the sunset for our happiness. If we could see the sunset, great; if not, that would be fine too. We would be happy following Jesus virtuously, with or without the sunset. We would be detached from the sunset, as St. John of the Cross would say.

Some Christians think that detachment of John's sort would prevent us from enjoying worldly goods. But this is not so. In fact, we often enjoy worldly goods even more if we do not desire them for our happiness than we would if we did desire them. How could this be? Simple. If we desired certain worldly goods for our happiness, we would probably pursue them anxiously. If we did not get them, we might be frustrated, angry, or otherwise emotionally upset. Even if we did get them, we might be afraid of losing them, or we might just get bored with them. Our anxiety, frustration, anger, fear, boredom, and other mental and emotional distress would make it hard to enjoy the worldly goods. As an old American proverb says, "He who lives in either desire or fear can never enjoy his possessions."[252]

We couples can enjoy dinner, a movie, a beautiful sunset, a career in real estate, a Harvard University education, and other worldly goods non-possessively when we have them without throwing a fit if we cannot have them. If we cannot have them, there are often plenty of other worldly goods to enjoy instead. Helen Keller modifies a popular American proverb to point out that "when one door of happiness closes, another opens; but often we look so long at the closed door that we do not see the one which has been opened for us."[253]

The problem for many of us relatively prosperous Americans is not that there are not enough worldly goods to go around. The problem is that we set our hearts on certain worldly goods, and then we stress ourselves and others out trying to get them in order to be conventionally happy. We stress ourselves and others out trying to get such things as jet-skiing adventures, Caribbean cruises, six-figure incomes, expensive washing machines with many settings, a trim figure, a fun evening out with our partner at a baseball game, pleasant feelings of inner peace during prayer, and golfing with friends five times a week.

When we look at the whole happiness picture, a Christian preferential motivation for worldly goods is *more* desirable than a conventional desirous motivation. For one thing, it is less stressful to prefer worldly goods than to desire them for our happiness. The more strongly we desire certain worldly goods for our happiness, the more stressed out and unhappy we are likely to be if we cannot get these good things. On the other hand, the more we prefer certain worldly goods without desiring them for our happiness, the less stressed out and unhappy we are likely to be if we cannot get them. The worldly goods are "small stuff," as psychiatric stress expert Richard Carlson puts it in his book, *Don't Sweat the Small Stuff*. According to Carlson, there are two rules for stress-free living: "Don't sweat the small stuff" and "It's all small stuff."[254]

The Chinese word "ta" translates loosely as not sweating the small stuff.[255] A person with "ta" takes things lightly. He is not upset if his favorite baseball team comes in last place or if his incompetent co-worker is promoted instead of him. His happiness does not depend upon these things—lucky for him!

As my son John said recently, most of the things that upset people are not that important.

CHRISTIAN APPRECIATION FOR WORLDLY GOODS

We couples can benefit tremendously by preferring worldly goods as small stuff instead of desiring them as big stuff that we need in order to be conventionally happy. For one thing, we often *appreciate* worldly goods more if we prefer them instead of desiring them for our happiness. St. John of the Cross points out that the more people desire worldly goods for their happiness, the more likely they are to chase anxiously after new worldly goods that they do not yet have, and then they may not appreciate as much the worldly goods that they already do have. John compares these people to little children who are "restless and hard to please, always whining to their mother for this thing or that, and never satisfied."[256]

The experience of never being satisfied with worldly goods is sometimes discussed in modern psychological terms of "adaptation." Adaptation involves getting used to things and taking them for granted, as sociologist Barry Schwartz puts it.[257] Lottery winners often get used to their lottery winnings as time passes, so they derive less and less pleasure from them.

A story about a rich American industrialist from the North and a fisherman from the South illustrates this point about appreciating what we have instead of whining about what we do not have. The Northern industrialist was horrified to see a Southern fisherman lying lazily by his boat. The industrialist asked the fisherman why he was not fishing, and the fisherman said that he had caught enough fish for the day. The industrialist said that if the fisherman fished more, he could earn more money, buy a motor for his boat, fish in deeper waters, catch more fish, earn still more money, buy nylon fish nets, buy more boats, earn even more money, and eventually become a rich man like the industrialist. The fisherman asked what he would do then. The industrialist said that then he could enjoy life. The fisherman replied, "What do you think I am doing right now?"[258]

FREEDOM FROM DEPENDENCY UPON WORLDLY GOODS

We are also less dependent upon worldly goods if we prefer them instead of desiring them for our happiness. The Southern fisherman did not desire more fish nets, boats, money, and other worldly goods for his happiness, so he did not depend upon these things. He was not "held captive" by his desires for these things, as St. John of the Cross would say.[259] I made a point like this as a high school sophomore in an extra credit essay critical of American values. I wrote that America "is supposedly free. It is supposed to be a very democratic nation. But how can one be free when one is bound by the rush for wealth and pleasure?" Years later my son Kevin wrote along these lines in a college admissions application:

> Movies and television shows teach us that we need to make a lot of money in order to be happy, but true happiness is not

having a lot of money, going to Disneyland, or driving a new sports car. True happiness is something that we take with us when we die. True happiness involves knowledge, virtues, and love.

We are also more *flexible* about worldly goods if we prefer them without desiring them for our happiness. We can usually take them or leave them. What if I plan to play tennis today, but it rains? No problem. I can be happy shopping with my wife Arnell instead. What if I plan to do research at the San Diego State University library tonight, but our son John and his wife Holly need a baby-sitter for their two-year-old son Jake, and Arnell will be out for the evening with her women's bridge group? No problem. I can be happy baby-sitting Jake this evening instead of researching at the library. And what if I have to change Jake's diapers? Maybe I could handle that too!

DEALING WITH MARITAL PROBLEMS & DIFFERENCES PEACEFULLY & LOVINGLY

Being flexible about worldly goods can help us couples deal with marital problems and decisions peacefully and lovingly. We can compromise easily about such things as whether to buy a Toyota sedan or a Ford sports utility vehicle (SUV). In fact, we enjoy compromising. We enjoy dealing with problems and making decisions peacefully and lovingly, considering our partner's interests as well as our own.

My wife Arnell and I tried to help our children deal with problems and make decisions peacefully and lovingly when they were growing up. Once I heard Wendy (age 8 at the time) and Michelle (age 4) disagreeing about who would get the last serving of chocolate ice cream. They both wanted the ice cream for themselves. I said that they should want the ice cream for their sister too. They should be happy whether they got the ice cream or their sister got it. I asked them why they were not each arguing for their sister to get the ice cream. Then I left them to settle the matter for themselves. I was trying to help them make their decisions lovingly—not to make their decisions for them.

I still don't know who got the chocolate ice cream. About a week later, though, I heard Wendy and Michelle arguing about a nickel that they had found on the dining room floor. I asked them good-naturedly if they remembered what I had said about the chocolate ice cream. They laughed, and Wendy said something like this: "We remember. We're *pretend* arguing about who gets to give the nickel to the other one."

Apparently Wendy and Michelle got my chocolate ice cream problem-solving and decision-making message. The message was that we do not need the last serving of chocolate ice cream and other worldly goods in order to be truly happy, with a virtuous Christian Happiness. We just need to deal with the last serving of chocolate ice cream and other worldly goods with love, wisdom, and other Christian virtues, as Jesus would have us do.

With love, wisdom, and other Christian virtues, we couples are happy being virtuous, Christ-like persons and treating our partner well—sharing, compromising, giving, receiving—without fighting about who gets the last serving of chocolate ice cream, or whether we watch the evening news or the football game, or whether we buy the Mazda Miata or the Honda Civic.

Of course we do need to decide who gets the last serving of chocolate ice cream. But that's no problem. We can share worldly goods so that sometimes we get them and other times our partner gets them. We can deal with this small stuff peacefully and joyfully, with little or no anxiety, disappointment, anger, or other mental and emotional distress.

WORLDLY GOODS AS SECONDARY SOURCES OF CHRISTIAN HAPPINESS

With Christian wisdom, we Christian couples understand that chocolate ice cream and most other worldly goods are small stuff compared to the big stuff of following Jesus virtuously and being united with God, as discussed above. St. Thomas Aquinas describes Christian wisdom as a higher, perfect form of wisdom ("prudence") that "counts as nothing all things of the world."[260] Aquinas would count beautiful paintings, friendships, and other worldly goods as "nothing" in the sense that they are not the primary, ultimate source of our happiness. God is the primary, ultimate source of our happiness, together with the love and other Christian virtues that come with being united with God. St. John of the Cross teaches that a person "has to withdraw his [possessive] affection from all [worldly things] in order to center it wholly upon God" as the primary, ultimate source of the person's happiness.[261]

We Christian couples can withdraw our *possessive, selfish affection* for worldly goods in order to put God first as the *primary, ultimate* source of our happiness. But we should not withdraw our *non-possessive, unselfish affection* for worldly goods as *secondary* sources of our happiness. We rightly enjoy beautiful paintings, sunsets, and other worldly goods non-possessively and unselfishly, as we just discussed.

Worldly goods are often very important secondary sources of our Christian Happiness. To understand why this is so, let's distinguish between a Basic Christian Happiness and a Joyful Christian Happiness. Basic Christian Happiness consists of God and virtue, with or without pleasant emotions. Joyful Christian Happiness, on the other hand, consists of God, virtue, and pleasant emotions too. When we couples enjoy beautiful paintings, friendships, and other worldly goods non-possessively in addition to following Jesus virtuously, we experience a Joyful Christian Happiness, not just a Basic Christian Happiness. What's more, we rightly seek the Joyful Christian Happiness for ourselves and our partner, as we will see in the next chapter when we deal with Basic and Joyful Christian Happiness in more detail. The point here is simply that worldly goods can be important secondary sources of our Christian Happiness.

CONSOLING WORLDLY GOODS

There is still another reason why we couples may often seek and enjoy beautiful paintings, friendships, and other worldly goods for our Christian Happiness. Sometimes worldly goods can help us become more loving, Christ-like, virtuously-happy persons, so we rightly seek and enjoy these helpful worldly goods. A good friend, for example, might help us grow in love, wisdom, and other Christian virtues, so we would rightly seek and enjoy his friendship not only for his sake, but also for our sake. He would be helping us pursue our Christian Happiness goal of following Jesus virtuously and being united with God in this life and eternally.

Psychological and spiritual goods in particular can often help us grow morally and spiritually. Our partner's thoughtfulness, compassion, forgiveness, and other psychological and spiritual goods can often help us become more thoughtful, compassionate, and forgiving in return.

Some Christian authorities on the spiritual life call worldly goods that help us follow Jesus virtuously "consolations." St. John of the Cross teaches that we rightly desire consoling worldly goods that can help us follow Jesus virtuously, especially during "beginning" stages of Christian moral and spiritual growth. John approved of the desires of some Carmelite friars and nuns for beautiful places to pray ("oratories"), beautiful religious images to use during their prayers, and other consoling worldly goods. John realized that beautiful places to pray and beautiful religious images could help the friars and nuns feel close to God during their prayers, and feeling close to God could help them grow in love, wisdom, and other Christian virtues. John explained:

> For beginners [in the moral and spiritual life] it is permissible and even fitting to find some sensible gratification and satisfaction in the use of images, oratories, and other visible objects of devotion so that with this pleasure they may renounce worldly things from whose taste they are not yet weaned or detached. This is what we do with a child when we desire to take something away from him; we give him another thing to play with so that he will not begin to cry when left empty-handed.[262]

We couples rightly desire and seek consoling worldly goods that could help us follow Jesus more virtuously. Here is another reason why seeking a virtuous Christian Happiness would not prevent us from enjoying a good, meaningful life with plenty of worldly goods.

PERSONAL STYLES OF CHRISTIAN LOVING

Ordinarily we couples may follow Jesus virtuously and still enjoy a good, meaningful life with plenty of worldly goods, as long as we do not put the worldly goods ahead of God and virtue, as discussed above. What's more, we may enjoy worldly goods that especially interest us, considering such things as our personality, cultural background, and individual gifts and talents. We may follow Jesus with our own personal Christian marriage discipleship, including our own personal style of Christian loving.

There is a lovely medieval story about a Christian minstrel who developed his personal style of Christian loving that reflected his outgoing personality and his individual singing, dancing, and tumbling talents. The story is titled "Our Lady's Tumbler." In the story, a Christian minstrel gives up his tumbling and dancing to become a monk. He cannot pray as seriously as the other monks do, however, so he thinks he is a failure. But then he decides to express his love for Jesus and Mary by doing what he does best, that is, by tumbling and dancing. He approaches a statue of Mary and says, "Lady, I set before you a fair play. This travail [work] I do for you alone; so help me God, for you Lady, and your Son. Think not I tumble for my own delight; but I serve you." Then he walks on his two hands, with his feet in the air and his head near the ground. He twirls his feet and weeps with his eyes, and he says, "Lady, I worship you with my heart, with body, feet and hands. [. . .] Now I am your minstrel. Others may chant your praises in the church, but here in the crypt will I tumble for your delight."[263]

Some years ago I suggested to my daughter Michelle, age 10 at the time, that her tumbling could be her prayer. Michelle had just gone to bed, and I heard strange thumping noises coming from her bedroom. She was practicing her gymnastics by turning cartwheels on the bed. I told her the story of Our Lady's Tumbler, and I suggested that her cartwheels could be her bedtime prayers. Then I added that maybe she could "pray" (cartwheel) a little more quietly!

CARL JUNG'S PERSONALITY TYPES

We couples can develop our personal style of Christian loving that reflects our personality, including our general "type" of personality. According to psychiatrist Carl Jung, human beings are born with different types of personalities, that is, different types of minds ("psyche"). Jung theorizes that all people inherit capacities for thinking, feeling, sensing, and intuiting. In this way, all people are the same and equal. But some people inherit greater capacities for thinking than others do, so they fall into the category of the thinking personality type. Other people inherit greater capacities for feeling, sensing, and intuiting, so they fall into the categories of the feeling personality type, the sensing personality type, and the intuiting personality type respectively.[264]

People inherit also psychological attitudes of extraversion and introversion, according to Jung. The extraverted attitude orients people's conscious mind outwards towards external things, such as nature and society. The introverted attitude orients people's conscious mind inwards towards themselves, including their own thoughts, feelings, sensations, and intuitions. Jung combines these extraverted and introverted attitudes with the four capacities for thinking, feeling, sensing, and intuiting, and he comes up with eight basic personality types: the extraverted thinking type, the introverted thinking type, the extraverted feeling type, the introverted feeling type, the extraverted sensing type, the introverted sensing type, the extraverted intuitive type, and the introverted intuitive type. Jung identifies more personality types, but let's keep it simple.

The Christian Happiness of Transformed Lovers 141

Let's look at Jung's descriptions of two of the eight basic personality types, that is, the extraverted feeling type and the extraverted sensing type. According to Jung, people with an extraverted feeling personality have the capacity for strong feelings, and they express their feelings outwardly. They develop strong emotional attachments to people, but they lose their attachments easily, so their feelings of love can easily turn into feelings of hatred. They need to control the ways that they act upon their emotions in their external conduct. They need also to rid themselves of negative emotions and develop more positive emotions. The majority of them are women, but some are men, according to Jung.[265]

People with an extraverted sensing personality type have the capacity for strong sense experiences of sight, hearing, smell, taste, and touch, according to Jung. They derive their sense experiences from the external world of nature and society, and they tend to express their sensations outwardly. They are sensual, pleasure-loving, and thrill-seeking. They are also hard-headed and practical because they deal mostly with concrete things that they can see, hear, smell, taste, and touch. They are not especially interested in inner mental, emotional, and spiritual experiences, so their thoughts and emotions are often shallow. A majority of them are men, but some are women, according to Jung.[266]

Jung stresses that no one personality type is better than any other type. According to Jung, we should develop our natural, inborn personality. We should not try to develop a different personality that is not natural for us. We should not try to be extraverts, for example, if we are naturally introverts.

To develop our natural personality, we can build on our natural personality strengths and deal with our natural personality weaknesses. A husband with an extraverted feeling personality could build on his natural personality strengths by expressing his strong feelings of love for his wife with warm, emotional displays of affection. He could deal also with his natural personality weaknesses, such as his tendency to express strong *unloving* feelings towards his wife with angry emotional attacks. He could use emotional management techniques to manage his unloving emotions. Better yet, he could gradually rid himself of his unloving emotions and become more loving emotionally, as discussed above (III,3).

Suppose that we human beings do have these natural, inborn personalities, and that we should develop our natural personality instead of trying to develop a different personality that is not natural for us. Then we couples should not try to change our partner's natural personality any more than we should try to change our own. An extraverted husband should not pressure his introverted wife to party with friends several evenings a week, and his wife should not pressure him to stay home every night without ever going out with friends. The husband and wife should build a loving relationship that accounts for their different personalities.

We couples can develop a personal style of Christian loving that fits us well, much as we can wear clothes that fit us well. As an African proverb says, "Borrowed trousers and garments never fit a man well; they are usually too tight or too loose. Proper fitting is achieved when one wears one's own dress."[267]

CONCLUSION

When all is said and done about Christian Happiness, the Good/Meaningful Life Objection to this happiness does not stand up to Christian scrutiny. Letting go of our desires for worldly goods in order to be happy following Jesus virtuously—with or without these worldly goods—does not prevent us from achieving and enjoying a good, meaningful life with plenty of worldly goods. In fact, paradoxically, the best way to achieve and enjoy a good, meaningful life with plenty of worldly goods is *to let go of our selfish desires for a conventionally good, meaningful life with plenty of worldly goods in order to be happy following Jesus virtuously, with or without these worldly goods!*

How could this be? Simple. Suppose that we desired a conventionally good, meaningful life with plenty of worldly goods in order to be conventionally happy. Then we would suffer from the frustration, the unpleasant emotions, the hurtful marital conflict, the weakening of Christian virtues, and all the other mental, emotional, moral, and physical distress that often comes with a desirous pursuit of worldly goods, as discussed above (II,2–4; III,2–4). We would not enjoy a conventionally good, meaningful life with plenty of worldly goods partly because we desired one so much for our Conventional Happiness. Author Eric Hoffer observes that the desirous pursuit of this conventional sort of happiness is *one of the main sources of unhappiness.*[268] As the Mexicans say, "He who wants it all will lose it all."[269]

Many defenders of Conventional Happiness admit that the desirous pursuit of a Conventional Happiness comes with frustration, anxiety, depression, and other unpleasant emotions a good deal of the time. These authorities define Conventional Happiness initially in terms of experiencing pleasant emotions with an absence of unpleasant emotions, but then they admit that few if any of us human beings can be completely happy in this conventional sense of feeling good emotionally. Psychologist Daniel Goleman writes, "It is not that people need to avoid unpleasant feelings to feel content, but rather that stormy feelings not go unchecked, displacing all pleasant moods. People who have strong episodes of anger or depression can still feel a sense of well-being if they have a countervailing set of equally joyous or happy times."[270]

This weak, watered-down, morally-deficient Conventional Happiness is nothing to write home to mother about.

When we look at the whole happiness picture, it is clear that the combined Good/Meaningful Life Objection to Christian Happiness applies more to Conventional Happiness than to Christian Happiness! It is our desirous pursuit of a Conventional Happiness that often prevents us from enjoying a truly good, meaningful, happy life. As an old American proverb says, it may cost something to be a Christian, but it costs more to be a sinner.[271]

chapter 2

Christian Happiness during Hard Times

WE COUPLES MAY ORDINARILY FOLLOW Jesus virtuously and enjoy a good, meaningful life with plenty of worldly goods too, as discussed above (IV,1). In this best-case scenario, God and virtue are sufficient for our happiness, but we enjoy plenty of worldly goods too. We have the best of both worlds.

THE HARDSHIPS OBJECTION TO CHRISTIAN HAPPINESS

What if we do not have the best of both worlds? What if we struggle with severe hardships, such as a painful cancer or an unfaithful spouse? Then it might seem that God and virtue would not be sufficient for our happiness. It might seem that we would experience anxiety, sorrow, anger, fears of death, or other unpleasant emotions that would prevent us from being completely happy with God and virtue. It might seem that we would need relief from our hardships *in addition to God and virtue* in order to be happy. At the very least, it might seem that we would need minimally good health and other sustaining goods in addition to God and virtue. I call this the HARDSHIPS OBJECTION to Christian Happiness in this life. Many scholars have raised an objection of this hardships sort not only to Christian Happiness in particular, but also to virtuous happiness in general, including ancient Greek concepts of virtuous happiness.[272]

The Hardships Objection to Christian Happiness may hit home for many of us couples. Many of us experience health problems, broken relationships, poverty, natural disasters, or other severe hardships at times, and we all experience death and taxes. It might seem that we would need relief from the hardships in order to be happy—in addition to God and virtue.

But this is not so. We can be happy with God and virtue even if we experience severe hardships. In fact, we need to turn to God and virtue for our happiness even more during hard times than we do during good times. The Hardships Objection to Christian Happiness does not stand up to Christian scrutiny. Let's see why this is so.

BASIC CHRISTIAN HAPPINESS & JOYFUL CHRISTIAN HAPPINESS

Critics of Christian Happiness object that many of us human beings could not be completely happy in the conventional sense that requires pleasant emotions if we struggled with severe hardships. This is true. But we could be completely happy in the Christian sense that does *not* require pleasant emotions. Christian Happiness consists essentially of following Jesus virtuously and being united with God, and we can follow Jesus virtuously and be united with God even if we experience sorrow, fears of death, or other unpleasant emotions during hard times.

To understand how we can be happy following Jesus virtuously during hard times, let's look more closely at the Basic Christian Happiness and Joyful Christian Happiness discussed above (IV,1). Both Basic and Joyful Christian Happiness consist essentially of God and virtue. Joyful Christian Happiness, however, includes pleasant emotions with an absence of unpleasant emotions, while Basic Christian Happiness does not necessarily include pleasant emotions with an absence of unpleasant emotions. Basic Christian Happiness may come with unpleasant emotions at times.

We couples might not always be joyfully happy following Jesus virtuously during hard times, but we could be basically happy, with a Basic Christian Happiness that does not require pleasant emotions. The Hardships Objection to Christian Happiness does not apply to this Basic Christian Happiness.

Many critics of Christian Happiness would probably reject this concept of a Basic Christian Happiness. They might insist that few if any of us human beings could be truly happy in any plausible sense of the word "happiness" if we suffered from severe hardships. But let's not turn up our noses at this Basic Christian Happiness. With this happiness, we are like Jesus in our moral character and conduct, with love, wisdom, courage, and other Christian virtues. We are also free from the problems that come with the Emotional Happiness of romantic lovers and the Conventional

Happiness of needs lovers, including the Christian Morality Problems, the Emotional Problems, and the Fantasy Problems discussed above (II,2–4; III,2–4; IV,1). The Basic Christian Happiness of transformed lovers is a pretty good deal compared to the Emotional Happiness of romantic lovers and the Conventional Happiness of needs lovers.

It makes good sense to characterize happiness more in terms of virtuous, Christ-like character and conduct than in terms of pleasant emotions. Happiness is the one primary, overall goal of human life that truly fulfills all of us human beings, and God, virtue, and goodness are much more fulfilling than pleasant emotions. Anglican clergyman Charles Kingsley observes,

> Did it ever strike you that goodness is not merely a beautiful thing, but by far the most beautiful thing in the whole world? So that nothing is to be compared for value with goodness; that riches, honor, power, pleasure, learning, the whole world and all in it, are not worth having in comparison with being good; and the utterly best thing for a man is to be good, even though he were never to be rewarded for it.[273]

There is more good news about Christian Happiness. Usually we couples can be *joyfully* happy following Jesus virtuously, not just basically happy. Usually we can follow Jesus virtuously, possess plenty of worldly goods, and feel good emotionally too, with a Joyful Christian Happiness, not just a Basic Christian Happiness.

Usually we couples would feel *better* emotionally with a Joyful Christian Happiness than we would with a Conventional Happiness. With a Joyful Christian Happiness, we would enjoy worldly goods non-possessively with pleasant emotions and an absence of frustration, anger, regret, and other unpleasant emotions. With a Conventional Happiness, on the other hand, we would suffer at times from the frustration, anger, regret, and other unpleasant emotions that often come with a desirous pursuit of worldly goods (III,2–3 above).

STRONGLY PREFERRING WORLDLY GOODS WITHOUT DESIRING THEM FOR OUR HAPPINESS

Some of us couples might still have doubts about Basic Christian Happiness. It might seem that we would rightly *desire* relief from a painful cancer or other hardships in order to be happy—in addition to desiring God and virtue. Then God and virtue would not be sufficient for our happiness.

This aspect of the Hardships Objection to Christian Happiness does not account adequately for a distinction between *conventional desires* for worldly goods that often come with Conventional Happiness, and *Christian preferences* for worldly goods that often come with Christian Happiness. Suppose that a husband *desired* the remission of a painful cancer in order to be conventionally happy with pleasant emotions and an absence of unpleasant emotions. Then the husband would not be completely happy with God and virtue; he would want the remission of his cancer too.

Suppose, on the other hand, that the husband *strongly preferred* the remission of his painful cancer without desiring the cancer remission for his happiness. Then he could be happy with God and virtue, with or without the remission of his cancer. He would not desire the remission of his cancer too.

We Christian couples can be happy following Jesus virtuously during hard times with a Basic Christian Happiness, at least, if not always a Joyful Christian Happiness. At the same time, we may strongly prefer the Joyful Christian Happiness to the Basic Christian Happiness for ourselves and our partner, and rightly so. We rightly prefer good health and other worldly goods that help us and our partner feel good emotionally. That's part of loving ourselves and our partner, and treating ourselves and our partner well.

It might seem that we are just playing with words when we distinguish between *desiring* relief from hardships for a Conventional Happiness and *strongly preferring* relief from hardships for a Joyful Christian Happiness. But we are not just playing with words. There are significant differences between conventional desires for relief from hardships and strong Christian preferences for relief from hardships. For one thing, strong Christian preferences for relief from hardships come with a faithful, loving, and courageous *acceptance* of the hardships. With Christian faith, we believe that God is the primary source of our happiness in this life and eternally; that God loves us; that Jesus suffered and died for us on the cross; that Jesus invites us to take up our cross every day and follow him (Luke 9:23); and that Jesus is the Way to happiness in this life and eternally. With this Christian faith, we would accept a painful cancer and follow Jesus faithfully and courageously along the Christian Way of the Cross.

Christian love would also help us accept a painful cancer or other hardships. With Christian love for God, we love God above all things as the one primary, ultimate source of our happiness. With Christian love for God, we would accept a painful cancer and follow Jesus lovingly and courageously along the Christian Way of the Cross.

VIRTUOUS EMOTIONS DURING HARD TIMES

Most of us couples would probably experience sorrow, fears of death, or other unpleasant emotions at times if we struggled faithfully, lovingly, and courageously with a painful cancer or other severe hardships, as discussed above. But at least the unpleasant emotions would not be negative, un-Christ-like emotions. We would not experience bitterness, anger, or other negative emotions. We would accept our hardships faithfully, lovingly, and courageously, with no un-Christ-like emotions.

With a Christian acceptance of hardships, the sorrow and other unpleasant emotions that we couples might experience could be virtuous, Christ-like emotions. St. Thomas Aquinas points out that it is a sign of goodness not only to be joyful in the presence of good, but also to be sorrowful in the presence of evil.[274] Aquinas quotes Matthew, "Blessed are they that mourn, for they shall be comforted (Matt. 5:5)."[275] Aquinas identifies evil not only with sin, but also with bodily pain (such as a painful cancer).

We couples may mourn compassionately and lovingly for ourselves and others during hard times. It is better to light one little candle of compassion and love during hard times than to curse the darkness.

Jesus experienced sorrow and other virtuous emotions shortly before his crucifixion instead of experiencing bitterness, anger, or other un-Christ-like emotions. Jesus's sorrow included a faithful, loving, and courageous acceptance of his impending crucifixion. Jesus took Peter and two sons of Zebedee to Gethsemane to pray, and he said to them:

> 'My soul is sorrowful to the point of death. Wait here and keep awake with me.' And going on a little further he fell on his face and prayed. 'My Father,' he said 'if it is possible, let this cup pass me by. Nevertheless, let it be as you, not I, would have it' (Matt. 26:36–40).

In this passage, Jesus strongly preferred not to suffer and die on the cross, but he did not selfishly desire, demand, and depend upon avoiding the suffering and death in order to fulfill himself and be happy. He was fulfilled and happy doing God his Father's will by faithfully, lovingly, and courageously suffering and dying for us on the cross.

We couples can be fulfilled and happy following Jesus virtuously along the Christian Way of the Cross with a Basic Christian Happiness, at least, if not always a Joyful Christian Happiness. Catholic spiritual director François Fénelon describes a basic Christian happiness of this virtuous sort that can be comforting during times of adversity. Fénelon writes:

> This hundredfold happiness which the true children of God possess amid all the troubles of this world consists in a peaceful conscience, freedom of spirit, a welcome resignation of all things to God, the joyful sense of his light ever growing stronger within their heart, and a thorough deliverance from all tyrannous fears and longings after worldly things.[276]

SEEKING A JOYFUL CHRISTIAN HAPPINESS

Most of us couples are troubled with hardships at times, so it is lucky for us that we can be happy in the midst of "all the troubles of this world," with a Basic Christian Happiness, at least, if not always a Joyful Christian Happiness. Of course most of us would prefer the Joyful Christian Happiness, and that's perfectly o.k. We rightly seek a Joyful Christian Happiness for ourselves and others, including our partner. We should treat ourselves and our partner well, and this involves getting good, enjoyable things that please us emotionally, like a Hawaiian vacation, not bad, unpleasant things that displease us, like a bankruptcy.

SEEKING VOLUNTARY HARDSHIPS

To seek a Joyful Christian Happiness, we should usually try to avoid hardships, as discussed above. Sometimes, though, we are morally obligated to take on hardships. A soldier might be morally obligated to put his life on the line to defend his country.

Sometimes we couples may voluntarily undertake hardships that could help us purify ourselves, treat our partner well, or improve our community.

Christian Happiness During Hard Times

We might fast during Lent, sacrifice our Saturday night bowling to help our wife clean house for her quilting party, or donate $1,000 to help shelter the homeless.

Many Christians have undertaken voluntary hardships unselfishly with a commendable love for God and neighbor. Some Christians, however, have undertaken voluntary hardships selfishly to impress others with their "piety" rather than to purify themselves or help others (Mt. 6:1–4).[277]

Sometimes Christians may seek voluntary hardships selfishly without realizing it. St. Thérèse of Lisieux wanted to suffer and die for Jesus as a heroic Christian martyr, but she realized later that her desire to be a martyr was selfish.[278] She wanted to love God *her* way, according to *her* will, by being a martyr. She was not completely content loving God *his* way, according to *his* will, even if he did not call her to be a martyr.

What was God's will for Thérèse?

God did not reveal to Thérèse that he wanted her to be a martyr. But he did reveal that he wanted her to love him and to love her neighbor as Jesus loves us. Thérèse came to realize that her Christian vocation was *love,* not necessarily martyrdom. Her Christian vocation included loving God and neighbor during her ordinary activities in her convent.[279]

God has revealed to all of us Christian couples that he wants us to love him and to love our neighbor as Jesus loves us. We are called to love our partner with a Christ-like transforming love during our ordinary marriage and family activities, much as Thérèse was called to love her fellow nuns with a Christ-like transforming love during her ordinary convent activities. Our Christian marriage vocation is love, together with faith, wisdom, and other Christian virtues.

ACCEPTING INVOLUNTARY HARDSHIPS LOVINGLY

We couples may seek voluntary hardships that can help us purify ourselves, treat our partner well, or improve our community, as discussed above. But let's not go overboard looking for voluntary hardships. Many *involuntary* hardships are bound to come our way in this real world with poverty, injustice, natural disasters, disease, and the list could go on to death itself.

There is something to be said for accepting involuntary hardships lovingly without going overboard looking for lots of voluntary hardships too. The Trappist monk Thomas Merton has observed that it is usually more praiseworthy to accept involuntary hardships lovingly than to accept voluntary hardships lovingly. After all, we choose the voluntary hardships ourselves. We might choose the hardships selfishly in order to impress others with our "devotion," to feel morally superior to others, or for other selfish reasons, as St. John of the Cross points out.[280] We do not choose involuntary hardships selfishly because we do not choose them at all.

CONCLUSION

When all is said and done about happiness and hardships in marriage and family life, we couples lose little by seeking a Christian Happiness instead of a Conventional Happiness. When we seek a Christian Happiness, we usually avoid hardships in order to treat ourselves and our partner well, much as we usually avoid hardships when we seek a Conventional Happiness. It is true that seeking a Christian Happiness does not prevent hardships from coming our way, but seeking a Conventional Happiness does not prevent this either.

As far as hardships go, we gain a lot by seeking a Christian Happiness instead of a Conventional Happiness. When we seek a Christian Happiness during hard times, we may still experience sorrow, fears of death, or other unpleasant emotions at times, but we accept our hardships faithfully, lovingly, and courageously, so we do not experience bitterness, anger, or other un-Christ-like emotions. When we seek a Conventional Happiness during hard times, on the other hand, we are less likely to accept our hardships, so we are more likely to experience bitterness, anger, or other un-Christ-like emotions.

Seeking a Christian Happiness helped me, my parents, my sisters, and my brother Johnny when he struggled with leukemia for over four years before he died shortly before his 16th birthday. Johnny lived about four years longer than his doctors had predicted. He won a United States National 13-and-under tennis doubles title during this time, and, much more importantly, he enjoyed a good, loving, happy life. My mother, Owenita Sanderlin, has described Johnny's life with leukemia in her book, *Johnny*, that was written mostly in Johnny's own words taken from his journals and family newsletter. When Johnny learned that the final attempt to cure his leukemia had failed, he said, "I wouldn't want to be anybody else in the world but me." Shortly before his death, he said to our parents, "There are two things I want. I want to live . . . but if I can't do that, I just want to go to heaven."[281]

With my Catholic faith, I believe not only that Johnny is in heaven with my mother, but also that my father, sisters, and I will be with Johnny forever in a loving reunion of our family. St. Catherine of Siena describes a loving reunion of Christians in heaven in her *Dialogue*. As a speaker in the *Dialogue*, Jesus says that souls who loved one another during their lifetime will love one another eternally:

> They [loving souls] rejoice and exult, sharing each other's goodness with loving affection, besides that universal good [God] which they all possess together. [. . .] And though they are all joined in the bond of charity, they know a special kind of sharing with those whom they loved most closely with a special love in the world, a love through which they grew in grace and virtue.[282]

The story of my brother Johnny's life with leukemia continues to inspire children and adults in San Diego and throughout the country. My father and I give copies of the book *Johnny* to children playing in the Johnny Sanderlin-Owenita Sanderlin memorial tennis tournament that is held in San Diego every year. Johnny lived a good, loving, courageous, happy Christian life.

chapter 3

A Generous but Non-Permissive Marital Love

WE COUPLES SHOULD USUALLY AVOID HARDSHIPS, including hardships that our partner selfishly tries to impose upon us. We should not sacrifice our interests so much that we let our partner get his or her way most of the time and control the relationship. We should not love our partner too permissively.

Christian love might seem too permissive. Jesus often describes Christian love in terms of self-denial and self-sacrifice, including a complete giving of oneself, even unto death. Jesus teaches that a person can have no greater love than to lay down his life for his friends (John 15:13). This self-sacrificial love might work well for marriage if both partners loved one another in this unselfish way, but what if just one partner did this? Then it might seem that the unselfish partner would let the selfish partner control the relationship. It might seem that the unselfish partner's love would be too permissive. I call this the PERMISSIVENESS OBJECTION to Christian love in marriage and other intimate relationships.

Christian love is not too permissive, however. In fact, Christian love is *less* permissive than needs love. In this chapter, let's see why this is so. Let's see how we couples can love our partner generously, but not too permissively.

A PERMISSIVENESS OBJECTION TO SELF-SACRIFICIAL CHRISTIAN LOVE

Psychotherapists Rosa Gil and Carmen Vazquez have raised a permissiveness objection to Christian love in marriage and other intimate relationships in their book, *The Maria Paradox*. Gil and Vazquez maintain that the self-sacrificial Christian marital love in popular "Old World" Hispanic-American culture is too permissive. They argue that many Catholic Hispanic-American women and other Catholic women of Latin descent ("Latinas") have loved their husbands too permissively.[283]

Gil and Vazquez describe this permissive Christian marital love in terms of "marianismo." Marianismo characterizes the ideal Latin woman, much as "machismo" characterizes the ideal Latin man. The model for the ideal Latin woman is the Virgin Mary. The ideal Latin woman, like the Virgin Mary, is self-sacrificial, chaste, and dutiful. The ideal Latin woman does not put her needs and desires ahead of her husband's needs and desires. She does not criticize her husband—not even for such things as alcoholism, drug addiction, and infidelity. She loves her husband too permissively.[284]

Gil and Vazquez are right that the self-sacrificial woman in popular Old World Hispanic-American culture loves her husband too permissively. Gil and Vazquez do not account adequately, however, for the positive character traits of this self-sacrificial Hispanic-American woman—especially compared to the thin, glamorous, sexually-liberated, self-indulgent woman that is often idealized in "New World" American culture. The New World American ideal for women seems to have influenced some teenage American girls to become anorexic, not to mention having sex by the age of 15 and possibly an abortion as well. Researchers at the U.S. Center for Disease Control and Prevention reported on March 11, 2008, that one out of every four American teenage girls has a sexually transmitted disease.[285] The Virgin Mary would not be a bad role model for these girls.

As a matter of fact, the Virgin Mary is an excellent role model for American girls with her self-sacrificial Christian love. We just need to understand Mary's self-sacrificial Christian love better than Gil and Vazquez seem to. Gil and Vazquez fail to distinguish adequately between their "marianismo" version of self-sacrificial Christian love in Hispanic-American culture and the authentic self-sacrificial Christian love that is envisioned in the Bible and other Christian classics. The authentic self-sacrificial Christian love is not too permissive.

Gil and Vazquez argue that the Virgin Mary is too "self-sacrificial" and permissive. But there is no Biblical evidence that Mary loved Joseph too permissively. There is no Biblical evidence that Mary permitted Joseph to mistreat or abuse her.

What's more, there is no Biblical evidence that Jesus loved people too permissively. Jesus did not love the scribes and Pharisees too permissively.

He warned them, "Alas for you, scribes and Pharisees, you hypocrites! You who shut up the kingdom of heaven in men's faces, neither going in yourselves nor allowing others to go in who want to" (Matt. 23:13).

Christian love is not too permissive. With Christian love for her husband, a wife would desire what is good for him, not what is bad for him. It would be good for him to be an unselfish, Christ-like person, and it would be bad for him to be a selfish, un-Christ-like person. If she loved her husband, she would stand up against his selfish conduct not only for her sake and for the sake of their relationship, but also for his sake. She would try to help him become a more Christ-like person to the extent that he was willing and able to do this.[286]

LIVING FOR OUR GOOD AS WELL AS OUR PARTNER'S GOOD

There is another reason why Christian love is not too permissive. Christian love includes self-love and love for God as well as neighbor-love. With Christian love for ourselves as well as our partner, we couples seek our good as well as our partner's good. The Buddha observes that there are four kinds of people:

> One who lives for his own good but not for the good of others; one who lives for the good of others but not for his own good; one who lives neither for his own good nor for the good of others; and one who lives both for his own good and for the good of others.[287]

With Christian love for ourselves as well as our partner, we couples build an equal, loving relationship that is good for both of us. We do not build an unequal, permissive/controlling relationship that is not good for either one of us.

A black woman Monique helped build a permissive/controlling relationship with her husband. She tried to make him happy by doing everything for him, but this did not work. She explained,

> I loved my husband so much. [. . .] All I could think about were things to make him happy. I would be running all over, buying and preparing his special dishes [. . .] I was always making it too easy for him and then getting angry because of it. There was too much give and not enough take.[288]

Monique thought that she was loving her husband generously by doing everything for him. The poet Ogden Nash would probably say that she was being stupid. Nash writes about the supposedly generous pig:

> The pig, if I am not mistaken,
> Supplies us sausage, ham, and bacon.
> Let others say his heart is big—
> I call it stupid of the pig.[289]

Monique was loving her husband not only stupidly, but also selfishly. She was doing everything for him largely for her own sake, that is, to get him to satisfy *her* desires for his attention and love. She thought that she was being unselfish, but she was being selfish. Realizing this might have helped her.

PERMISSIVE NEEDS LOVE COMPARED TO NON-PERMISSIVE TRANSFORMING LOVE

The Permissiveness Objection to Christian transforming love in marriage and other intimate relationships misses the mark, as discussed above. As a matter of fact, this objection applies more to a conventional needs love than to Christian transforming love! Needs lovers are often more permissive than transformed lovers. Let's see why this is so.

For starters, needs lovers are needier than transformed lovers, so they are more likely to be permissive. Needs lovers need their partner to help them get the worldly goods that they desire for their Conventional Happiness. They depend upon their partner for their happiness, so they need to be in their partner's good graces. They often try to please their partner so their partner will please them in return. But sometimes they may go overboard trying to please their partner. A wife with a poor body image did this. She wanted her husband to approve of her body in order to help her feel good about herself, so she did almost anything to please him. He complained about her small breasts, so she got breast implants even though she did not want them. He liked permanent tattoos, so she got permanent tattoos even though she hated them. She loved her husband too permissively partly because she needed him so much for her Conventional Happiness.

This wife was a pleaser. She went overboard trying to please her husband in order to get his approval and love, and he took advantage of this. He was a controller. Controllers are often attracted to pleasers, and vice versa. Psychologist Kevin Leman observes that a controlling husband with a pleasing wife may be the most common marriage partnership.[290] A controlling wife with a pleasing husband is common too.

Transformed lovers are not pleasers. They do not depend upon their partner for their virtuous Christian Happiness as much as needs lovers depend upon their partner for their Conventional Happiness. Transformed lovers are independent and self-sufficient. Their virtuous Christian Happiness comes mostly from within, that is, from being loving, virtuous, Christ-like persons mentally, emotionally, and spiritually.

Some psychologists and other authorities in modern times have envisioned a mature, self-sufficient, non-permissive love of a Christian transforming sort. Psychologist Abraham Maslow contrasts an unselfish, self-sufficient "being love" ("B-love") with a selfish, needy "dependency love" ("D-love")—somewhat as I have contrasted an unselfish, self-sufficient Christian transforming love with a somewhat selfish, dependent needs love and romantic love. According to Maslow, D-lovers need to be loved by others before they can love others in return. Their D-love is a "sickness," a "love-hunger," a "hole which has to be filled." They depend upon others for their happiness.[291]

B-lovers, on the other hand, do not depend upon others for their happiness nearly as much as D-lovers do. B-lovers are less needy, jealous, threatened, and anxious than D-lovers. They are also more self-sufficient, altruistic, and fostering.[292]

Transformed lovers, like B-lovers, do not depend upon others for their happiness nearly as much as needs lovers and romantic lovers do. Transformed lovers can be happy in the basic sense of following Jesus virtuously even if they experience severe hardships, such as an unfaithful spouse. They can experience a Basic Christian Happiness during hard times, if not a Joyful Christian Happiness.

Transformed lovers do not depend upon their partner for a Basic Christian Happiness, but they often *do* depend upon their partner for a Joyful Christian Happiness. A Christian transformed lover might not be joyfully happy if his wife had an affair with his best friend, filed for divorce, and complained to their children that he was fat, ugly, and boring. He might need a more faithful, loving wife in order to be joyfully happy—not to mention having a more trustworthy best friend too!

PERMISSIVE NEEDS LOVERS WITH CONVENTIONAL MORAL STANDARDS

There is another reason why needs lovers are more permissive than transformed lovers. Needs lovers have lower moral standards for their relationship. Many needs lovers believe that anger, fighting, and other conflict is inevitable and morally permissible in marriage and other intimate relationships, so they get mad at their partner at times, and they permit their partner to get mad at them. They accept anger, fighting, and other conflict in their relationship without objecting to these things. A wife brags that her husband has learned to accept her anger, so she can yell and scream at him, and he will still love her.[293]

Certainly we married couples *should* love our partner even if our partner is yelling and screaming at us. But it does not necessarily follow that we should permit our partner to continue yelling and screaming at us day in and day out without objecting to this. We do not have to settle for anger, fighting, and other hurtful conflict in our marriage relationship, including our marital communications. Our marital communications can be a loving marital art instead of a fighting martial art.

HELPING OUR PARTNER BECOME A MORE CHRIST-LIKE PERSON

Suppose that our partner communicates unlovingly and treats us poorly at times. Then we should try to help our partner communicate more lovingly, treat us better, and become a more Christ-like, virtuously-happy person to the extent that he or she is willing and able to do this. If we do not help our partner become a more Christ-like, virtuously-happy person, as our partner's soul-mate, who will?

Of course we should be careful about trying to help our partner treat us better and grow in love, wisdom, and other Christian virtues. We should not try to help our partner in these ways unless we are right that our partner is treating us poorly; unless we are treating our partner well at the time; unless we respond sensitively to our partner's concerns; unless we are loving and wise enough to provide helpful input; and unless our partner would be likely to respond positively to our input.

For the most part, we couples can help our partner become a more virtuous, Christ-like person simply by being virtuous, Christ-like persons ourselves. Example is infectious, so example is often the best "sermon."[294]

PERMISSIVELY VALIDATING OUR PARTNER'S UNLOVING EMOTIONS

There is another way that we can help our partner grow in love, wisdom, and other Christian virtues. We can refuse to support our partner's selfish, un-Christ-like behavior. The wife with the poor body image discussed above could refuse to get breast implants when her husband complained about her small breasts. She could tell him that his selfish, unloving complaints would not work.

Some marriage authorities do not advise couples strongly enough to resist their partner's selfish, unloving behavior, including such things as angry emotional outbursts. In fact, some marriage authorities advise couples to *validate* their partner's anger and other unloving emotions. In Greg's and Anne's supposedly model marriage (III,3 above), Greg validated Anne's anger when she was mad at him for not wearing his wedding ring. Greg said that it "made sense" that Anne was angry.

Certainly it was good for Greg to validate Anne's anger in some ways. It was good for Greg to assure Anne that he loved her just as she was, even when she got mad at him. It was good for Greg to tell Anne that he always wanted to know how she felt so he could respond to her feelings and concerns.

It was not good, however, for Greg to give Anne the impression that her anger "made sense" in the sense of being reasonable and morally acceptable. It was not reasonable or morally acceptable for Anne to attack Greg angrily for "betraying" her by not wearing his wedding ring. Anne did not know whether Greg was betraying her or not. She should have asked Greg why he was not wearing his ring before she jumped to any angry conclusions. For all she knew, Greg might have gained weight recently, and he might have taken off his ring to enlarge it, as noted above (III,3).

As it turned out, Greg was not betraying Anne by taking off his wedding ring any more than Anne was betraying him by using her maiden name. Anne was worried about Greg not wearing his wedding ring as a public sign of their marriage. In much the same way, Greg was worried about Anne not using her married name as a public sign of their marriage. Greg and Anne had similar concerns about the public signs of their marriage.

Greg could talk with Anne at some suitable time about working together to communicate reasonably and lovingly without resorting to angry verbal attacks or other unreasonable, unloving communications.

PERMISSIVELY PRAISING OUR PARTNER'S UNLOVING CHARACTER TRAITS & CONDUCT

Some "positive thinkers" in psychology and other disciplines advise couples not only to validate their partner's unloving emotions, but also to *praise* their partner's unloving emotions! Some of these "positive thinkers" advise couples to praise also their partner's character weaknesses in general, including such things as jealousy and stubbornness. Martin Seligman, a founder of "Positive Psychology," advises married couples to think positively about their relationship, including their partner's character weaknesses, *even if they would be unrealistic by doing this.* According to Seligman, marriage partners with the most positive "romantic illusions" about one another have the most stable and happiest relationships.[295] Seligman praises a woman who viewed her partner's jealousy positively without objecting to it. The woman said that her partner's jealousy showed "how important my presence is in his life."[296]

Seligman's Positive Psychology can be helpful. Seligman and other positive psychologists contribute significantly to psychology by dealing with what they consider to be optimal behavior in addition to abnormal and normal behavior. They rightly advise couples to appreciate their partner's character strengths without harping on his or her weaknesses. They rightly encourage couples to look for the good in their partner—much as St. Thomas Aquinas looked for the good in his friend when his friend called him to come see a flying ox outside the window (III,3 above).

We couples may benefit from some aspects of Positive Psychology, but we should not go for all of it, hook, line, and sinker. We should not think so "positively" about our partner that we avoid dealing honestly and realistically with our partner's character weaknesses. We should not mislead our partner into thinking that angry emotional outbursts, jealousy, and other selfish conduct and character traits are perfectly acceptable. We should help our partner acknowledge and deal with serious character weaknesses to the extent that he or she is willing and able to do this.

The woman with the jealous partner mentioned above was not doing her partner any Christian favors by being grateful for his jealousy without trying to help him overcome it. She said that her partner's jealousy made *her* feel important. But here she was thinking selfishly about her feelings and interests more than her partner's feelings and interests. How did her partner's jealousy make *him* feel? Jealousy is not a pleasant emotion, much less a virtuous, Christ-like emotion. The woman should have tried to help her partner overcome his jealousy and become a more virtuous, Christ-like person if he had been open to doing this.

Few Christians in the past have viewed jealousy positively as a sign of true love. During the 17th century an anonymous Dutch author and artist depicted jealousy as a bogeyman who was chasing Cupid. The inscription under the illustration reads: "Once you have acquired a taste for jealousy, lover, you will never overcome it. When jealousy conquers all, love must give way."[297]

Seligman praised another woman for thinking "positively" about her partner's obstinacy, or stubbornness. The woman said, "I respect him [my partner] for his strong beliefs, and it helps me have confidence in our relationship."[298]

This woman rightly appreciated the positive aspects of her partner's obstinacy. But she should have acknowledged and dealt with the negative aspects too. She described her partner's obstinacy in flattering terms of "having strong beliefs." But this is not an accurate description of obstinacy. Webster's dictionary defines obstinacy as a "firm and *usually unreasonable* [my italics] adherence to an opinion, purpose, or substance." Webster's dictionary associates obstinacy with being "perverse," "annoying," and "irksome." Roget's thesaurus associates obstinate people with hard-liners, hardheads, fanatics, zealots, bigots, reactionaries, and diehards.

This woman was not doing her obstinate partner any Christian favors by praising him for his obstinacy without trying to help him overcome it. She said that her partner's obstinacy gave *her* confidence in their relationship. But here she was thinking selfishly about her interests more than her partner's interests. How did her partner's obstinacy affect *him?* Obstinacy is not a universally admired character trait, much less a virtuous character trait. Obstinate people have trouble dealing with other people not only in their relationships, but also in their careers. They have trouble compromising and working things out as team players. They often need to overcome their obstinacy not only to become more virtuous, Christ-like persons, but also to become more well-liked, successful persons.

THE VIRTUOUS "PERMISSIVENESS" OF TRANSFORMED LOVERS

Suppose we couples understand that transformed lovers are not too permissive, as discussed above. Now it might seem that they are not permissive enough! It might seem that they would not permit their partner to be jealous, obstinate, or otherwise morally imperfect. But this is not so. They accept and love their partner as he or she is, however jealous, obstinate, or otherwise morally imperfect their partner may be. It's just that they also try to help their partner overcome serious character weaknesses and grow in love, wisdom, and other Christian virtues if their partner is open to this.

There is another reason why transformed lovers are permissive enough. They are permissive about the small stuff that we couples should be permissive about, such as our partner forgetting a phone message. Transformed lovers would permit their partner to forget a phone message without getting all hot and bothered about this. Transformed lovers are easy-going, low-maintenance lovers.

Needs lovers, on the other hand—and romantic lovers too—are not always permissive about the small stuff. Needs lovers desire certain worldly goods for their Conventional Happiness so much that they are often upset with themselves, their partner, and/or God if their desires for these worldly goods are frustrated. They are more demanding, high-maintenance lovers.

Here is some small stuff that high-maintenance romantic lovers and needs lovers have complained about in their somewhat demanding, needy relationships. In the first example, a high-maintenance husband complains about his wife serving dinner five minutes late, according to his wife's report on this:

1) "When dinner is five minutes late, he flies into a fury."[299]
2) "Guy criticizes everything about me. My tastes in clothes, my hairdo, even my Saturday art classes—one of my few pleasures."[300]
3) "You ought to see what she wears at home for me! Any old thing will do."[301]
4) "Now, she's forever nagging to drive our car, and she doesn't know beans about how to treat a car."[302]
5) "I don't want her keeping schedules for me and reminding me to buy a present for my brother, whose birthday is three months away."[303]
6) "When Stewart tries to help, he gets everything wrong. He takes Max to the park but forgets to take his hat or bottle of milk. He offers to watch him so I can lie down, but if Max cries, Stewart gives him juice even though it's right before dinner. Then he's not hungry when he's scheduled to eat."[304]

These high-maintenance romantic lovers and needs lovers should get off their partners' backs! Christian transformed lovers never think, reason, feel, or talk like this. They are "permissive" about all this small stuff. But they are not permissive about the big stuff of responding to their partner lovingly and following Jesus virtuously. They have their Christian priorities straight.

CONCLUSION

Some of us Christian couples may need to get our Christian priorities straight. We may need to be more permissive about the small worldly stuff and less permissive about the big Christian marriage discipleship stuff. The big Christian marriage discipleship stuff includes building an equal, loving relationship with our partner instead of an unequal, unloving, permissive/controlling relationship. French philosopher Albert Camus appeals for equal, loving relationships with friends and loved ones:

> Don't walk in front of me, I may not follow.
> Don't walk behind me, I may not lead.
> Walk beside me and be my friend.[305]

chapter 4

Virtuous Marriage Conduct

WE COUPLES FOLLOW JESUS BY TRYING TO become like him in our moral character and conduct, as discussed throughout this guide. In this chapter, let's look more closely at Christ-like moral conduct in marriage and family life.

To act like Jesus in our moral conduct, we couples need to treat our partner well—and let's not forget about treating ourselves well too. It is often easy to treat our partner *or* ourselves well in specific marriage situations. But it may not always be easy to treat both our partner *and* ourselves well at the same time—especially if we and our partner have competing interests and serious differences of opinion. As a wise person once said, many couples vow to become one when they marry, but then the trouble starts when they try to decide which one.[306]

How can we couples figure out how to treat our partner and ourselves well at the same time? Where can we turn for our moral marriage guidance?

We can turn to Christian ethics. In this chapter, let's see how Christian ethics can help us understand how to treat our partner and ourselves well in specific marriage and family situations.

GOD & REASON: THE TWO MAIN SOURCES FOR CHRISTIAN ETHICS

The two main sources for Christian ethics are God and reason. Some of us couples turn mostly to God for our moral guidance, and others turn mostly to reason. But we should turn both to God and reason.

First and foremost, we should turn to God. As a Catholic, I believe that Jesus, the Son of God, reveals the principles of Christian ethics in his public ministry. I find the ethical teachings of Jesus in the New Testament and in many Christian churches, especially the Catholic Church.

The ethical teachings revealed in the New Testament and in many Christian churches are *public* revelations that are available to all human beings. There are also *private* revelations that we individuals may receive from God privately. In this chapter, let's focus on the public revelations in the Bible, Christian church teachings, and other public sources.

We should turn not only to God for our moral guidance, but also to our God-given human reason. We can use our reason to understand the ethical principles that God reveals in the Bible and other public sources. We can use our reason to apply these ethical principles to specific marriage and family situations. We can use our reason to develop ethical principles that account for current knowledge and address current moral issues, such as stem cell research. We need to be sure, however, that the ethical principles that we develop with our reason are compatible with the ethical principles that God reveals in the Bible and other public sources.

We couples can grow in our moral reasoning, much as we can grow in our mathematical reasoning, scientific reasoning, and other types of reasoning. As far as our moral reasoning goes, we can grow from a positive-thinking romantic wisdom to a conventional needs wisdom and finally to a Christ-like transforming wisdom, as discussed throughout this guide. With transforming wisdom, we reason wisely about how to treat our partner and ourselves well in specific marriage and family situations. We understand Christian ethics.

A CHRISTIAN DISCIPLESHIP VIRTUE ETHIC

Christian ethics is a huge topic! Christians have developed many approaches to ethics from Biblical times to the present, including consequentialism, deontological ethics, agent-relative ethics, virtue ethics, and the list goes on. We could not cover Christian ethics adequately in a scholarly book, much less in this chapter. So let's just get a brief overview of Christian ethics, and let's begin by going straight to Christian virtue ethics.

Christian ethics is above all a virtue ethic. Virtue ethics dominated both Judeo-Christian and secular ethics from ancient Greek and Biblical times to the 18th century. The influence of virtue ethics declined in scholarly circles during the 18th, 19th, and 20th centuries, but recently virtue ethics has become fashionable once again. The time is right for strengthening today's Christian marriage guidance with an authentic Christian virtue ethic.

This guide helps recover from the Bible, St. Thomas Aquinas, St. John of the Cross, and other Christian sources an authentic Christian virtue ethic centered around the primary, overall Christian Happiness goal of following Jesus virtuously in this life and being united with God in this life and eternally. I call this virtue ethic a *Christian discipleship virtue ethic*.

In this chapter, let's look at the following four broad ethical principles that help provide an overview of this guide's Christian discipleship virtue ethic: 1) the Christian Virtuous Happiness Principle, 2) the Christian Deontological Constraints Principle, 3) the Christian Deontological Responsibilities Principle, and 4) the Christian Virtuous Permissions Principle.

THE CHRISTIAN VIRTUOUS HAPPINESS PRINCIPLE

The Christian Virtuous Happiness Principle is that we Christians should pursue the one primary, overall goal of our human and Christian life, that is, the Christian Happiness goal of following Jesus virtuously in this life and being united with God in this life and eternally. We follow Jesus virtuously in this life by becoming like Jesus in our moral character and conduct, with love, wisdom, faith, and other Christian virtues and gifts, as discussed throughout this guide. So we have been covering the Christian Virtuous Happiness Principle.

The Christian Virtuous Happiness Principle tells us couples to put God and virtue first in our marriage and family life. This principle reflects the teachings of Jesus and the apostles that we should seek first the kingdom of God for our happiness (Matt. 6:33); that we are happy in this life if God considers us righteous (Rom. 4:6–8); that we cannot serve God and mammon [worldly goods] (Matt. 6:24—NAB); that we should put away our old self and put on a new virtuous, Christ-like self (Eph. 4:22–24); that we should love one another as Jesus loves us (John 13:34; 1 Cor. 13:4–7); and that we should live the same kind of life that Jesus lived (1 John 2:5–6).

The Happiness principle reflects the teleological character of both secular and Christian virtue ethics. A teleological ethic is based on the principle that there is "only *one true goal* for all human life that is determined by the very nature of humanity," as Benedict Ashley puts it.[307] In this guide's teleological Christian virtue ethic, the one true Christian Happiness goal for all human life is God and virtue, that is, to follow Jesus virtuously in this life and to be united with God in this life and eternally.

We Christian couples should always put this God-and-virtue Christian Happiness goal first in our marriage and family life, ahead of all our other secondary goals. We should put God and virtue ahead of moving up the corporate ladder, looking beautiful or handsome, having fun with our spouse at a baseball game, developing and enjoying our God-given golfing talents, and other secondary goals. We should not pursue these secondary goals selfishly at the expense of God and virtue.

The Virtuous Christian Happiness Principle reflects the emphasis upon moral character in both secular and Christian virtue ethics. Virtue ethicists rightly criticize consequentialism and deontological ethics for emphasizing moral conduct and neglecting moral character. Virtue ethicists stress that it is not enough to act morally in our external conduct. We should also be good, virtuous persons in our inner character, including our intellect, will, and emotions. For example, we couples should love our partner as much as possible with a Christ-like transforming love that is always patient and kind, with no selfish anger, animosity, or other unloving, un-Christ-like emotions (II,3; III,3; IV,1 above).

Jesus is a virtue ethicist. Jesus calls us to be virtuous, Christ-like persons not only in our external conduct, but also in our inner character. It is not enough to refrain from committing murder in our conduct; we should not be angry with others in our character (Matt. 5:21–22). It is not enough to refrain from committing adultery in our conduct; we men should not lust after a woman in our character, including our emotions (Matt. 5:27–28). Jesus calls us to be poor in spirit, gentle, merciful, and pure in heart (Matt. 5:3–8). Jesus denounces the scribes and Pharisees for looking like good, honest men on the outside, but being full of hypocrisy and lawlessness on the inside (Matt. 23:27–28).

THE MORAL CONDUCT OBJECTION TO CHRISTIAN VIRTUE ETHICS

Some critics of virtue ethics object that virtue ethicists focus so much on moral character that they neglect moral conduct. These critics argue that virtue ethicists do not provide clear, objective, comprehensive ethical principles for guiding our conduct. I call this the MORAL CONDUCT OBJECTION to both secular and Christian virtue ethics.[308]

Some versions of virtue ethics do fail to provide adequate moral guidance for our conduct. But this guide's Christian discipleship virtue ethic does not fail to do this. The Happiness, Constraints, Responsibilities, and Permissions principles identified above provide comprehensive, objective moral guidance for our conduct. Let's see why this is so.

For starters, let's see how the Happiness principle could help guide the conduct of a wealthy, 43-year-old businessman, Christopher. Christopher gets mad at his wife Susan so often that he makes her physically ill. He tells their marriage counselor:

> Of course I'm upset about Susan. [...] When I come home, I expect my wife to have taken the time to prepare a decent meal. I do not consider greasy barbecued chicken to be a decent meal. [...] Susan just doesn't respect the things that are important to me. How could she allow a fourteen-month-old to munch crackers and spill juice on the Aubusson carpet? I am trying to provide her with a beautiful home and she shows no respect for that either.
>
> Since I'm paying a bloody fortune for this [house] renovation, I expect everything to be done perfectly.[309]

Susan tells the marriage counselor that Christopher is "such a perfectionist. [...] Nothing pleases him. [...] It's impossible to discuss anything with him. He can argue circles around me; I never know what to say."[310]

Susan would know what to say if she could apply the Happiness principle to Christopher's unloving marriage conduct. The Happiness principle would tell Christopher that he should let go of his selfish desires for home-cooked gourmet meals in order to be happy responding to Susan lovingly when she serves greasy barbecued chicken for dinner. The Happiness principle would tell Christopher to seek a Christian Happiness centered around being a virtuous, Christ-like person instead of a worldly happiness centered around satisfying his desires for home-cooked gourmet meals and other worldly goods.

The Happiness principle works with the Constraints, Responsibilities, and Permissions principles to provide lots of guidance for our conduct. Let's look at the Constraints and Responsibilities principles next.

THE DEONTOLOGICAL ASPECTS OF A CHRISTIAN DISCIPLESHIP VIRTUE ETHIC

The Deontological Constraints Principle and the Deontological Responsibilities Principle reflect the deontological aspects of this guide's Christian discipleship virtue ethic. Deontological ethics has flourished in the Western world from the 18th century to the present, beginning especially with the deontological ethic of the German philosopher Immanuel Kant (1724–1804). Deontologists, like consequentialists, focus on moral conduct more than moral character. Deontologists and consequentialists view moral conduct differently, however. Let's look at some of the differences.

Consequentialists determine the morality of an action by considering above all the consequences of the action. They consider how much overall good an action would be likely to produce and how much overall evil it would be likely to prevent or eliminate. Consequentialists hold that in our moral conduct we should act always to produce the greatest good for everyone overall without giving special consideration to our personal interests. For example, suppose that a terrorist held a bank teller, the teller's wife, and three bank customers hostage. Suppose that the terrorist demanded that the teller kill his wife, or else he the terrorist would kill all the hostages. Should the teller kill his wife?

Most consequentialists would argue that the teller *should* kill his wife. Then four persons would live (the teller and the three customers) instead of no persons living. The four lives saved would be a greater overall good than no lives saved.

Most deontologists, on the other hand, would say that the teller should not kill his wife. Deontologists do not determine the morality of an action by considering mostly the consequences of the action, including the "overall good" that the action might produce. Deontologists consider above all the nature of the action in itself. They hold that some actions are morally wrong in themselves, such as murder, adultery, and incest, and other actions are morally right in themselves, such as honoring one's father and mother. Deontologists hold that we should never perform an action that is morally wrong in itself—not even if we could produce a greater overall good of a consequentialist sort by doing so.

Most deontologists would argue that the teller's wife is an innocent person, and killing an innocent person is morally wrong in itself, so the teller should never do this, no matter what.

Jesus too would say that the teller should not kill his wife. Jesus teaches that we should obey the Ten Commandments, including the commandment not to commit murder.

This guide's Christian discipleship virtue ethic includes the Ten Commandments and other deontological principles for guiding Christian conduct.

GOD & REASON: THE TWO MAIN SOURCES FOR DEONTOLOGICAL PRINCIPLES

How can we couples know the deontological principles that should guide our conduct? We can know these principles from God and reason, the two main sources for Christian ethics. God has revealed in the Ten Commandments, for example, that we should not commit murder or adultery.

We can know the deontological principles that should guide our conduct also with our God-given reason. We can reason that we should not commit murder or adultery, and we can formulate reasonable principles, rules, laws, and commandments that tell us not to commit murder or adultery. These principles that tell us what we should *not* do are often called deontological constraints. We couples should obey deontological constraints.

Deontological ethical thinkers formulate principles, rules, laws, and commandments that tell us not only what we should not do (deontological constraints), but also what we should do. We should perform actions that are morally good in themselves, such as honoring our father and mother. These principles that tell us what we should do are often called deontological responsibilities. We couples should carry out our deontological responsibilities.

THE NATURAL LAW, INCLUDING THE TEN COMMANDMENTS

Many philosophers and other scholars identify deontological constraints and responsibilities with a universal natural law. The natural law includes moral principles, rules, laws, and commandments that identify actions that are morally wrong or morally right in themselves. It would be morally wrong for us couples to cheat on our income taxes, for example, and it would be morally right to love our partner as Jesus loves us.

We can know the natural law with our reason, according to St. Paul, St. Thomas Aquinas, and many other Christians. St. Paul taught that pagans could be holy because they could be led by their reason to obey the moral law that was "engraved in their hearts"—even if they had not heard about the Old Testament Law or the New Testament Law of Love. Paul wrote:

> It is not listening to the Law but keeping it that will make people holy in the sight of God. For instance, pagans who never

heard of the Law but are led by *reason* [my italics] to do what the Law commands, may not actually 'possess' the Law, but they can be said to 'be' the Law. They can point to the substance of the Law engraved on their hearts—[...] that is, their own conscience (Rom. 2:13–15).[311]

The natural law includes moral principles, rules, laws, and commandments, such as the Ten Commandments. But the natural law is not *just* a set of moral principles, rules, laws, and commandments. Catholic philosopher Jean Porter holds that the natural law is primarily "a fundamental capacity for moral judgment," that is, "a capacity or power to distinguish between good and evil."[312]

We couples have a natural capacity for moral discernment or, in other words, moral wisdom. We can realize our potential for moral wisdom by growing from a positive-thinking romantic wisdom to a conventional needs wisdom and finally to a Christ-like transforming wisdom, as discussed throughout this guide. With the transforming wisdom, we understand Christian ethics.

THE CHRISTIAN DEONTOLOGICAL CONSTRAINTS PRINCIPLE

Let's look more closely at the Christian Deontological Constraints Principle in this guide's Christian discipleship virtue ethic. The Constraints principle is that we Christians and all other human beings should obey deontological constraints, that is, the principles, laws, rules, and commandments that tell us that certain actions are morally wrong in themselves, so we should never perform them, no matter what.

Immature couples in distressed marriages are most likely to disobey deontological constraints. In a distressed marriage, Nick, his wife Kim, and their daughter all disobeyed the deontological constraint on lying. Nick lied to Kim for twenty years in order to hide his compulsive gambling. Kim lied to herself, her friends, and her relatives in order to "protect" Nick. Kim's daughter hid the truth in order to cover up Nick's gambling. She gave Nick her babysitting money to use for his gambling without telling her mother about this.[313]

Nick and Kim could begin to rebuild their marriage by dealing with the truth about Nick's gambling instead of lying to themselves and others about it.

The Christian Deontological Constraints Principle discussed above tells us couples what we should *not* do in our marriage and family life (constraints). Let's look now at what we *should* do (responsibilities).

THE CHRISTIAN DEONTOLOGICAL RESPONSIBILITIES PRINCIPLE

The Christian Deontological Responsibilities Principle is that we Christians and all other human beings should carry out our deontological responsibilities in reasonable ways, considering the circumstances. In short, we should act responsibly.

We have many deontological responsibilities. We should honor our father and mother (one of the Ten Commandments). We should treat others fairly (1 Thess. 2:10–12). We should treat others as we would like them to treat us (Matt. 7:12). We should pursue virtue.[314] We should love God with our whole heart, mind, and soul, and we should love our neighbor as Jesus loves us (Matt. 22:37–40; John 13:34).

Deontological responsibilities are often more general than deontological constraints. It may not always be easy to determine how to carry out our general deontological responsibilities in specific marriage and family situations. A husband Brandon might know generally that he should honor his aging mother who is struggling to make ends meet on her social security income. But how specifically should Brandon honor his mother in his external conduct? Should he help house her in a retirement home that provides long-term medical care even though he and his family would go deep into debt to do this? Should he invite his mother to live with him, his wife, and their three children in their crowded three-bedroom apartment even though his wife and children would have trouble with this?

It may be especially hard to determine how to carry out our responsibilities when we have competing responsibilities. Brandon has competing responsibilities to honor and care for his aging mother on one hand, and to love and care for his wife and children on the other hand. How should he handle these responsibilities?

For starters, Brandon should honor and love his mother, wife, and children internally in his heart, mind, and soul. Christian virtue ethics requires internal mental, emotional, and spiritual acts of honoring, loving, forgiving, and the like, as St. Thomas Aquinas points out. Aquinas writes that "the Kingdom of God consists chiefly in internal acts."[315] Aquinas refers to St. Paul (Rom. 14:16–17), "The kingdom of God does not mean eating or drinking this or that, it means righteousness and peace and joy brought by the Holy Spirit."[316]

Brandon should honor and love his mother, wife, and children not only internally in his character, but also externally in his conduct. He should carry out his responsibilities to honor and love his mother, wife, and children in reasonable ways that would reflect the kingdom of God within him.

There are usually many reasonable ways to carry out our responsibilities in any given situation, not just one reasonable way. Brandon could go deep into debt to house his mother in a retirement home. He could invite his mother to live with him and his family in their three-bedroom apartment. He could do something else entirely.

We couples might not always think of all the reasonable ways to carry out our responsibilities in specific situations. Suppose that a husband and wife with four children could not afford to make the mortgage payments on their 3,000 square-foot house in an upscale neighborhood even though the husband was working full-time and his wife was working part-time. The husband might think that he needed to get a second job on weekends even though he would stress himself out and risk another heart attack by doing this. The husband might not realize that he could stick to his one full-time job, sell his house, buy a less expensive house, and enjoy a responsible, loving life with his wife and children. This would be a reasonable thing to do.

The Christian Responsibilities Principle tells us couples to carry out our marriage and family responsibilities in reasonable ways, considering the circumstances, as discussed above. When we try to figure out how to carry out our responsibilities, we may consider our own interests as well as the interests of others, including our spouse. To understand how much we may take our own interests into consideration, let's go to the next principle in this guide's Christian discipleship virtue ethic, that is, the Christian Virtuous Permissions Principle. This principle permits us to pursue our personal interests with a good deal of freedom.

THE CHRISTIAN VIRTUOUS PERMISSIONS PRINCIPLE

We couples might need to sacrifice our personal interests at times in order to treat our partner well, with a self-sacrificial Christian marital love. But we might not need to sacrifice our interests as much as we might think. We have the Christian Virtuous Permissions Principle to thank for this. The Permissions principle is that we may pursue our individual interests freely as long as we comply with the Happiness, Constraints, and

Responsibilities principles discussed above, together with other principles that come with them.

The Permissions principle would ordinarily permit us couples to vacation in Paris or the Bahamas; to donate money for the homeless or for cancer research; to become an accountant or a teacher; and the list would go on. We could ordinarily do any of these things and follow Jesus virtuously too.

The Permissions principle would permit the husband Brandon discussed above to account for his personal interests when he was figuring out how to honor and care for his aging mother. Suppose that he was interested in spending more time with his wife and children, but he could not do this if his mother lived with them in their apartment. Then he would not be obligated to invite his mother to live with him and his family—as long as he honored his mother internally and carried out his responsibilities for her in some other reasonable way, considering the circumstances.

The Permissions principle permits us to pursue our interests with a good deal of freedom, but not too much freedom. The Permissions principle is not too subjective. We are not free to disregard the objective Happiness, Constraints, and Responsibilities principles discussed above that apply universally to all human beings. Brandon, for example, would not be morally permitted to cheat on his income taxes in order to get enough money to house his mother in a retirement home. Cheating is morally wrong in itself, so Brandon should never do this, no matter what.

A UNIVERSAL, COMMON-SENSE CHRISTIAN DISCIPLESHIP VIRTUE ETHIC

When all is said and done about Christian virtue ethics, the Moral Conduct Objection to Christian virtue ethics does not apply to this guide's Christian discipleship virtue ethic. This virtue ethic provides plenty of guidance for moral conduct with the objective Happiness, Constraints, Responsibilities, and Permissions principles discussed above. What's more, this virtue ethic is not weakened by the moral permissiveness and moral relativism of our times—unlike some modern ethics, including agent-relative ethics and some modern versions of virtue ethics.[317]

This guide's Christian discipleship virtue ethic makes good sense. Should we couples pursue the overall Christian Happiness goal of being unselfish, virtuous, Christ-like persons instead of being selfish, sinful, un-Christ-like persons (the Happiness principle)? By all means! Should we refrain from committing adultery, sexually abusing children, and performing other actions that are morally wrong in themselves (the Constraints principle)?

Certainly! Should we carry out our Christian marital, parental, and other responsibilities in reasonable ways, considering the circumstances (the Responsibilities principle)? To be sure! Should we be permitted to pursue our personal interests with a good deal of freedom, within objectively reasonable moral limits (the Permissions principle)? Yes indeed!

Here, then, is the least that every Christian couple should know about Christian ethics: 1) Seek a Christian Happiness centered around God and virtue (Happiness principle); 2) Do not do anything that is morally wrong in itself (Constraints principle); 3) Act responsibly (Responsibilities principle); 4) Treat yourself well in addition to treating others well, including your spouse (Permissions principle).

SELFISH MORAL REASONING

Some of us couples might understand the Happiness, Constraints, Responsibilities, and Permissions principles pretty well, but we still might not always apply these principles lovingly and wisely to specific marriage and family situations. Why not?

Selfishness, for one thing, including selfish moral reasoning. Our moral reasoning may be distorted at times by our selfish desires for worldly goods, together with the frustration, anger, and other unloving emotions that often come with these desires. St. Paul teaches that we need to put away our old self that is corrupted by *deceitful desires* in order to be renewed in our *mind* (Eph. 4:22–24). Thomas à Kempis observes in *Of the Imitation of Christ* that "we often judge of a thing according as we feel disposed towards it, and our judgement is distorted by our feelings."[318] An ancient Hindu sage writes in the *Bhagavad Gita*, "Just as a fire is covered by smoke and a mirror is obscured by dust, [. . .] knowledge is hidden by selfish desire. [. . .] Selfish desire is found in the senses, mind, and intellect, misleading them and burying wisdom in delusion."[319]

Some of us couples may reason selfishly at times in order to evade responsibility for our actions, much as automobile drivers in traffic accidents sometimes reason selfishly to evade responsibility for their accidents. Here is some selfish reasoning in accident reports that drivers completed for their insurance companies and that were circulated on the Internet:

    a) The telephone pole was approaching fast. I was attempting to swerve out of its path when it struck my front end.

b) The pedestrian had no idea which direction to run, so I ran over him.
c) To avoid hitting the bumper of the car in front, I struck the pedestrian.
d) As I approached the intersection, a stop sign suddenly appeared in a place where no stop sign had ever appeared before. I was unable to stop in time to avoid the accident.
e) My car was legally parked when it backed into another vehicle.
f) An invisible car appeared out of nowhere, struck my vehicle, and vanished.

Some married couples reason selfishly to evade responsibility for mistreating their partner. A husband George rationalized verbally attacking his wife Marge after having one beer too many. Marge complained to their marriage counselor that George would often have a few drinks at parties and then verbally attack her with "a hate-filled diatribe of cruel and vicious insults."[320] George defended himself:

> Marge's big complaint is that I sometimes get rowdy after partying and pop out with things that might have been better left unsaid. I occasionally do that—but I always apologize. A guy can't be held accountable for every remark he makes when he's had one beer too many, now, can he?[321]

Sure, George—and a guy can't be held accountable for being struck by an invisible car that came out of nowhere and then vanished, now, can he?

A married mother of three, Carey, reasoned selfishly to evade responsibility for her extra-marital affair. Carey had felt lonely most of her life, and she wanted to feel good. She rationalized her affair on the grounds that it made her feel good.[322]

SELFISH MORAL REASONING IN DISTRESSED MARRIAGES

George and Carey had distressed marriages. Couples in distressed marriages usually reason more selfishly than couples in normal marriages do. Psychologist Aaron Beck identifies eleven types of distorted thinking ("cognitive distortions") that are common in distressed marriages, including personalized reasoning, tunnel vision, arbitrary inferences, polarized thinking, negative labeling, and other distortions.[323]

With personalized reasoning, according to Beck, we couples reason self-centeredly that our partner's actions are directed at us personally even when this is not so. We view life egocentrically as a struggle between us and other people, including our partner. A husband took his wife's actions too personally when she came home from work. When she came home earlier than he did, he thought she was sending a message that she cared for the children more than he did. When she came home later than he did, he thought she was sending a message that she worked harder than he did.[324]

SELFISH MORAL REASONING IN NORMAL MARRIAGES

Couples in normal marriages reason less selfishly than couples in distressed marriages do, but they still reason a little selfishly at times. Many marriage authorities provide tips and techniques that can help us couples reason unselfishly about how to treat our partner and ourselves well. Psychologist Aaron Beck recommends a desire-rating technique that can help us reason unselfishly in our marital decision-making. Suppose that a husband and wife used this technique to decide whether to eat at Jimmy's Restaurant or Anthony's Sea Food Grotto. The husband might rate his desire to eat at Jimmy's a 5 on a 10-point scale, and his wife might rate her desire to eat at Anthony's a 9. The 9 would beat the 5, so the husband and wife could decide to eat at Anthony's, and that could be a reasonable thing to do.

We couples could use this desire-rating technique unselfishly, but we could also use it selfishly, often without realizing it. Psychologist Aaron Beck creates a dialogue to show how a married couple, Cliff and Judy, could use this desire-rating technique effectively to decide where to spend Christmas. Beck does not seem to realize, however, that Cliff and Judy ("he" and "she") use the desire-rating technique somewhat selfishly. Here is the dialogue:

> *He:* I wonder if we might skip going to your parents this year? I've been awfully tired lately and would appreciate having a breather around Christmas. If we want to celebrate, we can do it with my folks [who live just around the corner].
> *She:* I would really like to see my parents this year.
> *He:* You know we went there last year, and we've already seen them twice this year.

She: I know. But it's not really Christmas unless I'm with my parents.
He: How important is it to go to your parents this year?
She: On a ten-point scale, it's a ten. How important is it for you to stay home?
He: On a ten-point scale, I guess it's about a five.
She: I guess the tens have it. [She laughs.]
He: I guess you're right.[325]

The problem here is that "he" and "she" (Cliff and Judy) use the desire-rating technique somewhat selfishly. Judy uses the technique to get what she wants without considering Cliff's interests much if at all. She pays little attention to Cliff's interest in staying home for Christmas this year to get a breather. She could at least tell Cliff that she would like him to get a breather this year. But she just insists that *she* wants to visit her parents for Christmas this year, with a strong 10-rated desire. She says that it is not really Christmas unless she is with her parents, so it seems that she must spend *every* Christmas with her parents. She does not seem willing to compromise. She does not even bring up the possibility of inviting her parents to visit Cliff and her for Christmas. With a compromise like this, she and Cliff could stay home for Christmas, Cliff could get a breather, and she could be with her parents too.

Cliff is a little selfish too. He pays little attention to Judy's interest in seeing her parents more often. He could at least tell Judy that he would like her to see her parents more often. But he just points out that he and Judy have already visited her parents twice this year. He pursues his interest in staying home to get a breather without expressing much concern for Judy's interests.

The problem with this desire-rating technique is that selfish, controlling people would probably use this technique selfishly at times, especially if they were married to a permissive partner. They might rate many of their desires selfishly as strong 9's and 10's, while their partner might rate many of his or her desires "unselfishly" or permissively as weak 1's and 2's. Then the selfish, controlling partner would get his or her way most of the time.

UNSELFISH, DESIRELESS MORAL REASONING

We couples should reason unselfishly about how to treat our partner and ourselves well, considering our partner's interests as well as our own.

To reason unselfishly, we should put away or at least disregard selfish desires for worldly goods. The wealthy businessman Christopher discussed above should have put away or at least disregarded his selfish desire for a clean Aubusson carpet so that it would not have distorted his reasoning about his wife Susan "letting" their child spill juice on the carpet (IV,4). Christopher should have reasoned more unselfishly that Susan could not always prevent their child from spilling juice on the carpet, that juice on the carpet is small stuff, and that it would be unreasonable and unloving for him to get mad at Susan about this.

Suppose that we couples put away our selfish desires for worldly goods so the desires would not distort our moral reasoning. Then we could reason unselfishly or, in other words, desirelessly. Then our mind would not be corrupted by deceitful desires for worldly goods, as St. Paul puts it (Eph. 4:22–24).

This Christian concept of unselfish, desireless moral reasoning is somewhat similar to philosopher Immanuel Kant's concept of pure reason and psychologist Abraham Maslow's concept of "desireless perception." According to Maslow, extraordinarily mature, self-actualized people perceive reality and reason about reality objectively. Their perceptions and reasoning are not distorted by their desires, needs, and emotions. They have "desireless perception."[326]

Most people perceive reality and reason about reality subjectively a good deal of the time, according to Maslow. Their perceptions and reasoning are often distorted by their desires, needs, and emotions.[327] Suppose that a husband viewed his wife subjectively in a need-determined way that reflected his desires and perceived needs for money and sex. In other words, suppose that he viewed his wife subjectively and needfully as a money-giver and sex partner. Then he would reason selfishly at times about how to use his wife for his financial gain and sexual gratification.[328] He would not reason unselfishly about how to treat his wife well.

We couples may need to let go of selfish desires for worldly goods at times in order to reason unselfishly about treating our partner well.

BECOMING LIKE JESUS IN OUR CHARACTER BY ACTING LIKE JESUS IN OUR CONDUCT

We have been focusing in this chapter on acting like Jesus in our marriage and family conduct. Now let's connect this Christ-like conduct to the Christ-like character that has been discussed throughout this guide. Let's see how acting like Jesus in our conduct can help us become like Jesus in our character.

The more we couples act like Jesus with loving, wise, Christ-like conduct, the more we develop the *habits* of acting in these ways. In other words, we develop Christ-like *character traits,* or *virtues.* We become increasingly virtuous, Christ-like persons not only in our conduct, but also in our character.

We do not need to complain about not having enough time to become increasingly virtuous, Christ-like persons in our busy marriage and family life. We may not have as much time as we would like for religious retreats and other "spiritual" activities that could help us grow morally and spiritually, but that's o.k. We can become increasingly virtuous, Christ-like persons in our character by acting like Jesus in our conduct during our ordinary marriage and family activities. Our ordinary marriage and family activities can be moral and spiritual exercises that help us become increasingly virtuous, Christ-like persons.[329]

We do not need to retreat to a monastery, convent, or mountain cabin for prayer, fasting, and a traditional contemplative life in order to become increasingly virtuous, Christ-like persons. We can become increasingly virtuous, Christ-like persons in our own home by acting with love, wisdom, and other Christian virtues in our busy marriage and family life. Our home can be our spiritual monastery, convent, or mountain cabin.

Of course it can help us couples to get out of the house from time to time for a peaceful, prayerful religious retreat—or maybe just for a quiet, reflective walk in the park.

CONCLUSION

This guide's Christian discipleship virtue ethic includes loving and wise ethical principles that can help us couples understand how to treat our partner and ourselves well in our marriage and family life. We should keep these principles in mind during our ordinary marriage and family activities instead of putting them on the back burners. As St. Paul puts it, we should fill our minds with "everything that is good and pure, everything that we love and honour, and everything that can be thought virtuous or worthy of praise" (Phil. 4:4–9).

Our loving and wise ethical thoughts can help us Christian couples grow in our Christian marriage discipleship. Our loving and wise ethical *thoughts* can become loving and wise *feelings;* our loving and wise thoughts and feelings can become loving and wise *words;* our loving and wise words can become loving and wise *actions;* our loving and wise actions can become a loving and wise *character;* finally, our loving and wise character can become our *Christian destiny* of following Jesus virtuously in this life and being united with God in this life and eternally. An anonymous author once wrote:

> Watch your thoughts, for they become words.
> Watch your words, for they become actions.
> Watch your actions, for they become habits.
> Watch your habits, for they become character.
> Watch your character, for it becomes your destiny.[330]

Let's go to the next chapter for some loving and wise ethical thoughts about money that could help some of us couples deal with our family money effectively, treat our partner and ourselves well, and become increasingly virtuous, Christ-like persons all at the same time.

chapter 5

Virtuous Marriage Money Management

We Christian couples are called to follow Jesus with love, wisdom, and other Christian virtues during our ordinary marriage and family activities, doing such things as managing our money and dealing with the housework. Managing our money lovingly and wisely in our conduct can help us become increasingly loving, wise, Christ-like persons in our character (IV,4 above). What's more, we have a moral responsibility to manage our money lovingly and wisely in order to treat our partner well and follow Jesus virtuously. Suppose that a husband self-indulgently used all the family savings to buy a new Porsche convertible, and there was no money left for his wife's dental care. He would not be treating his wife well or following Jesus virtuously. Money management is an important part of Christian marriage discipleship.

Many Christians during the worldwide financial crisis that came to a head in 2008 began to realize that responsible money management was an important aspect of their Christian faith. Many Christian churches and other religious groups ordained or appointed "financial missionaries," "stewardship pastors," and others with the "mission" of preaching and teaching about responsible money management.[331]

SELFISHNESS: A MAJOR CAUSE OF MONEY PROBLEMS

To understand how to manage our money lovingly and wisely, we couples need to understand what can prevent us from doing so. What can cause money problems?

There are many causes of money problems, such as unemployment, unexpected medical bills, and growing up in poverty with a mother on welfare and an absentee, drug-addicted father. But selfishness is the Number One cause of money problems for many of us reasonably prosperous middle-class Americans, according to financial advisor Henry Brock in his *Guide to Money Happiness*. Brock points out that some couples go deep into debt trying to satisfy their desires for material goods that they cannot afford and do not need. Their money problems often put stress on their marriage and sometimes lead to divorce. It has been said that money problems contribute to 75% of all divorces.[332]

A wife Linda desired material goods for her Emotional Happiness so much that she became a shopaholic. Her husband Bob complained to their marriage counselor:

> Linda casually mentioned that she once charged more than our credit limit—but she didn't bother to say that her purchases put us eleven thousand dollars in debt! Eleven thousand dollars! I had to go crawling to her old man and ask for help. How do you think that made me feel? [...] The way Linda spends money is like a disease. She never keeps receipts, charges here and there, never records her checks. Before she realizes it, she's blown a fortune.[333]

Linda not only shopped selfishly; she also reasoned selfishly about her shopping. She tried to evade responsibility for her addictive shopping, much as some automobile drivers try to evade responsibility for their accidents (IV,4 above). Linda would not admit that she was a shopaholic and that she was treating Bob poorly with her addictive shopping. Linda told their marriage counselor: "Well, I admit I sometimes spend more than I should, but I'm certainly not a compulsive shopper. What does Bob expect from me? I need a little happiness, a little release in my life."[334]

Linda did not take to heart the words of the author of Ecclesiastes that "no one who loves money can ever have enough, and no one who loves wealth enjoys any return from it. This too is futility" (Eccles. 5:10—REB).

Linda has plenty of shopaholic company. There may be over 10 million compulsive shoppers in the United States.[335]

SELF-DESTRUCTIVE SPENDING

Why are there so many American shopaholics? For one thing, our American consumer society encourages and facilitates self-destructive spending, as psychologist Stuart Wyse points out in his book, *Going Broke: Why Americans Can't Hold On to Their Money*. Wyse writes that self-destructive spending is encouraged and facilitated by the proliferation of such things as credit cards, advertising, shopping malls, home shopping channels, Internet shopping, telephone orders with the use of toll-free numbers, state lotteries, casino gambling, sports gambling, stock market day trading, and home loans with no down payments.[336]

It has become easier to buy things in recent years, at least until the worldwide economic crisis emerged in 2008. What's more, there are more things to buy. There are automobiles with computerized guidance systems, home entertainment centers, computers, printers, camcorders, video games, fax machines, cell phones with monthly fees, homeowner's association fees, fitness center fees, face-lifts, laser hair removal, lip and wrinkle fillers, and the list could go on. And what about all the money spent maintaining, storing, repairing, cleaning, and dealing in other ways with all this stuff? How can we couples come up with the time and money for all this stuff on top of the time and money that we need for food, shelter, transportation, health care, and other necessities?

Many Americans not only *desire* more things than ever before; they also think that they *need* more things. In 1973, 26% of Americans called home air conditioning a necessity; in 1996, 51%; and in 2006, 70%.[337] In 2006, 90% of Americans considered a clothes washer a necessity, 83% considered a clothes dryer a necessity, and 68% considered a microwave a necessity.[338]

Many Americans who "needed" all these things were not able to afford them during the world economic crisis that emerged in 2008. Some Americans suffered mentally and emotionally from what journalist Robert Samuelson calls "affluent deprivation." Affluent deprivation is not poverty. Affluent deprivation is a mental and emotional state of feeling poorer than we were before. We feel that we cannot afford all the things that we had before, so we are dissatisfied and disgruntled.[339]

FOLLOWING JESUS DURING HARD ECONIMIC TIMES

We couples do not have to be dissatisfied and disgruntled during hard economic times, even if we cannot afford the computerized automobile guidance systems and other material goods that we had before. We can follow Jesus virtuously and be happy during bad economic times as well as good ones.

Jesus can help us manage our money wisely during hard economic times. More specifically, Jesus can help us overcome the selfishness that lies at the root of many money problems. He can help us let go of selfish desires for material goods so that we will not be tempted to buy material goods that we cannot afford and do not need. He teaches that we should not store up treasures for ourselves on earth, for where our treasure is, there will our heart be also (Matt. 6:19–21). In this passage, he warns us not to "set our hearts" on worldly treasures, that is, not to desire them for our happiness.

ACHIEVING A GOOD MARRIAGE & FAMILY LIFE WITH MATERIAL GOODS

It might seem that letting go of selfish desires for material goods might require us couples to give up material goods too much. But this is not necessarily so. We can often let go of selfish desires for material goods without necessarily giving up the material goods themselves. It is our selfish desires for material goods that sometimes frustrate us, weaken our marital love, and prevent us from following Jesus virtuously—it is not the material goods themselves, as discussed above (IV,1). When we follow Jesus virtuously, we ordinarily work, save money, shop, and accumulate material goods, much as we always do. Ordinarily we may follow Jesus virtuously and enjoy a good marriage and family life with plenty of material goods too.

Following Jesus virtuously might even help some of us become wealthy. Wisdom ("prudence") is the basis of riches, as a Mexican proverb says.[340] Greed, selfishness, and other vices, on the other hand, can prevent us from becoming wealthy. "The greedy person ends up empty-handed," as another Mexican proverb says.[341]

The proverbial wisdom that virtues can lead to wealth and vices can lead to poverty is expressed in an early German "comic strip" that was written and illustrated by a Protestant artist, Hans Burgkmaier the Elder, during the 16th century. The comic strip is titled, "How the Poor Man Becomes Rich and the Rich Man Poor." The captions for the strip's seven illustrations read: 1) Poverty brings Humility, 2) Humility brings Improvement, 3) Improvement brings Riches, 4) Riches bring Arrogance, 5) Arrogance brings Envy, 6) Envy brings Discord, 7) Discord brings back Poverty.[342]

SAVING MONEY BY BUYING STRIPPED-DOWN ECONOMY CARS

Suppose that we couples let go of selfish desires for material goods in order to be happy following Jesus virtuously, with or without the material goods. Then we would not be tempted to pursue the material goods selfishly at the expense of God and virtue, as discussed above. And that's not all. Letting go of selfish desires for material goods could help us save money, avoid money problems, and enjoy a reasonably prosperous marriage and family life. My wife Arnell and I have avoided money problems, saved money, and been financially successful over the years partly because we have not desired lots of material goods for our happiness. We have not desired expensive cars with air conditioning, power steering, and other extras, for example. We have purchased stripped-down economy cars with no extras—no air conditioning, no power steering, and no radios (although we often bought and installed radios for about $100 after we bought the cars).

We bought the cars new when the dealers advertised them as "loss leaders" in the local newspapers at prices that were often below the dealer's cost. We paid cash for the cars to avoid financing costs, and we drove each car well over 100,000 miles before buying a new car.

Of course it is perfectly o.k. to buy expensive cars. There is no commandment or other deontological constraint that we human beings must not buy expensive cars. The point here is simply that Arnell and I have saved money and gained financially by buying stripped-down economy cars for well over 35 years instead of buying medium-sized, moderately-priced cars with lots of extras. How much did we gain from 1970 to 2002, not even counting the years since then?

ABOUT A THIRD OF A MILLION DOLLARS!

To put this another way, Arnell and I would have *spent* about a third of a million dollars more if we had bought the medium-sized cars instead of the economy cars. The third of a million dollars would have been the "opportunity costs" of buying the medium-sized cars instead of the economy cars. Opportunity costs are the costs of choosing one option instead of another option, such as the option of buying the more expensive cars instead of the less expensive cars.

Let's see more specifically how Arnell and I gained about a third of a million dollars from 1970 to 2002 by buying the stripped-down economy cars. We bought a Ford Fairlane 500 in 1970, a Plymouth Volare in 1976, a Mazda GLC in 1980, a Toyota Tercel in 1985, a Toyota Tercel in 1986, a Nissan Sentra in 1989, a Nissan Sentra in 1995, and a Nissan Sentra in 1996.

Let's see first how much money we gained by buying the stripped-down Toyota Tercel in 1986 instead of buying a medium-sized Toyota Celica with lots of extras. Then we can add the total financial gains for all eight cars.

The new 1986 Toyota Tercel cost $4,688, as advertised in the *Los Angeles Times* on July 26, 1986. A new Toyota Celica Coupe with extras was advertised on the same day for $9,488, so we saved $4,800 by buying the Tercel instead of the Celica ($9,488 minus $4,688)—not even counting the extra taxes for the Celica.

Suppose that Arnell and I had invested the initial $4,800 savings on the Tercel from 1986 to 2002 with an annual 8% rate of return. We would have made about $15,226.

Arnell and I saved more money because the smaller Tercel with the manual transmission and no air conditioning got about 10 more miles per gallon than the larger Celica with the automatic transmission and air conditioning. We used about 3,571 gallons of gas to drive the Tercel about 125,000 miles (125,000 divided by 35 mpg). In comparison, we would have used about 5,000 gallons of gas to drive the Celica about 125,000 miles (125,000 divided by 25 mpg). So we saved about $1,429 on gas during the five years that we drove the Tercel—figuring that the cost of gas averaged $1 a gallon. Think how much more we would have saved with $4-a-gallon gas!

Suppose that we had invested our gasoline savings ($1,429) from 1991 to 2002 with an 8% annual rate of return. We would have made about $3,598.

We saved more money on automobile insurance, annual registration fees, and car maintenance and repair expenses during the five years that we drove the car. These costs would have been higher for the more expensive Celica with the extras. I estimate conservatively about $1,000 a year savings on insurance, registration fees, and maintenance and repairs for a total savings of about $5,000 for the five years. Suppose that we had invested these savings from 1991 to 2002 with an annual 8% rate of return. We would have made about $12,591.

How much did Arnell and I gain financially by buying the Tercel instead of the Celica? About $33,163.

In the same ways, we gained about $52,072 on the 1970 Ford Fairlane, about $39,762 on the 1976 Plymouth Volare, about $38,553 on the 1980

Mazda GLC, about $32,952 on the 1985 Toyota Tercel, about $29,858 on the 1989 Nissan Sentra, about $23,694 on the 1995 Nissan Sentra, and about $22,181 on the 1996 Nissan Sentra. That's a total of about $272,181. And let's not forget about $20,000 that we gained by buying these cars with cash instead of financing them, including savings on financing costs and interest payments. So we gained a grand total of about $292,181.

That's how Arnell and I gained close to a third of a million dollars without winning the lottery!

There are websites and other sources for checking the annual ownership costs for cars before we buy them (for example, www.edmunds.com).

Of course we couples do not need to buy economy cars and gain about a third of a million dollars in order to be happy loving one another and following Jesus virtuously. We could be happy loving one another and following Jesus virtuously with medium-sized cars with air conditioning and other extras, with or without nearly a third of a million dollar savings.

As a matter of fact, Arnell and I gained *more* than a third of a million dollars from our car savings because we invested some of the savings and some of our other savings in California real estate, including several single-family rental houses. We passed along some of our financial gains to our tenants. We did not ordinarily raise the rent while the same tenants rented a house, so our rents were usually significantly below market—especially for tenants who rented one of our houses for four or five years or more. Rents in their neighborhood often went up, but their rent ordinarily stayed the same, so some of them saved about $300 to $500 a month, that is, about $3,600 to $6,000 a year. We tried to treat our tenants well. We believe that promoting social justice begins at home, including the ways that we treat our neighbors in our ordinary activities, including our business activities.

Arnell and I have always agreed on financial matters for the most part, so it has not been hard to manage our money together. And "together" is a key word. We have always made decisions together about money, parenting, housework, and other aspects of our marriage and family life. As far as the money goes, it has not mattered that for a good many years Arnell worked full-time at home to help raise our children without getting a salary for this, while I always earned a salary for teaching college full-time. All of our money has always been our family money, and Arnell and I have always decided together what to do with it.

CONCLUSION

The Duwamish Indians say, "I love a people who do not live for the love of money."[343] Suppose that we couples do not live for the love of money. Suppose that we live for the love of God and neighbor, including our marriage partner. Then we will manage our money lovingly and wisely. Money will be a good servant for us, not a bad master.[344] Henry Brock explains that money is a bad master when we are preoccupied with getting it, when we "forfeit our freedom to debt," and when we try anxiously to keep up with the Joneses.[345] John D. Rockefeller says that money is a good servant when we use it for the good of our fellow man in keeping with our conscience.[346]

We couples lose little and gain a lot by managing our money lovingly and wisely. Doing this helps us treat our partner well, avoid money problems, and follow Jesus virtuously. And it can often help us save money and enjoy a good marriage and family life with plenty of material goods too.

chapter 6

Union with God in Marriage & Family Life

SUPPOSE THAT WE COUPLES GROW FROM a romantic love for our partner to a conventional needs love and finally to a Christ-like transforming love, together with other virtues that ordinarily come with the love, as discussed throughout this guide. The love and other virtues help make us happy in this life not only in the sense of being virtuous, Christ-like persons, but also in the sense of being united with God in a limited way. We have been focusing on the virtue component of Christian Happiness in this life. Let's look now at the union-with-God component.

The union-with-God component of Christian Happiness is dealt with thoroughly in the Christian contemplative and mystical traditions. Christian contemplatives and mystics, however, are not influential in today's mainstream marriage guidance. They may seem to be out of touch with marriage and family life. They write about such things as abandonment to God, the vanity of the world, and the spiritual marriage between the soul and God. But they are not out of touch. We couples just need to understand them better and apply some of their insights to marriage and family life.

We have already been applying Christian contemplative and mystical insights to marriage and family life throughout this guide. St. John of the Cross, St. Teresa of Avila, and other Christian contemplatives and mystics have helped us understand how we can follow Jesus virtuously during our ordinary marriage and family activities. These contemplatives and mystics have helped us understand the virtue component of Christian marriage discipleship. Now let's see how they can help us understand the union-with-God component of this discipleship.

In this chapter, we will find that following Jesus virtuously during our ordinary marriage and family activities helps unite us with God in a limited way in this life and prepares us to be united with God eternally. We will find that Christian marriage discipleship is indeed a holy calling!

THE CHRISTIAN WAY TO BE UNITED WITH GOD

The Christian Way for us Christian couples to be united with God in this life and then eternally is to follow Jesus with love, wisdom, faith, and other Christian virtues, as discussed throughout this guide. Jesus teaches, "Those who love me will keep my word, and my Father will love them, and we will come to them and make our home with them" (John 14:23—NRSV). St. John teaches: "His [God's] commandments are these: that we believe in the name of his Son Jesus Christ and that we love one another as he told us to. Whoever keeps his commandments lives in God and God lives in him" (1 John 3:23–24).

Saints, sages, and other holy men and women in the world's great religions have taught that love for God and neighbor helps unite us with God, or, in other words, Ultimate Reality. St. John of the Cross teaches that Christian faith, hope, and especially love ("charity") are the means and the preparation for uniting us with God in a limited way in this life and then eternally.[347] Krishna, an Incarnation of the Hindu God, teaches that "by loving me he comes to know me truly; then he knows my glory and enters into my boundless being."[348] The Fox Indians say, "When you have learned about love, you have learned about God."[349]

ORDINARY UNION WITH GOD & EXTRAORDINARY UNION WITH GOD

Some of us couples might think that loving our partner during our ordinary marriage and family activities would not necessarily help unite us with God. We might think of union with God mostly in terms of raptures, visions, and other extraordinary mystical experiences. But we can be united with God by loving our partner during our ordinary marriage and family activities without necessarily being gifted with extraordinary mystical experiences. To understand why this is so, let's distinguish between an ordinary union with God with love and grace, and an extraordinary union with God with love, grace, *and* extraordinary mystical experiences too. St. John of the Cross, Teresa of Avila, and some other saints and mystics have distinguished in this way between an ordinary union with God and an extraordinary union with God.

St. John of the Cross distinguishes between an ordinary union with God with love and grace, and an extraordinary union with God with an inflaming of love.[350] We are united with God with love and grace by the Christian theological virtues of faith in our intellect, hope in our memory, and especially love in our will ("charity").[351] The love includes God's divine love and our human love. When we experience God's love, we become *like* God without actually becoming God. John, following St. Thomas Aquinas, holds that union with God is a union of likeness. There is a likeness of love between our love and God's love. Our love is not like God's love in the sense of being *equal* to it. Our love is like God's love in the sense of *imitating* it.[352]

We Christian couples imitate God's love by loving God and neighbor as Jesus loves us, as discussed throughout this guide.[353] With this Christ-like love, we live in God and God lives in us, as St. John puts it (1 John 3:23–24). We experience an ordinary union with God with love and grace even if we do not experience an extraordinary union with God with an "inflaming of love" that includes extraordinary mystical experiences.

We Christian couples could experience an extraordinary union with God with an inflaming of love. With the extraordinary union, we are united with God by the Christian theological virtues of faith, hope, and love, just as we are with the ordinary union. Union with God always includes faith, hope, and love, according to St. John of the Cross. But the extraordinary union with God includes also extraordinary mystical experiences, such as "divine touches." We couples might be gifted with the mystical experiences, but then again, we might not be, as St. Teresa of Avila points out.[354]

ORDINARY UNION WITH GOD AS THE PRIMARY GOAL OF CHRISTIAN MARRIAGE DISCIPLESHIP

Should we Christian couples desire and seek an ordinary union with God with love and grace in this life, or an extraordinary union with God with an inflaming of love? What should be the immediate goal of our Christian marriage discipleship?

It might seem that we should desire and seek an extraordinary union with God in this life. The extraordinary union is a more advanced stage of Christian marriage discipleship than the ordinary union, for the most part. We experience God more directly and intensely in the extraordinary union than we do in the ordinary union, as St. John of the Cross points out.[355] But this does not necessarily mean that we should desire and seek the extraordinary union instead of the ordinary union. The fact of the matter is that we should desire and seek the ordinary union with God, *with or without extraordinary mystical experiences!* We should love God unconditionally without selfishly desiring and demanding mystical experiences in this life in return for our love.

The love, wisdom, and other Christian virtues that help unite us Christian couples with God with love and grace are even more important for our moral and spiritual fulfillment than the mystical experiences that come with union with God with an inflaming of love. St. Teresa of Avila points this out:

> Progress [moral and spiritual] has nothing to do with enjoying the greatest number of consolations in prayer, or with raptures, visions or favours [often] given by the Lord. [. . .] The other things I have been describing are current coin, an unfailing source of revenue and a perpetual inheritance. [. . .] I am referring to the great virtues of humility, mortification and an obedience so *extremely* strict that we never go an inch beyond the superior's orders.[356]

St. John of the Cross teaches likewise that we Christians should desire and seek an ordinary union with God with love and grace in this life without desiring and seeking mystical experiences too. John writes in a letter to a friend:

> What do you think serving God involves other than avoiding evil, keeping His commandments, and being occupied with the things of God as best we can? When this is had, what need is there of other [supernatural] apprehensions or other lights and satisfactions. [. . .] What need is there [. . .] other than to walk along the level road of the law of God and of the Church and live only in dark and true faith and certain hope and complete charity, expecting all our blessings in heaven [. . .] hoping for everything in heaven?[357]

SELFISH DESIRES FOR MYSTICAL EXPERIENCES

In one sense, morally speaking, ordinary union with God with love and grace is a more advanced stage of Christian marriage discipleship than extraordinary union with God with an inflaming of love. How could this be? With the ordinary union with God, we would love God and neighbor, including our partner, with a Christ-like transforming love *even though we were not gifted with mystical experiences.* It would be more praiseworthy, morally speaking, to love God and neighbor if we did *not* receive consoling mystical experiences in return for our love than it would be if we *did* receive these experiences—as St. Teresa of Avila,[358] St. John of the Cross,[359] and others have pointed out. Thomas à Kempis makes this point in *Of the Imitation of Christ*:

> It is not hard to despise all human consolation when we have divine. But it is a great thing [...] to be able to forgo all comfort, both human and divine, and to be willing to bear this heart's exile for God's honour, and seek oneself in nothing, nor regard one's own deserts. What great thing is it, if you be cheerful and devout when grace comes? This hour is desired by all men. He rides very pleasantly who is carried by the grace of God. [...] Therefore, when God gives spiritual consolation, receive it with thanksgiving; but know that it is God's gift, and not any desert [merit] of your own.[360]

St. John of the Cross points out that we can desire mystical experiences and other spiritual consolations selfishly, as noted briefly above (III,2). John writes:

> They [supposedly spiritual persons] feed and clothe their natural selves with spiritual feelings and consolations instead of divesting and denying themselves of these for God's sake. [...] When some of this solid, perfect food (the annihilation of all sweetness in God—the pure spiritual cross and nakedness of Christ's poverty of spirit) is offered them in dryness, distaste, and trial, they run from it as from death and wander about in search only of sweetness and delightful communications from God.

Such an attitude is not the hallmark of self-denial and nakedness of spirit, but the indication of a "spiritual sweet tooth."[361]

John Wesley, founder of the Methodist reform movement within the Church of England during the 18th century, likewise understood that desires for joyful spiritual feelings in this life can be selfish. Wesley recalled that he experienced joyful spiritual feelings during beginning stages of his faith, but he learned later that faith involves above all "victory over sin," not just joyful spiritual feelings. He learned that victory over sin might come with joyful spiritual feelings, but then again, it might not.[362]

Mother Teresa was seldom gifted with joyful spiritual feelings or other divine consolations from the age of 49 or 50 until her death at age 86. On the contrary, she experienced a great deal of mental, emotional, and spiritual darkness during these years, including painful experiences of the absence of God. But that was perfectly o.k. with her. She came to "love the darkness" as her opportunity to share the darkness and suffering that Jesus experienced along the Way of the Cross. Mother Teresa said that she was "happier than ever" during her times of darkness and suffering.[363]

ORDINARY UNION WITH GOD IN EVERYDAY MARRIAGE & FAMILY LIFE

We couples can be united with God with love and grace during our ordinary marriage and family activities while doing such things as sharing the housework, going out for dinner and a movie, and getting up at 5 a.m. to check the baby for the third time since midnight. We may not rise up ecstatically into the air and hear the voice of Jesus when we check the baby at 5 a.m. for the third time during the night, but that's o.k. We just need to check the baby and do other ordinary marriage and family things with a Christ-like transforming love for our partner, for our children, and for God.

Suppose that we couples love God, our partner, and our children during our ordinary marriage and family activities, and we are not gifted with extraordinary mystical experiences of God's presence. That's o.k. We can still have faith and trust that God is with us, loving us, even during the most trying times of our life. The dreamer in the poem "Footprints" by Mary Stevenson learned that God was present during the most trying times of his or her life. The dreamer noticed that there were two sets of footprints in the sand during most of his or her life, that is, the dreamer's footprints and God's footprints. But there was only one set of footprints during the saddest times of the dreamer's life. The dreamer complained to God that

God had not been there during these trying times. God replied, "I love you and I would never leave you. [...] When you see only one set of footprints, it was then that I carried you."[364]

THE IMPORTANCE OF HUMAN LOVE FOR HELPING UNITE US WITH GOD

We Christian couples can have faith and trust that God is with us, carrying us, loving us, even if we do not see his footprints in the sand during the most trying times of our life, and even if we are not gifted with mystical experiences of his love. God does love us, for sure. We just need to love God in return, and we need to love our neighbor, not only with God's love, but also with our own human love. We should not underestimate the importance of our human love for God and neighbor in our loving union with God. Let's see what St. John of the Cross says about this.

John holds that our human love for God and neighbor helps unite us with God in this life and helps prepare us to be united with God eternally. John uses a God/sun metaphor to explain how our human love for God and neighbor helps unite us with God. John compares God to the sun and our soul to a window. The sun shines on the window and illuminates the window with its light. Likewise God shines on our soul and illuminates our soul with his divine being, including his love. God transforms our soul with his love so that we are united with God in a limited way in this life.[365]

God does not ordinarily transform us without calling upon us to participate in our transformation with our own faith, hope, love, and other virtues. God does not force himself upon us, as if we had no free will to accept or reject him. We do have a free will to accept or reject God. We accept God with our faith, love, and other Christian virtues. We reject God with our sinfulness, including faithlessness, hopelessness, hatred, and selfishness.

John compares our sinfulness to the smudges and smears on the window of our soul in his God/sun metaphor. The smudges and smears prevent the window from being completely illuminated and transformed by the sun's light. Likewise the smudges and smears of sinfulness on our soul ordinarily prevent our soul from being completely transformed by God's divine being, including his love—even though God could and often does transform us in spite of our sinfulness. John explains:

> A ray of sunlight [God's love and grace] shining upon a smudgy window [our soul] is unable to illumine that window completely and transform it into its own light [God's love and

grace]. It could do this if the window were cleaned and polished. The less the film and stain are wiped away, the less the window will be illumined; and the cleaner the window is, the brighter will be its illumination. [. . .] If the window is totally clean and pure, the sunlight will so transform and illumine it that to all appearances the window will be identical with the ray of sunlight and shine just as the sun's ray.[366]

John goes on to compare the sun to God and the window to the soul:

The soul upon which the divine light of God's being is ever shining, or better, in which it is always dwelling by nature, is like the window. [. . .] A man makes room for God by wiping away all the smudges and smears of creatures [including selfish desires for worldly goods], by uniting his will perfectly to God's [including God's will that we love one another as Jesus loves us].[. . .] When this is done the soul will be illumined by and transformed in God.[367]

A child told her parents at church that the light shining through the stained glass windows was God's love.

We couples can "make room for God" by wiping away the smudges and smears of sinfulness that darken our soul. We can "make room for God" by putting away our old sinful self and putting on a new, more faithful, loving, Christ-like self. With our new self, we let God illuminate our soul and transform us with his love. We participate in our moral and spiritual transformation with our faith, love, and other Christian virtues. Our virtues help prepare and dispose us to be transformed by God and thereby united with God.

SELF-EMPTYING MARITAL LOVE

Let's look more closely at the Christian transforming love for our partner and for God that helps unite us Christian couples with God. To purify and perfect our human love for our partner, we let go of selfish desires for worldly goods in order to love our partner unselfishly without desiring and demanding the worldly goods in return for our love. In other words, we "empty our will" of selfish desires for worldly goods in order to love our partner unselfishly, as St. John of the Cross would say.[368]

The wealthy businessman Christopher discussed above could empty his will of his selfish desires for home-cooked gourmet meals every night in order to respond to his wife Susan more lovingly when she serves greasy barbecued chicken for dinner (IV,4).

We couples can put away our selfish desires for worldly goods and purify our love for our partner and for God during our ordinary marriage and family activities every bit as much as contemplative Christians can put away their selfish desires for worldly goods and purify their love for God and neighbor during their times set aside for prayer. French Catholic theologian Jean-Pierre de Caussade (1675–1761) writes in his spiritual classic, *Abandonment to Divine Providence*:

> People trying to be holy would be saved a lot of trouble if they were taught to follow the right path, and I am writing of people who lived [sic] ordinary lives in the world. [. . .] Now, you who read this [. . .] must realize that I am asking nothing extraordinary from you. All I want is for you to carry on as you are doing and endure what you have to do—but change your attitude to all these things. And this change is simply to say "I will" to all that God asks. What is easier? For who could refuse obedience to a will so kind and good? By this obedience we shall become one with God.[369]

A LOVING CHRISTIAN "EQUATION" FOR UNION WITH GOD

We couples need to understand the importance of purifying our human love for our partner and for God in our everyday marriage and family life. In one sense, the extent to which we are united with God in this life depends more on actively purifying our human love for God and neighbor than on passively receiving God's love, according to St. John of the Cross. John uses his God/sun metaphor to explain why this is so:

> The extent of the illumination [union with God in this life] is not dependent upon the ray of sunlight [God's love] but upon the window [the soul, including our human love]. If the window is totally clean and pure, the sunlight will so transform and illumine it that to all appearances the window will be identical with the ray of sunlight and shine just as the sun's ray.[370]

John continues, "When the soul completely rids itself of what is repugnant and unconformed to the divine will [for example, faithlessness, hopelessness, selfishness, and other sinfulness], it [the soul] rests transformed in God through love."[371]

John's point is that the extent to which we are transformed by God in this life ordinarily depends more upon us, the window, than upon God, the sun. Why? Because God the sun is *always* shining on the window of our soul with his love and grace. God's love and grace is the *constant factor* in John's metaphorical "equation" for union with God in this life. Our human faith, hope, and love, on the other hand, are the *variable factors* in this "equation." We do not always purify our human faith, hope, and love.

Here is John's "equation" for union with God in this life: God's divine love and grace [the constant factor] + our human faith, hope, and love [the variable factors] = union with God in this life in the theological virtues of faith, hope, and charity (love).[372]

To be united with God, then, we couples need to purify our human faith, hope, and love by ridding ourselves of faithlessness, hopelessness, hatred, and other smudges and smears of selfishness and sinfulness that often prevent God from transforming us completely with his love and grace. John explains,

> God [ordinarily] communicates Himself more to the soul more advanced in love, that is, more conformed to His will. [. . .] A man has nothing more to do than strip his soul of these natural contrarieties [sic] and dissimilarities [to God, including God's will] so that God Who is naturally communicating himself to it [the soul] through nature may do so supernaturally through grace.[373]

Of course we couples cannot purify ourselves without God's grace. But we can purify ourselves *with* God's grace. John writes that "a person should insofar as possible strive to do his part in purifying and perfecting himself" in order to prepare for union with God. John assures us that God will heal us of whatever ills we are unable to overcome through our own efforts.[374]

John would probably agree with St. Thomas Aquinas that purifying our human faith, hope, love, and other virtues can not only *prepare* us for being united with God eternally; purifying these virtues can help us "merit" eternal union with God in a very limited way. Aquinas emphasizes that we cannot merit eternal union with God *without grace* because no natural human act can merit a supernatural reward.[375] But we can merit union with God *with grace* in two limited ways, that is, *condignly* and *congruously*.

First, we can merit eternal life condignly, that is, by strict standards of justice, insofar as our meritorious actions proceed from the grace of the Holy Spirit. In this case, the grace of the Holy Spirit makes our actions meritorious.

Second, we can merit eternal life congruously, insofar as our meritorious actions proceed not only from the grace of the Holy Spirit, but also from our own free will. In this case, we do not merit eternal life condignly, that is, by strict standards of justice, because no natural human act of our will can merit a supernatural reward. But we do merit eternal life congruously, that is, by an *equitable justice* whereby it is fitting, but not necessary, that God should reward us for our faith, hope, love, and other virtues. Aquinas explains that it is fitting that "if a man does what he can, God should reward him according to the excellence of his power."[376] In fact, Jesus promises that if we love him, he and his Father *will* come to us and make their abode with us (John 14:23).

We Christian couples should not sell ourselves short with negative, self-deprecating thoughts that we cannot do much to purify our marital love and other Christian virtues during our ordinary marriage and family activities. The good news of the Gospels is that we can do a great deal to purify our love and other Christian virtues during our ordinary marriage and family activities, with God's help. We have the human and Christian potential to love God above all things and to love our partner as Jesus loves us. To the extent that we do these things, Jesus and his Father will come to us and make their abode with us.

And there is more Gospel good news! Jesus and his Father will often come to us and make their abode with us even when we fall short in our efforts to purify our love, wisdom, and other Christian virtues. We can have faith and trust that God the Father, Son, and Holy Spirit loves us, forgives us repentant sinners, and carries us during the most trying times of our life.

CHRISTIAN MARRIAGE DISCIPLESHIP AS A HOLY CALLING

When all is said and done about being united with God in marriage and family life, we couples do not need to withdraw from our ordinary marriage and family activities and wait passively for God to gift us with mystical experiences that could unite us with God in an inflaming of love. With the help of Jesus, we can be united with God with love and grace by actively purifying our love for our partner and for God during our ordinary marriage and family activities, with or without mystical experiences. With the help of Jesus, we can purify our love for our partner and for God by doing such things as contentedly letting our partner forget a phone message, lovingly eating greasy barbecued chicken for dinner, and wisely letting our partner miss another freeway exit without getting all hot and bothered about this. When we purify our love for our partner and for God in these little ways during our ordinary marriage and family activities, we prepare ourselves to be united with God in a limited way in this life and then eternally. Our Christian marriage discipleship is indeed a holy calling!

CONCLUSION TO PART IV

Now that you readers have acquainted yourselves with Christian marriage discipleship, this is a good time to check your own discipleship. You could use the Christian Marriage Discipleship Check-Up Worksheet in Appendix A for help doing this. If you complete the worksheet, you could use the reflection questions in the conclusions of Parts II, III, and IV of this guide. The reflection questions can help you relate the material in Parts II, III, and IV to your Christian marriage discipleship. Here are six reflection questions for this Part IV on the transforming stage of Christian marriage discipleship:

1) To what extent do you seek a Christian Happiness centered around God and virtue in your marriage and family life instead of an Emotional Happiness or a Conventional Happiness (IV,1)? Explain your answer with examples from your marriage experiences.
2) To what extent do you respond lovingly to your partner and follow Jesus virtuously during hard times as well as good times (IV,2)? Explain your answer with examples from your marriage experiences.
3) To what extent do you love your partner virtuously instead of loving him or her in a permissive or controlling way (IV,3)? Explain your answer with examples from your marriage experiences.

4) To what extent do you treat your partner and yourself well with virtuous, Christ-like marriage conduct (IV,4)? Explain your answer with examples from your marriage experiences.
5) To what extent do you manage your family money lovingly and wisely (IV,5)? Explain your answer with examples from your marriage experiences.
6) To what extent are you preparing yourself for union with God by purifying and perfecting your marital love and other Christian virtues during your ordinary marriage and family activities (IV,6)? Explain your answer with examples from your marriage experiences.

Conclusion

We have explored the Christian Way to be happily married by following Jesus in the Biblical sense of becoming like Jesus in our moral character and conduct, with love, wisdom, and other Christian virtues during our ordinary marriage and family activities. It may not be easy to become like Jesus with a new, Christ-like Transformed Self. Many of us may need to put away our old Romantic Self and/or our old Needs Self in order to put on a new Transformed Self. We may need to walk away mentally and emotionally from the familiar romantic and needy places that we have called home in order to walk with Jesus faithfully, hopefully, and lovingly through the dark Christian woods where the liquid silver voices of the birds call us to a greater love and happiness than we have known before.

Let's not be afraid to walk with Jesus through these dark woods towards a greater love and happiness than we have known before. In these dark woods, we discover the Garden of Love in our soul where God the Father, Son, and Holy Spirit is always with us, loving us, forgiving us, guiding us. In this Garden of Love, we and our partner love and cherish one another for all the days of our lives. In this Garden of Love, we and our partner are united with God now and forever. In this Garden of Love, we and our partner live happily ever after.

Appendix A
Christian Marriage Discipleship Check-Up

To CHECK YOUR CHRISTIAN MARRIAGE DISCIPLESHIP, complete the Christian Marriage Discipleship Check-Up Worksheet below. You may reproduce multiple copies of the worksheet for yourself and your partner. Completing the worksheet and discussing it with your partner can help you and your partner share your ideas about following Jesus with love, wisdom, and other Christian virtues during your ordinary marriage and family activities.

When you complete the worksheet, be positive and hopeful about yourself and your partner. But be honest and humble too. Identify areas of your marriage and family life where you could follow Jesus more virtuously as well as areas where you are already following Jesus virtuously. Take to heart what St. Augustine says, "Do you wish to rise? Begin by descending. You plan a tower that will pierce the clouds? Lay first the foundation of humility."[377]

Suppose that you are so humble that you identify lots of problems with your Christian marriage discipleship. That's o.k. Take pride in your humility. You are taking two giant steps towards overcoming the problems. First, you are humbly acknowledging the problems instead of sweeping them under the rug. Second, you are identifying the problems wisely as moral, Christian discipleship problems that sometimes prevent you from responding to your partner lovingly, following Jesus virtuously, and being virtuously happy. It is hard to work out your moral problems if you do not identify them wisely.

The romantic lover Bill discussed above (I,1) did not identify his moral jet-skiing problem wisely. He thought the problem was that his wife Maria would not jet-ski with him, so he tried to get her to jet-ski with him, and he got mad when she would not do this. The real problem, though, was Bill's selfishness, together with his low self-esteem and other mental and emotional problems. Bill needed to deal with his selfishness in order to respond to Maria more lovingly and follow Jesus more virtuously.

Suppose you acknowledge your moral problems and identify them wisely. It still might not be easy to deal with them. That's o.k. Do not try to deal with all your moral problems in one fell swoop today, tomorrow, or by the end of the year. Deal with your moral problems gradually over the years at your own pace and God's pace. For the most part, you can deal with moral problems gradually when they come up, with as much love, wisdom, and other Christian virtues as possible at the time. You would often need to deal with the problems anyway, so you might as well deal with them with as much love, wisdom, and other Christian virtues as possible, as Jesus would like you to do, and as your partner probably would too.

You can work out many moral problems by doing one positive, growth-oriented thing during your ordinary marriage and family activities. That is, focus positively on putting away your old Romantic Self or Needs Self and putting on a new, increasingly loving, Christ-like, virtuously-happy self. Then many of your moral problems may gradually fade away. This is the Christian marriage discipleship way to deal with moral problems, build a strong marriage, and live happily ever after.

You may complete the Christian Marriage Discipleship Check-Up Worksheet now that begins on the next page.

Appendix A: Christian Marriage Discipleship Check-Up

CHRISTIAN MARRIAGE DISCIPLESHIP CHECK-UP WORKSHEET

DIRECTIONS: Complete Parts I and II of this worksheet. In your answers to the questions in Part I, identify one or two general points about your relationship with your partner, and then illustrate each point with an example from your marriage experiences. For Question A below on communicating with your partner, for example, you could make the general point that you criticize your partner too much, and then you could give an example of criticizing your partner's cooking yesterday.

To get ideas for answering the worksheet questions, you could think of specific problems in your relationship, including *differences of opinion* with your partner and *decisions* that have been difficult to make together. These problems may not seem to be moral problems. They may seem to be financial problems, housecleaning problems, or other types of problems. But often they are moral problems too. Have you dealt with these problems with as much love, wisdom, patience, and other Christian virtues as possible? Have you used some of these problems as stepping-stones to responding to your partner more lovingly and becoming a more loving, Christ-like, virtuously-happy person yourself?

PART I: QUESTIONS

A. How much do you *communicate* with Christian love & wisdom in your marriage relationship? Describe your conduct in this area.

    a. Loving & wise communications: _____

    aa. Not so loving & wise communications: _____

B. How much do you use *money* with Christian love & wisdom in your marriage relationship? Describe your conduct in this area.

    b. Loving & wise use of money: _____

    bb. Not so loving & wise use of money: _____

C. How much do you deal with *friends & relatives* (for example, in-laws, a former spouse) with Christian love & wisdom in your marriage relationship? Describe your conduct in this area.

    c. Loving & wise conduct involving friends & relatives: _____
_____

    cc. Not so loving & wise conduct involving friends & relatives: _____
_____

D. How much do you deal with *your personality or your partner's personality* with Christian love & wisdom in your marriage relationship? Describe your conduct in this area.

    d. Loving & wise conduct in the personality area: _____
_____

    dd. Not so loving & wise conduct in the personality area: _____
_____

E. How much do you deal with *gender, cultural, or religious differences* with Christian love & wisdom in your marriage relationship? Describe your conduct in this area.

    e. Loving & wise handling of gender, cultural, or religious differences: _____
_____

    ee. Not so loving & wise handling of gender, cultural, or religious differences: _____
_____

F. How much do you deal with *sex & intimacy* with Christian love & wisdom in your marriage relationship? Describe you conduct in this area.

    f. Loving & wise conduct in the sex & intimacy area: _____
_____

    ff. Not so loving & wise conduct in the sex & intimacy area: _____
_____

G. How much do you deal with *housework or other family work* with Christian love & wisdom in your marriage relationship? Describe your conduct in this area.

Appendix A: Christian Marriage Discipleship Check-Up 215

  g. Loving & wise conduct in the area of housework or other family work: _____

  gg. Not so loving & wise conduct in the area of housework or other family work: _____

H. How much do you deal with *your education or career, or your partner's education or career* with Christian love & wisdom in your marriage relationship? Describe your conduct in this area.

  h. Loving & wise conduct in the area of education & careers: _____

  hh. Not so loving & wise conduct in the area of education & careers: _____

I. How much do you deal with *prayer, worship, or other religious activities* with Christian love & wisdom in your Christian marriage discipleship? Describe your conduct in this area.

  i. Dealing with religious activities lovingly & wisely: _____

  ii. Not dealing with religious activities lovingly & wisely: _____

J. How much do you raise your children with Christian love & wisdom in your *parenting conduct* (if applicable). Describe your conduct in this area.

  j. Loving & wise parenting conduct: _____

  jj. Not so loving & wise parenting conduct: _____

PART II: DISCUSSION

DIRECTIONS: After you and your partner complete Part I, discuss your answers. Sometimes you might disagree with your partner's description of his or her conduct. For example, suppose your partner wrote that he always uses money wisely, but you disagree. That's o.k. The main purpose of your discussion is not to agree on everything, much less to solve all your problems and deal with all your differences in one fell swoop. The main purpose is to share your ideas about following Jesus with love, wisdom, and other Christian virtues in these specific areas of your marriage and family life.

You and your partner could help each other answer some of the questions, if you like. Suppose a wife could not think of any unloving and unwise conduct in the area of housework, but her husband could. Suppose her husband thought that she was treating him inconsiderately when she served dinners ten minutes late, as she did last Monday night. Her husband could suggest that she add "late dinners" to her worksheet as an example of "not so loving and wise conduct" in the area of housework.

The wife should not add the "late dinners" to her worksheet, however, if she did not agree with her husband that she served dinner late at times. What's more, even if she agreed that she sometimes served dinners late, she still might not think that she was treating her husband inconsiderately when she did this. She might think that her husband was being overly scrupulous, hypercritical, and demanding about dinners being served exactly on time.

After you and your partner discuss your answers to the questions in Part I of this worksheet, write a brief summary of your discussion and share your summary with your partner. Your summary could include any interesting or important points that came up during your discussion.

Your summary of your discussion of your responses in Part I of this worksheet:

_____
_____
_____
_____
_____
_____
_____

Appendix A: Christian Marriage Discipleship Check-Up

PERMISSIONS: Readers have permission to reproduce multiple copies of this Appendix A, including the "Christian Marriage Discipleship Check-Up Worksheet," from David Sanderlin, *The Christian Way to be Happily Married*. www.TheChristianWaytobeHappilyMarried.com.

Appendix B
Group Discussion Questions

This appendix includes group discussion questions for the Introduction to this marriage guide and each one of the guide's chapters. Copies of this appendix, including the discussion questions, may be reproduced for use in group discussions.

Teachers, facilitators, students, and other leaders and participants in classes, workshops, and other groups that deal with marriage, Christian ethics, Christian spirituality, and related areas may use the discussion questions as they see fit. A large class or other large group could be broken down into smaller groups (about 4 to 8 members per group) in order to facilitate discussion within the smaller groups. Then a leader in each group could share his or her group's ideas with the other groups.

During the group discussions, engaged and married couples may refer to their personal engagement or marriage experiences *if and only if* their partner enthusiastically approves of this.

DISCUSSION QUESTIONS

Introduction (questions pertaining to this book's Introduction)
1. Summarize this marriage guide's Christian discipleship approach to being happily married, and comment on this approach.
2. Relate this book's Christian discipleship approach to being happily married to your engagement or marriage, or to engagements or marriages in general in the United States or other countries.

Part I, Chapter 1. Christian Happiness.

1. Summarize one of the author's major points about Christian Happiness, and comment on this point.
2. Relate the author's discussion of Christian Happiness to your engagement or marriage, or to engagements or marriages in general.

Part I, Chapter 2. The Christian Way to Happiness.

1. Summarize one of the author's major points about the Christian Way to happiness, and comment on this point.
2. Relate the author's discussion of the Christian Way to happiness to your engagement or marriage, or to engagements or marriages in general.

Part II, Chapter 1. The Emotional Happiness of Romantic Lovers.

1. Summarize one of the author's major points about the Emotional Happiness of romantic lovers, and comment on this point.
2. Relate the author's discussion of the Emotional Happiness of romantic lovers to your engagement or marriage, or to engagements or marriages in general.

Part II, Chapter 2. The Christian Morality Problem with Emotional Happiness.

1. Summarize one of the author's major points about the Christian Morality Problem with Emotional Happiness, and comment on this point.
2. Relate the author's discussion of the Christian Morality Problem with Emotional Happiness to your engagement or marriage, or to engagements or marriages in general.

Part II, Chapter 3. The Emotional Problem with Romantic Love.

1. Summarize one of the author's major points about the Emotional Problem with romantic love, and comment on this point.
2. Relate the author's discussion of the Emotional Problem with romantic love to your engagement or marriage, or to engagements or marriages in general.

Part II, Chapter 4. The Fantasy Problem with Romantic Wisdom.

1. Summarize one of the author's major points about the Fantasy Problem with romantic wisdom, and comment on this point.
2. Relate the author's discussion of the Fantasy Problem with romantic wisdom to your engagement or marriage, or to engagements or marriages in general.

Part III, Chapter 1. The Conventional Happiness of Needs Lovers.

1. Summarize one of the author's major points about the Conventional Happiness of needs lovers, and comment on this point.
2. Relate the author's discussion of the Conventional Happiness of needs lovers to your engagement or marriage, or to engagements or marriages in general.

Part III, Chapter 2. The Christian Morality Problem with Conventional Happiness.

1. Summarize one of the author's major points about the Christian Morality Problem with Conventional Happiness, and comment on this point.
2. Relate the author's discussion of the Christian Morality Problem with Conventional Happiness to your engagement or marriage, or to engagements or marriages in general.

Part III, Chapter 3. The Emotional Problem with Needs Love.

1. Summarize one of the author's major points about the Emotional Problem with needs love, and comment on this point.
2. Relate the author's discussion of the Emotional Problem with needs love to your engagement or marriage, or to engagements or marriages in general.

Part III, Chapter 4. The Fantasy Problem with Needs Wisdom.

1. Summarize one of the author's major points about the Fantasy Problem with needs wisdom, and comment on this point.
2. Relate the author's discussion of the Fantasy Problem with needs wisdom to your engagement or marriage, or to engagements or marriages in general.

Part IV, Chapter 1. The Christian Happiness of Transformed Lovers.
1. Summarize one of the author's major points about the Christian Happiness of transformed lovers, and comment on this point.
2. Relate the author's discussion of the Christian Happiness of transformed lovers to your engagement or marriage, or to engagements or marriages in general.

Part IV, Chapter 2. Christian Happiness during Hard Times.
1. Summarize one of the author's major points about Christian Happiness during hard times, and comment on this point.
2. Relate the author's discussion of Christian Happiness during hard times to your engagement or marriage, or to engagements or marriages in general.

Part IV, Chapter 3. A Generous but Non-Permissive Marital Love.
1. Summarize one of the author's major points about a generous but non-permissive marital love, and comment on this point.
2. Relate the author's discussion of a generous but non-permissive marital love to your engagement or marriage, or to engagements or marriages in general.

Part IV, Chapter 4. Virtuous Marriage Conduct.
1. Summarize one of the author's major points about virtuous marriage conduct, and comment on this point.
2. Relate the author's discussion of virtuous marriage conduct to your engagement or marriage, or to engagements or marriages in general.

Part IV, Chapter 5. Virtuous Marriage Money Management.
1. Summarize one of the author's major points about virtuous marriage money management, and comment on this point.
2. Relate the author's discussion of virtuous marriage money management to your engagement or marriage, or to engagements or marriages in general.

Appendix B: Group Discussion Questions

Part IV, Chapter 6. Union with God in Marriage and Family Life.

1. Summarize one of the author's major points about union with God in marriage and family life, and comment on this point.
2. Relate the author's discussion of union with God in marriage and family life to your engagement or marriage, or to engagements or marriages in general.

PERMISSIONS: Readers have permission to reproduce multiple copies of this Appendix B, including the group discussion questions, from David Sanderlin, *The Christian Way to be Happily Married*. www.TheChristianWaytobeHappilyMarried.com.

Notes

Abbreviations

A	*Ascent of Mount Carmel*	John of the Cross
N	*The Dark Night*	John of the Cross
SC	*The Spiritual Canticle*	John of the Cross
LF	*The Living Flame of Love*	John of the Cross
ST	*Summa Theologica*	Thomas Aquinas

INTRODUCTION

1. Vern McLellan, *The Complete Book of Practical Proverbs & Wacky Wit* (Wheaton: Tyndale, 1996) 145.
2. Michael G. Lawler, *Family: American and Christian* (Chicago: Loyola, 1998) ix.
3. Barbara Dafoe Whitehead, *The Divorce Culture* (New York: Knopf, 1997).
4. Martin L. Gross, *The Psychological Society: A Critical Analysis of Psychiatry, Psychotherapy, Psychoanalysis and the Psychological Revolution* (New York: Simon-Touchstone, 1979).
5. Stephen Prothero, *American Jesus: How the Son of God Became a National Icon* (New York: Farrar, 2003) 11.
6. Margaret Pepper, ed., *The Harper Religious & Inspirational Quotation Companion* (New York: Harper, 1989) 77.

7 Benedict XVI (Joseph Cardinal Ratzinger), *Truth and Tolerance: Christian Belief and World Religions*, trans. Henry Taylor (San Francisco: Ignatius, 2004) 117–144. Benedict XVI (Joseph Cardinal Ratzinger), *Values in a Time of Upheaval*, trans. Brian McNeil (New York and San Francisco: Crossroad and Ignatius, 2006) 138–160.
8 Thomas à Kempis, *Of the Imitation of Christ*, 1954, trans. Justin McCann (New York: New American Library of World Literature-Mentor, 1957) Book One, Chapter 1.
9 John Paul II, *Man and Woman He Created Them: A Theology of the Body*, trans. Michael Waldstein (Boston: Pauline, 2006) No. 88, Sections 1–2; p. 69. For a comprehensive treatment of the concept of the imitation of Christ in the Christian tradition, see Edouard Cothenet, et. al., *Imitating Christ*, trans. Simone Inkel and Lucy Tinsley, with a Preface by John L. Boyle (St. Meinrad: Abbey, 1974).
10 John Paul II, *Novo Millennio Ineunte*, Apostolic Letter, Jan. 6, 2001, Nos. 30, 31, 33, from http://www.vatican.va/holy_father/john_paul_ii/apost_letters/ documents/hf_jp-ii_apl_20010106_novo-millenio-ineunte_en.html. See Ralph Martin, *The Fulfillment of All Desire: A Guidebook for the Journey to God Based on the Wisdom of the Saints* (Steubenville: Emmaus Road, 2006) 2–3.
11 Cathy Lyon Grossman, "Benedict's April Visit to the USA Includes Silence, Prayer, and a Piano," *USA Today* 28 Feb. 2008: 7D.
12 Robert Moynihan, ed., *Let God's Light Shine Forth: The Spiritual Vision of Pope Benedict XVI* (New York: Doubleday, 2005) 119.
13 Arthur M. Brazier, "Bishop Arthur M. Brazier," *Marriage—Just a Piece of Paper?*, eds. Katherine Anderson, Don Browning, and Brian Boyer (Grand Rapids: Eerdmans, 2002) 192.
14 Laurence J. Peter, quotation from Michael Moncur, *The Quotations Page*, 31 March 2009, http://www.quotationspage.com.
15 Whitehead 194. See Robert N. Bellah, et. al., *Habits of the Heart: Individualism and Commitment in American Life* (New York: Harper-Perennial, 1986).
16 Melvyn Kinder and Connell Cowan, *Husbands and Wives: Exploding Marital Myths/Deepening Love and Desire* (New York: Potter, 1989) 104.
17 Kinder 104.
18 Dana Mack, "Educating for Marriage, Sort Of," *First Things* March 2001: 18–20.

[19] C. Kevin Gillespie, *Psychology and American Catholicism: From Confession to Therapy?* (New York: Crossroad, 2001) 4–5.
[20] Matthew Kelly, *Rediscovering Catholicism: Journeying Toward Our Spiritual North Star* (Cincinnati: Beacon, 2002) 62.
[21] Bernard Shaw, *Androcles and the Lion, Overruled, Pygmalion,* 1914 (New York: Dodd, 1930) xiii.
[22] Psychologist Martin Seligman, for example, identifies marital love with romantic love and needs love without saying much about love of a transforming sort. See Martin E.P. Seligman, *Authentic Happiness: Using the New Positive Psychology to Realize Your Potential for Lasting Fulfillment* (New York: Simon-Free Press, 2002) 187–188.
[23] Julia Annas, *The Morality of Happiness* (New York: Oxford UP, 1993) 426–465. Annas compares some ancient Greek and Roman ethical theories that identify virtue with happiness with modern ethical theories that envision a subjective happiness that often conflicts with morality.
[24] Jill Smolowe, "Intermarried ... with Children," *Time,* Special Issue, Fall 1993: 64.
[25] Smolowe 64.
[26] Paul VI, *Ecclesiam Suam,* Encyclical, August 6, 1964, No. 108, http:// www.vatican.va/holy_father/paul_vi/encyclicals/documents/hf_pvi_enc_06081964_ecclesiam_fr.html.
[27] *The New Testament of the Jerusalem Bible* (Garden City: Doubleday, 1966). Also *The New Jerusalem Bible* (New York: Bantam Doubleday Dell-Darton, 1985), rpt. in *The Complete Parallel Bible: Containing the Old and New Testaments with the Apocryphal/Deuterocanonical Books* (New York: Oxford UP, 1993).
[28] *The New Revised Standard Version Bible* (New York: Division of Christian Education of the National Council of the Churches of Christ in the United States of America, 1989), rpt. in *The Complete Parallel Bible.*
[29] *The Revised English Bible* (Oxford UP and Cambridge UP, 1989), rpt. in *The Complete Parallel Bible.*
[30] *The New American Bible* (Washington, D.C.: Confraternity of Christian Doctrine, 1986, 1991), rpt. in *The Complete Parallel Bible.*
[31] Anne Fremantle, ed., *The Protestant Mystics* (New York: New American Library-Mentor, 1965) 129.
[32] See Thomas à Kempis I,1.

PART I, INTRODUCTION

33 Richard P. McBrien, *Catholicism*, rev. ed. (New York: HarperCollins, 1994) 857.

PART I, CHAPTER 1

34 McBrien 924.
35 Bill Coleman and Patty Coleman, *Only Love Can Make It Easy: Leader's Guide for Marriage Preparation*, 3rd ed. (Mystic: Twenty-Third, 1997) 41–58.
36 Kelly 61.
37 Kelly 61.
38 Douglas V. Porpora, *Landscapes of the Soul: The Loss of Moral Meaning in American Life* (Oxford: Oxford UP, 2001) 3.
39 Bennett Kelley, ed., *Saint Joseph Baltimore Catechism: The Truths of Our Catholic Faith Clearly Explained and Illustrated with Bible Readings, Study Helps and Mass Prayers* (New York: Catholic Book, 1962–1969) Lessons 1, 3–5.
40 "The Mystery of Happiness: Who Has It . . . How to Get It. With John Stossel," *20/20*, ABC, Executive Producer Victor Neufeld, ABC Transcript #85, 4 Sept. 1997: 2.
41 "Mystery of Happiness" 3.
42 Claudia Wallis, "The New Science of Happiness," *Time* 17 Jan. 2005: A2–A9.
43 See Sonja Lyubomirsky, *The How of Happiness: A New Approach to Getting the Life You Want* (New York: Penguin, 2007).
44 Robert A. Emmons, *The Psychology of Ultimate Concerns: Motivation and Spirituality in Personality* (New York: Guilford, 1999) 44. Leslie J. Francis, Susan H. Jones, and Carolyn Wilcox, "Religiosity and Happiness: During Adolescence, Young Adulthood, and Later Life," *Journal of Psychology and Christianity* 19.3 (Fall 2000): 249.
45 Rosalind Hursthouse, *On Virtue Ethics*, 1999 (Oxford: Oxford UP, 2001) 10.
46 Thomas Aquinas, *Summa Theologica*, rev. ed., 1920, 5 vols., trans. Fathers of the English Dominican Province (Westminster: Christian Classics, 1981), Vol. 2, Part I–II, question 4, articles 6–8 (I–II,q.4,a.6–8). See Robert Sokolowski, *Moral Action: A Phenomenological Study* (Bloomington: Indiana UP, 1985) 202–203.

47 Vernon J. Bourke, *Augustine's Love of Wisdom: An Introspective Philosophy* (West Lafayette: Purdue UP, 1992) 179ff.
48 Frank S. Mead, ed., *The Encyclopedia of Religious Quotations* (Old Tappan: Revell-Spire, 1976) 311.
49 Mead 315.
50 Brian Kolodiejchuk, ed., *Mother Teresa: Come Be My Light* (New York: Doubleday, 2007) 18.
51 Octavio A. Ballesteros and Maria del Carmen Ballesteros, *Mexican Sayings: The Treasure of a People* (Austin: Eakin, 1992) 61.
52 Julia Annas, "Should Virtue Make You Happy?", *Apeiron: A Journal for Ancient Philosophy and Science* XXXV.4 (December 2002): 1–19. Deal W. Hudson, *Happiness and the Limits of Satisfaction* (Lanham: Rowman, 1996) xi, 151–157. Jean Porter, *Nature as Reason: A Thomistic Theory of the Natural Law* (Grand Rapids: Eerdmans, 2005) 141–203. Thomas Aquinas, *Virtue: Way to Happiness*, trans. Richard J. Regan (Scranton: Scranton UP, 1999). R. Scott Smith, *Virtue Ethics and Moral Knowledge: Philosophy of Language after MacIntyre and Hauerwas* (Burlington: Ashgate, 2003). Daniel McInerny, *The Difficult Good: A Thomistic Approach to Moral Conflict and Human Happiness* (New York: Fordham UP, 2006).
53 Henry Foster, *Life Secrets: Spiritual Insights of a Christian Physician*, ed. Hal M. Helms (Orleans: Living Library, 1995) 106.
54 Mead 78.
55 Richard F. Heller and Rachael F. Heller, *Healthy Selfishness: Getting the Life You Deserve Without the Guilt* (Des Moines: Meredith, 2006) 11–18.
56 Heller 19–20.
57 Christopher Lasch, *The Culture of Narcissism: American Life in an Age of Diminishing Expectations* (New York: Norton, 1978). Jean Twenge, *The Narcissism Epidemic: Living in the Age of Entitlement* (New York: Simon, 2009).

PART I, CHAPTER 2

58 McBrien 184–194. See Benedict M. Ashley, *Living the Truth in Love: A Biblical Introduction to Moral Theology* (New York: St. Pauls-Alba, 1996) 96–98.

[59] John of the Cross, *The Ascent of Mount Carmel, The Collected Works of St. John of the Cross*, trans. Kieran Kavanaugh and Otilio Rodriguez, with Introductions by Kieran Kavanaugh (Washington, D.C.: ICS, 1979) Book One, Chapters 1–3 (A1,1–3); Book Two, Chapters 4–9 (A2,4–9). John of the Cross, *The Living Flame of Love, Collected Works*, Stanza 2, No. 33 (LF,2,33).

[60] Gerald G. May, *The Dark Night of the Soul: A Psychiatrist Explores the Connection Between Darkness and Spiritual Growth* (New York: HarperCollins-HarperSanFrancisco, 2005) 84–85. See also Mary Ann Fatula, "The Holy Spirit Hidden in the Experience of Human Weakness," *Spirituality Today* 36.2 (Summer 1984): 109–122.

[61] David Sanderlin, "Charity According to St. John of the Cross: A Disinterested Love for Interesting Special Relationships, Including Marriage," *Journal of Religious Ethics* 21.1 (Spring 1993): 87–115. David Sanderlin, "Faith and Ethical Reasoning in the Mystical Theology of St. John of the Cross: A Reasonable Christian Mysticism," *Religious Studies* 25.3 (Sept. 1989): 317–333. David Sanderlin, "Charity in the Dark Night of St. John of the Cross: The Human Experience of Union with God through Love," *Carmelus* 36 (1989): 10–43.

[62] Thorstein Veblen, *The Theory of the Leisure Class: An Economic Study of Institutions* (New York: New American Library, 1953).

[63] John of the Cross A1,3–4.

[64] Dietrich Bonhoeffer, *Discipleship*, 2002, ed. Geffrey B. Kelly and John D. Godsey, trans. Barbara Green and Reinhard Krauss (Minneapolis: Fortress, 2003) 43–44.

[65] Toni Sciarra Poynter, *From This Day Forward: Inspirations for Couples* (New York: HarperCollins, 2001) 163.

[66] Allen Klein, ed., *The Love and Kisses Quote Book: 500 Quotations To Snuggle Up To* (New York: Gramercy, 2006) 67.

[67] François Fénelon, *Fénelon's Letters to Men and Women*, ed. Derek Stanford (Westminster: Newman, 1957) 66.

[68] Barbel Inhelder and Jean Piaget, *The Growth of Logical Thinking from Childhood to Adolescence: An Essay on the Construction of Formal Operational Structures*, trans. Anne Parsons and Stanley Milgram (New York: Basic Books, 1958).

[69] Lawrence Kohlberg, *Essays on Moral Development*, 3 vols. (New York: Harper, 1981–1986).

[70] James W. Fowler, *Stages of Faith: The Psychology of Human Development and the Quest for Meaning* (New York: Harper, 1981).
[71] Ballesteros 51.
[72] McBrien 1067.
[73] John Flanagan, ed., *First Steps to Jesus: A New Prayer Book for First Holy Communion*, illus. Vincent Summers (New York: Regina, 1953) 9.
[74] McBrien 1067.

PART II, CHAPTER 1

[75] Richard Layard, *Happiness: Lessons from a New Science* (New York: Penguin, 2005) 12. Alex A. Lluch and Helen Eckmann, *Simple Principles to Enjoy Life and Be Happy* (San Diego: WS, 2008) 5–6, 18, 217–218.
[76] Mortimer J. Adler, *Desires Right & Wrong: The Ethics of Enough* (New York: Macmillan, 1991) 25–36.
[77] Catherine Siskos, "The Good Life Index," *Kiplinger's Personal Finance Magazine* January 1988: 81.
[78] Kim Casali, "Love is . . .," private Sanderlin family collection. See Kim Casali, *"Love is . . ."* (New York: Abrams, 2005).
[79] Jack Canfield and Mark Victor Hansen, *Dare to Win* (New York: Berkley, 1994) ix, xiii.
[80] Canfield xiii–xiv.
[81] Canfield 100–102.
[82] See McBrien 1065–1066.
[83] Francis de Sales, *Introduction to the Devout Life*, 1949, trans. and ed. John K. Ryan (Garden City: Doubleday-Image, 1955) First Part, I (p. 35). See Martin, 105.
[84] Francis de Sales, First Part, I. See E.W. Trueman Dicken, *The Crucible of Love: A Study of the Mysticism of St. Teresa of Jesus and St. John of the Cross* (New York: Sheed, 1963) 38–41.

PART II, CHAPTER 2

[85] David Van Biema and Jeff Chu, "Does God Want You To Be Rich?", *Time* 18 Sept. 2006: 50.
[86] Van Biema 50.

[87] Susan Heitler, *The Power of Two: Secrets to a Strong & Loving Marriage* (Oakland: New Harbinger, 1997) 191–192.
[88] Aaron T. Beck, *Love is Never Enough: How Couples Can Overcome Misunderstandings, Resolve Conflicts, And Solve Relationship Problems Through Cognitive Therapy*, 1988 (New York: HarperCollins-HarperPerennial, 1989) 56–57.
[89] Beck 56–57.
[90] Kinder 83–84.
[91] Joan Jacobs Brumberg, *The Body Project: An Intimate History of American Girls* (New York: Random-Vintage, 1998) 122.
[92] Brumberg 120–122.
[93] Brumberg 120–121.
[94] Brumberg 121–122.
[95] Brumberg xxi.
[96] Brumberg xxi.
[97] Gwendolyn Goldsby Grant, *The Best Kind of Loving: A Black Woman's Guide to Finding Intimacy*, 1995 (New York: HarperCollins-HarperPerennial, 1996) 48–50.
[98] Naomi Wolf, *The Beauty Myth: How Images of Beauty Are Used Against Women* (New York: Doubleday-Anchor, 1996) 12, 17.
[99] Wolf 86–88.
[100] Wolf 88. See also Elena Conis, "Feed the soul, trim the fat," *Los Angeles Times* 10 July 2006: F1+.
[101] Javier Abad and Eugenio Fenoy, *Marriage: A Path to Sanctity*, 2nd ed. (Manila: Sinag-Tala, 2002) 72.
[102] Abad 73.
[103] Wolfgang Mieder, Stewart A. Kingsbury, and Kelsie B. Harder, eds., *A Dictionary of American Proverbs* (New York: Oxford UP, 1992) 41. See the Old Testament, Prov. 31:30.

PART II, CHAPTER 3

[104] Daniel Goleman, *Emotional Intelligence* (New York: Bantam, 1995) 292.
[105] Klein 59.
[106] Jill Sherwin, *Quotable Star Trek* (New York: Pocket Books, 1999) 113.
[107] Andrea Hopkins, *The Book of Courtly Love: The Passionate Code of the Troubadours* (San Francisco: HarperCollins-HarperSanFrancisco, 1994) 18.
[108] Thomas Moore, *Care of the Soul: A Guide for Cultivating Depth and Sacredness in Everyday Life* (New York: HarperCollins, 1992) 78.
[109] McLellan 144.
[110] Howard J. Markman, Scott M. Stanley, and Susan L. Blumberg, *Fighting for Your Marriage: Positive Steps for Preventing Divorce and Preserving a Lasting Love*, rev. ed. (San Francisco: Jossey-Bass/Wiley, 2001) 134.
[111] Markman 134–136.
[112] Frances de Sales Third Part, VIII.
[113] Mieder 387.
[114] Mardy Grothe, *Oxymoronica: Paradoxical Wit and Wisdom from History's Greatest Wordsmiths* (New York: HarperCollins-HarperResource, 2004) 57.
[115] Grothe 58.
[116] Barry Schwartz, *The Paradox of Choice: Why More is Less*, 2004 (New York: Harper Perennial, 2005) 2–3.
[117] Schwartz 9–10.
[118] Schwartz 2–3.
[119] Schwartz 147.
[120] Schwartz 147–148.
[121] Schwartz 147–148.
[122] Schwartz 120–121.
[123] Schwartz 182.
[124] Schwartz 182.
[125] Thomas Hardy, *Jude the Obscure*, ed. Irving Howe (Boston: Houghton, 1965) 57.

PART II, CHAPTER 4

[126] Grant 70–75.
[127] Grant 70–75.
[128] Ballesteros 4.
[129] "Mystery of Happiness" 6.
[130] "Mystery of Happiness" 8.
[131] Robert Nozick, *The Examined Life: Philosophical Meditations* (New York: Simon-Touchstone, 1990) 106.
[132] Mieder 57.

PART III, INTRODUCTION

[133] Grothe 49.
[134] Clyde Francis Lytle, *Leaves of Gold: An Anthology of Prayers, Memorable Phrases, Inspirational Verse and Prose*, rev. ed. (Williamsport: Coslett, 1948) 36.

PART III, CHAPTER 1

[135] Emmons 43–44.
[136] Emmons 4.
[137] Tim Mulgan, *The Demands of Consequentialism* (Oxford: Clarendon, 2001) 173.
[138] Emmons 48–49.
[139] Emmons 48.
[140] Emmons 48.
[141] Emmons 48–49. Lyubomirsky 42–47.
[142] Emmons 48.
[143] "Mystery of Happiness" 4–5.
[144] Schwartz 106.
[145] Emmons 47–49.
[146] Emmons 47–49.
[147] Harville Hendrix, *Getting the Love You Want: A Guide for Couples*, 1988 (New York: HarperCollins-HarperPerennial, 1990) 265–267.
[148] Hendrix 3–238.
[149] Hendrix 90–92.

Notes

PART III, CHAPTER 2

[150] Emmons 72.
[151] Emmons 72.
[152] Emmons 76.
[153] Emmons 78.
[154] George Davis, *Love Lessons: African Americans and Sex, Romance, and Marriage in the Nineties* (New York: Morrow, 1998) 70.
[155] Howard Rheingold, *They Have a Word for It: A Lighthearted Lexicon of Untranslatable Words & Phrases*, 1988 (Louisville: Sarabande, 2000) 202–203.
[156] Jean M. Twenge, *Generation Me: Why Today's Young Americans Are More Confident, Assertive, Entitled—and More Miserable Than Ever Before* (New York: Free Press, 2006) 44–103.
[157] Twenge 68–69.
[158] John Gottman, with Nan Silver, *Why Marriages Succeed or Fail* (New York: Simon, 1994) 155.
[159] John of the Cross A2,7,5.
[160] Emmons 85.
[161] Emmons 86.
[162] Emmons 43–47. Annas, "Virtue" 15–16. L.W. Sumner, "Happiness Now and Then," *Apeiron: A Journal for Ancient Philosophy and Science* XXXV.4 (December 2002): 24–25.
[163] For example, see Lyubomirsky, including her "Subjective Happiness Scale," 32–33. Daniel Gilbert, *Stumbling on Happiness*, 2006 (New York: Random, 2007) 71–77. Holly J. Morris, "Happiness Explained," *U.S. News & World Report* 3 Sept. 2001: 49.
[164] Francis 246.
[165] Annas, "Virtue." Hudson 40. Porter 141–230. Thomas Aquinas, *Virtue.*
[166] Thomas Aquinas S.T. I–II,q.65,a.1–5.
[167] Thomas à Kempis I,6.
[168] *Tao Te Ching, Tao Te Ching; Chuang-tzu; Wen-tzu; The Book of Leadership and Strategy: Sex, Health, and Long Life*, trans. Thomas Cleary (Boston: Shambala, 1999), no. 46. My translation from Andrew Wilson, ed., *World Scripture: A Comparative Anthology of Sacred Texts*, 1991 (St. Paul: Paragon, 1995) 295.
[169] Emmons 68.

[170] Emmons 69–70.
[171] Wilson 638–673. Dorothy Berkley Phillips, Elizabeth Boyden Howes, and Lucille M. Nixon, eds., *The Choice is Always Ours: An Anthology on the Religious Way, Chosen from Psychological, Religious, Philosophical and Biographical Sources* (New York: Smith, 1948) 109–164.
[172] See John of the Cross A1,1–3; A3,24–27.
[173] John of the Cross, *The Dark Night, Collected Works* Book Two, Chapters 1–3 (N2,1–3).
[174] John of the Cross N2,1–3.
[175] John of the Cross A3,19,7. See also A1,13,11; A2,6,4; A2,7,6–7.

PART III, CHAPTER 3

[176] Steven W. Vannoy, *The 10 Greatest Gifts I Give My Children: Parenting from the Heart*, 1994 (New York: Simon-Fireside, 1994) 149.
[177] Editors of the *Ladies' Home Journal* with Margery D. Rosen, *Can This Marriage Be Saved? Real-Life Cases from the Most Popular, Most Enduring Women's Magazine Feature in the World* (New York: Workman, 1994) 132.
[178] Ron Adler and Neil Towne, *Looking Out/Looking In: Interpersonal Communication*, 2nd ed. (New York: Holt, 1978) 338.
[179] Hendrix 235.
[180] Thomas à Kempis II,3.
[181] Stanford M. Lyman, *The Seven Deadly Sins: Society and Evil* (New York: St. Martin's, 1978).
[182] Kinder 107.
[183] Robert Sokolowski, *The God of Faith and Reason: Foundations of Christian Theology* (Notre Dame: U of Notre Dame P, 1982) 56–58.
[184] Aristotle, *The Nicomachean Ethics of Aristotle*, trans. David Ross, 1925 (London: Oxford UP, 1954) Book VII,1; also I–VI, VII,2–9. Sokolowski, *God* 56–58.
[185] Aristotle VII, 2–9; also I–VI.
[186] Aristotle VII, 1–9.
[187] John of the Cross A3,16,2.
[188] John of the Cross A3,16,1. See Dt. 6:5.
[189] Thomas Aquinas S.T. I–II,q.24,a.1; I,q.81,a.3.

[190] Thomas Aquinas S.T. I–II,q.24,a.1–3; I,q.78,a.1; I,q.80,a.1.

[191] Thomas Aquinas S.T. I–II,q.24,a.1. Augustine, *The City of God*, trans. Marcus Dods, intro. Thomas Merton (New York: Modern Library, 1950) Book XIV, Chapter 7.

[192] Thomas Aquinas S.T. I–II,q.24,a.3.

[193] Simon G. Harak, *Virtuous Passions: The Formation of Christian Character* (New York: Paulist, 1993).

[194] William Shakespeare, *Venus and Adonis, The Complete Works of Shakespeare*, ed. Hardin Craig (New York: Scott, 1951) Line 799.

[195] Klein 65.

[196] John of the Cross, *The Spiritual Canticle, Collected Works* Stanza XIX, No. 3 (SC XIX,3).

[197] John Paul II, *Man and Woman* Nos. 129–130.

[198] John Paul II, *Man and Woman* No. 39,1; Nos. 24–63.

[199] John Paul II, *Man and Woman* No. 129,1; No. 58.

[200] Rosen 22–23.

[201] Redford Williams and Virginia Williams, *Anger Kills: Seventeen Strategies for Controlling the Hostility That Can Harm Your Health* (New York: Random-Times, 1993) 25–60.

[202] Basavanna, *Vacanas* 248, from Wilson 656.

[203] Earl Ubell, "The Deadly Emotions," *Parade* 11 Feb. 1990: 4–5. Author John Cloud observes that the most exciting mental health research today deals with preventing mental illness instead of just treating it. See John Cloud, "Staying Sane: May Be Easier Than You Think," *Time* 22 June 2009:72.

[204] Francis de Sales Third Part, 8.

[205] Williams xiii.

[206] Williams 100–104.

[207] C. Terry Warner, *Bonds That Make Us Free: Healing Our Relationships; Coming to Ourselves* (Salt Lake City: Shadow Mountain, 2001) 71.

[208] Williams 103.

[209] Mieder 19.

[210] Guy A. Zona, *The Soul Would Have No Rainbow If the Eyes Had No Tears* (New York: Simon, 1994) 28.

[211] Jacques Maritain, *St. Thomas Aquinas*, trans. and rev., Joseph W. Evans and Peter O'Reilly (Cleveland: World-Meridian, 1958) 41. Maritain's version of the story differs slightly from the version that I have read elsewhere.

[212] McLellan 151.
[213] Mieder 19.
[214] Mieder 18.
[215] Howard Markman, Scott Stanley, and Susan L. Blumberg, *Fighting for Your Marriage: Positive Steps for Preventing Divorce and Preserving a Lasting Love* (San Francisco: Jossey-Bass, 1994) 1.
[216] Hendrix 204.
[217] Hendrix 218.
[218] Hendrix 218.
[219] Hendrix 218.
[220] Hendrix 219.
[221] John Taylor, "Divorce is Good for You," *Esquire* May 1997:52.
[222] Maureen Sherwood, "'An Emptiness I Didn't Know Existed'," *Esquire* May 1997: 60–61.

PART III, CHAPTER 4

[223] Twenge 2.
[224] Twenge 2.
[225] Gottman 66.
[226] See Whitehead 53–106.
[227] John W. Jacobs, *All You Need is Love and Other Lies about Marriage: A Proven Strategy to Make Your Marriage Work, from a Leading Couples Therapist* (New York: HarperCollins, 2004) 31.
[228] Wilkie Au and Noreen Cannon, *Urgings of the Heart: A Spirituality of Integration* (New York: Paulist, 1995) 36–37.
[229] John of the Cross A3,28,4–5.
[230] Grothe 157.
[231] Owenita Sanderlin, "Saints in Their Lives," *Woman's World* Nov. 1954: 27–30.
[232] John A. Coleman, "Conclusion: After Sainthood?", *Saints and Virtues*, ed. John Stratton Hawley (Berkeley: U of California P, 1987) 206.
[233] John Coleman 206.
[234] Beck 376.
[235] "Take the Perfectionist Test," *Oprah: The Oprah Winfrey Show* (Chicago: Harpo Productions, 1999) 6 July 1999:2.
[236] "Take the Perfectionist Test" 1.

[237] Hendrix 189–190.
[238] Thérèse of Lisieux, *The Autobiography of St. Thérèse of Lisieux: The Story of a Soul*, trans. John Beevers (Garden City: Doubleday-Image, 1957) 142–143.
[239] Grothe 44.
[240] Meredith Brooks, "Bitch," *Blurring the Edges*, Capital Records, 1997.
[241] Teresa of Avila, *The Book of Her Life: Spiritual Testimonies, Soliloquies*, trans. Kieran Kavanaugh and Otilio Rodriguez, 2nd ed. (Washington, D.C.: ICS, 1987) Chapter 4, No. 7 (Ch. 4,7). See Martin 20.
[242] Teresa of Avila, *Life* Ch. 5,3.
[243] Teresa of Avila, *Life* Ch. 5,3.
[244] Teresa of Avila, *The Way of Perfection*, trans. and ed. E. Allison Peers (Garden City: Doubleday-Image, 1964) Chapter 41 (Ch. 41). See Martin 21.
[245] Jack Kornfield and Christina Feldman, eds., *Soul Food: Stories to Nourish the Spirit and the Heart* (New York: HarperCollins-HarperSanFrancisco, 1996) 184.
[246] François Fénelon, *The Royal Way of the Cross*, ed. Hal M. Helms (Brewster: Paraclete, 1982) 62.
[247] *Tao Te Ching*, trans. Cleary, No. 41 (p. 29).
[248] William Faulkner, "Barn Burning," *The Penguin Collected Stories of William Faulkner* (New York: Penguin, 1985) 24–25.
[249] William Johnston, ed., *The Cloud of Unknowing and the Book of Privy Counseling* (Garden City: Doubleday-Image, 1973) 111.

PART IV, CHAPTER 1

[250] Lawrence J. Jost, "Introduction," *Apeiron: A Journal for Ancient Philosophy and Science* XXXV.4 (December 2002): ix–xxxiii. Sumner 21–23. Gilbert 33–40.
[251] John of the Cross A3,20,1–3.
[252] Mieder 145.
[253] Robert I. Fitzhenry, ed., *The Harper Book of Quotations*, 3rd ed. (New York: HarperCollins, 1993) 192.
[254] Richard Carlson, *Don't Sweat the Small Stuff... and It's All Small Stuff: Simple Ways to Keep the Little Things from Taking over Your Life* (New York: Hyperion, 1997.)
[255] Rheingold 144–145.

[256] John of the Cross A1,6,6.
[257] Schwartz 167.
[258] Kornfield 285.
[259] John of the Cross A3,20,3.
[260] Thomas Aquinas S.T. I–II,q.61,a.5; II–II,q.47,a.13. Josef Pieper, *The Four Cardinal Virtues: Prudence, Justice, Fortitude, Temperance*, 1954–1959 (New York: Harcourt, 1965) 38–40.
[261] John of the Cross A2,6,4.
[262] John of the Cross A3,39,1.
[263] David Herlihy, ed., *Medieval Culture and Society* (New York: Harper, 1968) 295.
[264] C.G. Jung, *Psychological Types*, revision R. F. C. Hull of translation by H. G. Baynes (Princeton: Princeton UP, 1971) 330–407. See David Sanderlin, *Putting on the New Self: A Guide to Personal Development and Community Living* (Westminster: Christian Classics, 1986) 45–51.
[265] Jung 356–359.
[266] Jung 363–366.
[267] Wilson 505.
[268] Grothe 88.
[269] Ballesteros 24.
[270] Goleman 57.
[271] Mieder 99.

PART IV, CHAPTER 2

[272] Annas, *Morality* 426–435.
[273] Lytle 41.
[274] Thomas Aquinas S.T. I–II,q.39,a.1–2.
[275] Thomas Aquinas S.T. I–II,q.39,a.2.
[276] Fénelon, *Royal* 59–60.
[277] John of the Cross A3,28,5.
[278] Thérèse of Lisieux 154.
[279] Thérèse of Lisieux 154–155.
[280] John of the Cross A3,28.
[281] Owenita Sanderlin, *Johnny* (New York: A.S. Barnes, 1968) 152–153.
[282] Catherine of Siena, *Catherine of Siena: The Dialogue*, trans. Suzanne Noffke (New York: Paulist, 1980) 82–83.

PART IV, CHAPTER 3

[283] Rosa Maria Gil and Carmen Inoa Vazquez, *The Maria Paradox: How Latinas Can Merge Old World Traditions with New World Self-Esteem*, 1996 (New York: Berkley-Perigree, 1997) 7–9, 80–82.
[284] Gil 7–8.
[285] Lindsey Tanner, "1 in 4 Teenage Girls Has STD, Study Reports," *San Diego Union-Tribune* 12 Mar. 2008: A1+.
[286] See Sanderlin, "Charity in the Dark Night," 19–21.
[287] *Anguttara Nikaya. Numerical Discourses of the Buddha: An Anthology of Suttas from the Anguttara Nikaya*, trans. Nyanaponika Thera and Bikkhu Bodhi (Lanham: Rowan-AltaMira, 1999) 4.73 (p. 104).
[288] Grant 159.
[289] Ogden Nash, *Parents Keep Out: Elderly Poems for Youngerly Readers*, illus. Barbara Corrigan (Boston: Little, 1951) 53.
[290] Kevin Leman, *The Pleasers: Women Who Can't Say No* (New York: Dell, 1992) 159.
[291] Abraham H. Maslow, *Toward a Psychology of Being*, 1968, 3rd ed. (New York: Wiley, 1999) 47–49.
[292] Maslow 47–49.
[293] Hendrix 235.
[294] Mieder 187.
[295] Seligman 200.
[296] Seligman 200.
[297] Carsten-Peter Warncke, ed., *Théâtre d'Amour: Complete Reprint of the Coloured Emblemata Amatoria of 1620* (Koln: Taschen, 2004) folio 39.
[298] Seligman 200.
[299] Rosen 59.
[300] Rosen 60.
[301] Rosen 61.
[302] Rosen 62.
[303] Rosen 74.
[304] Rosen 116.
[305] Albert Camus, quotation from Michael Moncur, *The Quotations Page*, 31 March 2009, http://www.quotationspage.com.

PART IV, CHAPTER 4

[306] McLellan 151.
[307] Ashley 129.
[308] See David Solomon, "Internal Objections to Virtue Ethics," *Ethical Theory: Character and Virtue*, eds. Peter A. French, Theodore E. Uehling, Jr., and Howard K. Wettstein (Notre Dame: U of Notre Dame P, 1988) 432–433, 437–439.
[309] Rosen 166–167.
[310] Rosen 165–166.
[311] See Thomas Aquinas S.T. I–II,q.91,a.2; S.T. I–II,q.100,a.3.
[312] Porter 13.
[313] Rosen 26–28.
[314] Craig A. Boyd, *A Shared Morality: A Narrative Defense of Natural Law Ethics* (Grand Rapids: Brazos, 2007) 241.
[315] Thomas Aquinas S.T. I–II,q.108,a.1,reply obj.1.
[316] Thomas Aquinas S.T. I–II,q.108,a.1,reply obj.1
[317] Christine Swanton, *Virtue Ethics: A Pluralistic View* (Oxford: Oxford UP, 2003) 177–197. Michael Slote, *Goods and Virtues*, 1983 (Oxford: Clarendon, 1989) 39–59. For an introductory critique of relativism, see Francis J. Beckwith and Gregory Koukl, *Relativism: Feet Firmly Planted in Mid-Air* (Grand Rapids: Baker, 1998).
[318] Thomas à Kempis I,14.
[319] *Bhagavad Gita*, trans. Eknath Easwaran, with chapter introductions, Diana Morrison (Petaluma: Nilgiri, 1985) 3.38–3.41. My translation from Wilson 294.
[320] Rosen 78.
[321] Rosen 82.
[322] Laura Schlessinger, *How Could You Do That?!: The Abdication of Character, Courage, and Conscience*, 1996 (New York: HarperCollins-HarperPerennial, 1997) 241–242.
[323] Beck 159–169.
[324] Beck 166–167.
[325] Beck 311–312.
[326] Maslow 45–47. Duane Schultz, *Growth Psychology: Models of the Healthy Personality* (New York: Van Nostrand, 1977) 69.
[327] Maslow 45–47.
[328] Maslow 46.

[329] See Donald Nicholl, *Holiness*, 1981 (New York: Paulist, 1987) 87.
[330] Anonymous, *Thinkexist.com*, 31 March 2009, http://www.thinkexist.com.

PART IV, CHAPTER 5

[331] James H. Burnett, "Religious Counselors Advise Churchgoers on Finances," *San Diego Union-Tribune* 12 April 2009: C3.
[332] Henry S. Brock, *Your Complete Guide to Money Happiness* (Carson City: Legacy, 1997) 31.
[333] Rosen 219–220.
[334] Rosen 217.
[335] Shankar Vedantam, "Compulsive Buyers May Top 10 Million in U.S.," *San Diego Union-Tribune* 16 Oct. 2006: A1.
[336] Stuart Vyse, *Going Broke: Why Americans Can't Hold On to Their Money* (New York: Oxford UP, 2008).
[337] Vyse 153.
[338] Vyse 153.
[339] Robert J. Samuelson, "A Darker Future for Us," *Newsweek* 10 Nov. 2008: 28.
[340] Ballesteros 26.
[341] Ballesteros 24.
[342] David Kunzle, *The Early Comic Strip: Narrative Strips and Picture Stories in the European Broadsheet from c. 1450 to 1825* (Berkeley: U of California P, 1973) 208.
[343] Zona 21.
[344] Brock 40.
[345] Brock 40.
[346] Brock 40.

PART IV, CHAPTER 6

[347] John of the Cross A2,6,6; A1,7,1.
[348] *Bhagavad Gita* 18.55.
[349] Zona 122.
[350] John of the Cross LF,1,15–16.
[351] John of the Cross A2,6,1–6; A3,30,4–5; N2,21,11; LF,1,12–13.

[352] John of the Cross A2,5,3. Thomas Aquinas S.T. I–II,q.19,a.9, reply obj. 1. See Sanderlin, "Charity in the Dark Night" 33–34.
[353] John of the Cross A2,5,3. See Sanderlin, "Charity in the Dark Night" 32–33.
[354] Teresa of Avila, *Way* 127.
[355] John of the Cross LF,1,12–17.
[356] Teresa of Avila, *Way* 131–32. See Sanderlin, "Charity in the Dark Night" 37.
[357] John of the Cross, "Letter 19," *Collected Works* 699. John of the Cross A2,7,11; LF,3,47.
[358] Teresa of Avila, *Way* 127.
[359] John of the Cross A2,7,8–11.
[360] Thomas à Kempis II,9.
[361] John of the Cross A2,7,4–5.
[362] Fremantle 133.
[363] Kolodiejchuk 3–4, 20, 208–210.
[364] Mary Stevenson (Zangare), "Footprints in the Sand," *Footprints in the Sand*, 31 March 2009, http://www.footprints-inthe-sand.com.
[365] John of the Cross A2,5,6.
[366] John of the Cross A2,5,6.
[367] John of the Cross A2,5,6.
[368] John of the Cross A2,6,4–6.
[369] Jean-Pierre de Caussade, *Abandonment to Divine Providence*, trans. John Beevers (Garden City: Doubleday-Image, 1975) 34–35.
[370] John of the Cross A2,5,6.
[371] John of the Cross A2,5,3.
[372] John of the Cross A2,6,1; LF,3,47.
[373] John of the Cross A2,5,4. See Sanderlin, "Charity in the Dark Night" 30.
[374] John of the Cross N1,3,3.
[375] Thomas Aquinas S.T. I–II,q.114,a.2.
[376] Thomas Aquinas S.T. I–II,q.114,a.3.

APPENDIX A

[377] Grothe 161.

Permissions

Continued from the copyright page:

"A Poet Offering his Book to a Lady" for the Reader's Dedication page from *Codex Manesse*. Ms. Pal. Germ. 848, fol. 110r. Used by permission of Heidelberg University Library. www.ub.uni-heidelberg.de.

Material throughout the marriage guide from *The Jerusalem Bible*, copyright © 1966 by Darton, Longman & Todd, Ltd., and Doubleday, a division of Random House, Inc. Reprinted by permission.

Material in the Introduction, note 1 (n.1); Part II, Chapter 3, note 109 (II,3,n.109); III,3,n.212; and IV,4,n.306 from Vern McLellan, *The Complete Book of Practical Proverbs & Wacky Wit*, copyright © 1996 by Vern McLellan. Used by permission of Tyndale House Publishers, Inc. All rights reserved.

Material in I,2; III,2; III,3; and IV,1,2,3,6 from John of the Cross, *The Collected Works of St. John of the Cross*, trans. Kieran Kavanaugh and Otilio Rodriguez, copyright © 1964, 1979, 1991 by Washington Province of Discalced Carmelites, ICS Publications. Used by permission of the Washington Province of Discalced Carmelites, ICS Publications, 2131 Lincoln Road, N.E., Washington, DC, 20002-1199, USA. www.icspublications.org.

Material in I,1,n.44 and especially in III,1–2 from Robert Emmons, *The Psychology of Ulimate Concerns: Motivation and Spirituality in Personality*, copyright © 1999 by Guilford Press. Used by permission of Guilford Press.

Material in I,2,n.73 from John Flanagan, ed., *First Steps to Jesus: A New Prayer Book for First Holy Communion,* no copyright notice. Used by permission of Malhame/Regina Press.

Material in II,2,n.87 from Susan Heitler, *The Power of Two: Secrets to a Strong & Loving Marriage,* copyright © 1997 by Susan Heitler. Reprinted by permission of New Harbinger Publications, Inc.

Material in II,3,n.110–111 and III,3,n.215 from Howard J. Markman, Scott M. Stanley, and Susan L. Blumberg, *Fighting for Your Marriage,* 1st ed., copyright © 1994 by Jossey-Bass, Inc., and revised ed., copyright 2001 by John Wiley & Sons, Inc. Used by permission of John Wiley & Sons, Inc.

Material in III,1,n.147–149; III,3,n.179; III,3,n.216–220; and III,4,n.237 from Harville Hendrix, *Getting the Love You Want: A Guide for Couples,* copyright © 1988 by Harville Hendrix. Used by permission of Henry Holt and Company.

Material in III,3,n.210; IV,5,n.343; and IV,6,n.349 from Guy A. Zona, *The Soul Would Have No Rainbow If The Eyes Had No Tears: And Other Native American Proverbs,* copyright © 1994 by Guy A. Zona. Used by permission of Simon & Schuster.

Material in III,4,n.246 and IV,2,n.276 from François Fénelon, *The Royal Way of the Cross,* copyright © 1982 by The Community of Jesus. Used by permission of Paraclete Press. www.paracletepress. com. 1-800-451-5006.

"The Pig" in IV,3,n.289 from Ogden Nash, *Parents Keep Out: Elderly Poems for Youngerly Readers,* copyright © 1933 by Ogden Nash. Reprinted by permission of Curtis Brown, Ltd.

"Footprints in the Sand" in IV,6,n.364, copyright © 1984 by Mary Stevenson and 2003–2009 by Footprints-inthe-Sand.com. Used by permission of Richard Bartel, www.Footprints-inthe-Sand.com.

Acknowledgments

I THANK ABOVE ALL MY WIFE, Arnell, and our children, Wendy, John, Michelle, and Kevin, for their love and support during my writing of this book and for all the days of our lives together.

Professionally I give special thanks to Ralph Martin, leader in Catholic renewal movements and author of many important books on Catholic spirituality and worship, for generously using his time to review drafts of my marriage guide and provide helpful input and support—even though I was a complete stranger when I first contacted him about my guide. I have always been tremendously impressed with Mr. Martin's publications, including *A Crisis of Truth: The Attack on Faith, Morality and Mission in the Catholic Church*, which I read shortly after its publication in 1983, and a recent guide to the Catholic Christian moral and spiritual life, *The Fulfillment of All Desire*. Mr. Martin's publications have always reflected an authentic Catholic Christian orthodoxy, a strong commitment to moral and spiritual renewal, and a deep personal faith—a rare combination indeed. Mr. Martin's support has been very helpful and is greatly appreciated.

I thank Fr. Kieran Kavanaugh, O.C.D., translator, editor, and commentator of *The Collected Works of St. John of the Cross* and *The Collected Works of St. Teresa of Avila*. Fr. Kavanaugh generously took the time to review my manuscript and provide helpful input and support. My copy of Fr. Kavanaugh's translations of the works of St. John of the Cross is torn and tattered with use from the 1970's to this day.

I am especially grateful for the long-time support and friendship of Joan Carsola, leader of the lay Carmelites in San Diego for many years, and Marilyn Marshall, a licensed Marriage and Family Therapist and a member of the Secular Franciscan Order. Mrs. Carsola and Ms. Marshall have contributed significantly to San Diego's Catholic community with their teaching, counseling, spiritual advising, and other activities.

I am grateful to Lynne Pittard, artist, President/CEO, Visual Arts Network, for her permission to use the full image of her painting, "Two White Doves," for my book's cover, with a couple's silhouette added to the image of the painting. I think the world of Mrs. Pittard's paintings that capture the beauty of God's creation and reflect Mrs. Pittard's Christian values and personal faith. I love the Christian theme in "Two White Doves," with God guiding followers of Jesus with His light and the two white doves. Mrs. Pittard does a great job promoting Christian values in her paintings, teachings, and business activities shared on the web at www.visualartsnetwork.tv and www.LynnePittard.com.

I thank others with expertise in Christian marriage, spirituality, ethics, and other areas whom I have contacted in the writing of this marriage guide, including Janice and Don Keith; Peggy and Ralph Skiano; Norbert J. Rigali, S.J.; Don S. Browning; Margaret McCarthy; Jean Porter; Rev. Robert Sokolowski; Robert Emmons; and Barbara Dafoe Whitehead.

About the Author

David Sanderlin earned an interdisciplinary Ph.D. in Medieval Studies from the University of Notre Dame that included courses in theology, philosophy, literature, history, and other disciplines dealing with the Christian society and culture of medieval Europe. Dr. Sanderlin wrote his doctoral dissertation on student life in a Christian college at the University of Paris during the Middle Ages.

Upon graduating from Notre Dame, Dr. Sanderlin taught full-time in the History Department at California State University, Northridge, and then in the Humanities and English Departments at Miramar College in San Diego until his recent retirement. Dr. Sanderlin's college teaching included courses covering the Christian culture of medieval Europe; Christianity and Western Culture; the humanities; English composition; and critical thinking, including ethical reasoning.

Dr. Sanderlin has focused on Christian culture, ethics, spirituality, and personal growth in much of his teaching, research, and writing. His publications include a Christian guide to personal growth, *Putting on the New Self: A Guide to Personal Development & Community Living* (published by Christian Classics) and several scholarly articles on the spirituality and ethics of St. John of the Cross, including "Charity According to St. John of the Cross: A Disinterested Love for Interesting Special Relationships, Including Marriage" (published by Scholars Press in the *Journal of Religious Ethics*); "Charity in the Dark Night of St. John of the Cross: The Human Experience of Union with God through Love" (published by the Carmelite Institute in Rome in the journal *Carmelus*); and "Faith and Ethical Reasoning in the Mystical Theology of St. John of the Cross: A Reasonable Christian Mysticism" (published by Cambridge University Press in the journal *Religious Studies*). Some of Dr. Sanderlin's other books, articles, and pamphlets include *Writing the History Paper* (Barron's Educational Series) and *The Mediaeval Statues of the College of Autun at the University of Paris* (Mediaeval Institute, University of Notre Dame).

In addition to his college teaching, research, and writing, Dr. Sanderlin is active in his church and community. He has done such things as teaching in the teaching training program in the Catholic diocese of San Diego; offering workshops on the spirituality of St. John of the Cross and other Christian topics; establishing a Catholic Newman Club for Christian students at a local community college; helping edit marriage preparation materials for the Catholic diocese of San Diego; and holding non-profit Christian book sales in his parish after Sunday Masses.

Dr. Sanderlin resides in El Cajon, California, with his wife Arnell. David and Arnell dated in high school and married during David's junior year at U.C.L.A. David and Arnell have four children, Wendy, John, Michelle, and Kevin, and ten grandchildren. David and Arnell enjoy seeing their children and grandchildren for babysitting, dinners out, birthday parties, holidays, family vacations, and other family get-togethers.

As far as hobbies go, Arnell enjoys playing bridge (the card game), and David enjoys playing tennis. When David attended U.C.L.A., he was a member of the U.C.L.A. NCAA National Championship tennis team, and he was ranked among the top 20 men's tennis players in the United States. When he graduated from U.C.L.A., he stopped playing competitive tennis in order to devote himself to his education, teaching, writing, and, above all, to his wife Arnell and their growing family.